THE
GOOSE CREEK BRIDGE

Gateway to Sacred Places

10-19-13

To my friends Dale and Darlene with warm regards!
Michael J. Heitzler

Michael J. Heitzler, Ed.D.

authorHOUSE®

AuthorHouse™ LLC
1663 Liberty Drive
Bloomington, IN 47403
www.authorhouse.com
Phone: 1-800-839-8640

Published by AuthorHouse   07/25/2013

ISBN: 978-1-4772-5540-7 (sc)
ISBN: 978-1-4772-5539-1 (hc)
ISBN: 978-1-4772-5538-4 (e)

Library of Congress Control Number: 2012917295

Praise for Author

"...the books I read a lot and leaned on in writing this novel was the two volumes of *'Goose Creek: The Definitive History'* by Michael Heitzler." Bret Lott, author of *Hunt Club,* Charleston Post and Courier, January 7, 2012.

"The Goose Creek Bridge is a brilliantly researched and written account of South Carolina. This is a must read for any serious student of United States history." D. Clayton Meadows, Military Writers Association of America, American Authors Association, Author of "Of Ice and Steel," and "Epitaph."

"I want to reiterate my belief as a student of lowcountry history and as a book publisher that the work has an important place in South Carolina's literature." Alexander Moore, Acquisitions Editor, University of South Carolina Press.

CONTENTS

Introduction

The Goose Creek Bridge is the gateway to the Saint James, Goose Creek Parish in South Carolina and the church, cemeteries, chapels, and sanctuaries within. This work chronicles the bridge as it conveyed congregants to the pews of the church on selected Easter Sundays during every era of the three-hundred year saga and describes from that perspective, key personalities and their salient institutions transcending centuries in a small but critically important section of South Carolina.

This narrative sparks the interests of residents of the Greater Charleston section of South Carolina, particularly teachers of all levels of social studies. Scholars will find an in-depth description of the Yamassee War from the perspective of those residing in its vortex. It chronicles English soldiers chasing wily patriots on both sides of the aging bridge and three generations later, young black warriors of the United States Army with equally youthful white officers camping near the overpass. This comprehensive account explains the trauma of wars and the aftermaths, as well as the impact of public roads, taverns, rail lines and the durable values of the old and new south upon the rural people, and their aged institutions.

Foreword

Goose Creek is a community in the Charleston, South Carolina hinterland that fundamentally shaped the early political, agricultural and social history of South Carolina. The St. James, Goose Creek Parish, one of the original ten civil and ecclesiastical subdivisions of South Carolina established in 1706, was the sanctioned setting for the St. James, Goose Creek Church, The Chapel of Ease at the "camp," and a chapel of ease at Wassamassaw, plus schools, cemeteries and a parsonage. All of these sites were born from the toils of the Carolina frontiersmen and persisted for centuries. This publication is a study of the parish, beginning during the frontier era when the Yamassee War set the stage for the ascension of sacred places. The author conveys the reader across the Goose Creek Bridge and to the front door of the parish church and its rural chapels during every era, and vividly explains the ascension of those houses of prayer as they transition across three centuries.

About The Author

Michael James Heitzler earned a Doctor of Education Degree from the University of South Carolina. He is a Fulbright Scholar and a retired school administrator of the Berkeley School District, South Carolina. He has served as Mayor of the City of Goose Creek since 1978. He is the author of *Historic Goose Creek, South Carolina, 1670-1980,* published in 1983 by Southern Historical Press, Easley, South Carolina, and *Goose Creek, a Definitive History,* volume I published in 2005 and volume II published in 2006, by the History Press, Charleston, South Carolina. The Berkeley Chamber of Commerce published his work, *George Chicken, Carolina Man of the Ages* in 2011 and the City of Goose Creek and the South Carolina Historical Society published several of his articles in recent years.

Relevant Historic Markers:

The author collaborated with the City of Goose Creek and the South Carolina Department of Archives and History to erect historic markers at locations described in *The Goose Creek Bridge, Gateway to Sacred Places*. The following list gives the titles and locations of the markers pertaining to each of the chapters.

Chapter Number and Title – Historic Marker Title and Location

CHAPTER 1: THE GOOSE CREEK BRIDGE

Goose Creek Bridge: The marker stands at the intersection of Naval Ammunition Depot Road (NAD Road) and The Oaks Avenue, Goose Creek, South Carolina.

CHAPTER 2: THE YAMASSEE WAR AT GOOSE CREEK

Boochawee Plantation: The marker stands in Greenview Park in the Greenview neighborhood subdivision at 340 East Pandora Drive, Goose Creek, South Carolina.

Button Hall Plantation: The marker stands at the entrance to the City of Goose Creek Municipal Park, near the Public Works Facility and hydro-pillar, at 200 Brandywine Boulevard, Goose Creek, South Carolina.

Howe Hall Plantation: The marker stands at Dogwood Park, 680 Liberty Hall Road, Goose Creek, South Carolina.

Native American Trading Path/Goose Creek Men: The marker stands at the entrance to City Hall at the Marguerite H. Brown Municipal Center, 519 North Goose Creek Boulevard, Goose Creek, South Carolina.

Oaks Plantation: The marker stands near the front gate of the Oaks Plantation at 130, The Oaks Avenue, Goose Creek, South Carolina.

St. James, Goose Creek Chapel of Ease: The marker stands on Old Highway 52 at Avanti Lane, one mile north of the southern intersection of James Rozier Boulevard (South Carolina Highway 52) and Old South Carolina Highway 52, north of the City of Goose Creek, South Carolina.

Yamassee War, 1715: The marker stands near the entrance to the Foster Creek Park, 300 Foster Creek Road, Goose Creek, South Carolina.

CHAPTER 3: GATEWAY TO SACRED PLACES

Crowfield Plantation: The marker stands at the circular drive near the front door of the Crowfield Golf and Country Club at 300 Hamlet Circle in the Hamlets neighborhood of the City of Goose Creek.

A French Huguenot Plantation: The marker stands near 102 Dasharon Drive in the Hamlets Subdivision of the City of Goose Creek.

Springfield Plantation: The marker stands on the front lawn of Boulder Bluff Elementary School at 400 Judy Drive in the Boulder Bluff Neighborhood of the City of Goose Creek.

Wassamassaw: The marker stands near the Wassamassaw Baptist Church, and Cemetery, on Wassamassaw Road, ½ mile north of the intersection of State Road (South Carolina State Highway 176) and Jedburg/Cooper Store Road (South Carolina StateHighway 16), Berkeley County.

CHAPTER 4: ST. JAMES, GOOSE CREEK CHURCH

Thorogood / Mount Holly Plantation: The marker stands aside the Alcoa Mount Holly Aluminum Plant eastern entrance road, one hundred yards from its intersection with James Rozier Boulevard (South Carolina State Highway 52), Goose Creek, South Carolina.

Steepbrook Plantation: The marker stands near the southern entrance to Hanahan Elementary School, on Railroad Boulevard in the City of Hanahan, South Carolina.

White House Plantation: The marker stands on Marsh Creek Road at Magazine 3ATX 239 on Joint Base Charleston (Naval Weapons Station), above the "neck" of the Goose Creek flow way in Goose Creek, South Carolina.

Windsor Hill Plantation: The marker stands near the intersection of Windsor Hill Road and Ashley Phosphate Road near the Cathedral of Praise, 3790 Ashley Phosphate Road, North Charleston, South Carolina.

CHAPTER 5: LITTLE PLACES

CHAPTER 6: THE BRIDGE IS TORN ASUNDER

Medway Plantation: The marker stands on the north lawn of the Goose Creek Community Center near the intersection of Old Mount Holly Road and Goose Creek Boulevard, Goose Creek, South Carolina.

Liberty Hall Plantation: The marker stands at 100 Adler Drive near its intersection with Liberty Hall Road, Goose Creek, South Carolina.

CHAPTER 7: PRELUDE TO RECONSTRUCTION

The Elms: The marker stands at the entry road to Charleston Southern University, Exit 205B on I-26 and University Avenue, North Charleston, South Carolina.

Casey (Caice/Cayce): The historic marker stands on the front lawn of the Goose Creek branch of the Berkeley County Library, 325 Old Moncks Corner Road, Goose Creek, South Carolina.

CHAPTER 8: RECONSTRUCTION AND BEYOND

Mount Holly Station: The marker stands aside North Goose Creek Boulevard near the entrance to the Goose Creek Community Center north of the Marguerite H. Brown Municipal Center, 519 North Goose Creek Boulevard, Goose Creek, South Carolina.

CHAPTER 9: THE OLD PARISH IN THE NEW SOUTH

Howe Hall School: The marker stands near the front door of the Howe Hall School of the Arts on Howe Hall Road.

CHAPTER 10: THE CITY AND THE SACRED PLACES

The St. James, Goose Creek Church marker stands in the parking circle near the church cemetery at 100 Vestry Lane, Goose Creek. The secluded church setting is contiguous to Goose Creek Primary School at 200 Foster Creek Road in the City of Goose Creek, South Carolina.

ADDITIONAL MARKERS:

The South Carolina Department of Archives and History, as part of the South Carolina Historic Highway marker program, erected a historic marker indicating the location of the St. James, Goose Creek Church. It stands on Snake Road near the entrance to the church site in the City of Goose Creek. The Otranto Garden Club erected a marker designating the site of Otranto Plantation. The marker stands on Otranto Road East, at the entrance to Otranto residential neighborhood in the City of Hanahan.

Author's Notes

The term "Goose Creek" changes meaning according to context. It refers to a watershed, a creek, and sometimes a municipality. The watershed is located in Berkeley, Charleston, and Dorchester Counties in South Carolina and consists primarily of the central creek and its tributaries. The watershed occupies 38,766 acres (sixty square miles) of the lower coastal plain. The average slope of the terrain is 1% with a range of 0-2%. Ancrum Swamp and Huckhole Swamp flow into Blue House Swamp to form the headwaters of Goose Creek. A dam creates the Goose Creek Reservoir for a potable water supply. The waters of Goose Creek are fresh from its headwaters to the Goose Creek Reservoir Dam and brackish downstream from the reservoir. Turkey Creek flows into Goose Creek downstream of the reservoir in the City of Hanahan. Old Goose Creek drains into Goose Creek aside Joint Base Charleston as does New Tenant Pond, Brown Pond, and Logan Pond before the creek flows into the Cooper River.

The spelling for some place names, indigenous tribes, and families vary across usage, time and locale. The author employs a consistent spelling for each throughout the document. For example, he uses "Pocotaligo" and "Yamassee" although there are alternative spellings. He uses "Boochawee" although variant spellings such as "Boochaw" appear on some land records. The tribe and place name, "Wassamassaw," is a palindrome with alternate spellings. Similarly, a variant for "Mount Holly," is "Mt. Holly." Multiple spellings for "Thorogood" appear in the records including Thorough-good, Thorrowgood, and Thurgood. The author consistently uses "Schenckingh" and "Fleury" for the family names with several spelling variants. In addition, he spells the place, "Charleston," throughout the publication although "Charles Towne" and "Charles Town" are appropriate spellings during periods before the American Revolution.

There are two "Strawberry Chapels" in the Charleston hinterland. The colloquial reference to "Strawberry Chapel," in this publication indicates the brick cruciform chapel erected at the "camp," between the 22 and 23-mile markers on "Old Highway 52," (Road to Moncks Corner), in the St. James, Goose Creek Parish. "St. James, Goose Creek Chapel of Ease" is the appropriate title for this place, but some refer to the place as "Strawberry." The little community called "Strawberry," near the camp, acquired its popular moniker when the Northeastern Railroad Company erected a depot with that title in 1854. The depot was tagged, "Strawberry Station," because it stood near the Road to Strawberry Ferry, today's Cypress Garden Road. The Chapel of Ease near Strawberry is not to be confused with the Strawberry Chapel of Ease north of the Cooper River in St. John's Parish.

Finally, the name of the little Baptist Church erected at the camp, aside the ruins of the St. James, Goose Creek Chapel of Ease, at the 22-mile marker changes across time. Originally named, "Bethlehem Baptist Church," the congregation changed its name to "St. James Baptist Church" before the outbreak of the Civil War and named it "Groomsville Baptist Church" in 1890 after the congregation moved the structure to a village of clustered residences and businesses at Groomsville.

Acknowledgements

The author appreciates Goose Creek City Council, Berkeley County Council, North Charleston City Council, Hanahan City Council, St. James, Goose Creek Vestry, the Saint James, Goose Creek Parish Tea Ladies, the Rotary Club of Goose Creek, and Alcoa Mount Holly Aluminum, for purchasing and erecting historic markers relevant to this publication. The author also thanks the South Carolina Public Service Authority, (Santee Cooper) for its long-time support of the "Historic Goose Creek Legacy Project," a special initiative of Goose Creek City Council for the people of Goose Creek. The author appreciates the artistry of Ann Yarborough, the assistance of Lin Sineath, as well as the skillful editing of Nancy Paul Kirchner.

List of Figures

Figure 2.2: A plat shows the Goose Creek Bridge, the main road into Goose Creek, the house and out buildings of the Oaks Plantation and the parsonage.

Figure 2.3: A map describes a section of South Carolina in 1729.

Figure 2.4: A section of the Abernathie and Walker Map drawn in 1785, describes a section of the Road to Moncks Corner near the 23-mile stone.

Figure 2.5: A section of the Abernathie and Walker Map, describes a section of the road in Goose Creek and the Road to Moncks Corner.

Figure 2.6: The Henry Mouzon Map describes the St. James, Goose Creek Parish in 1775.

Figure 2.7: A partial plat describes a section of Chicken's Plantation (later named Cedar Grove).

Figure 2.8: A map describes a section of South Carolina in 1747.

Figure 2.9: A photograph shows Chapel Swamp.

Figure 2.10: A plat made from a survey in 1784 describes the "Remains of Old Settlement Mr. Chicken[']s."

Figure 2.11: A photograph shows a section of Wassamassaw Swamp.

CHAPTER 3: GATEWAY TO SACRED PLACES

Figure 3.1: A photograph shows the eastern avenue to George Chicken's plantation.

Figure 3.2: A photograph shows the St. James, Goose Creek Church.

Figure 3.3: A photograph shows the stucco Cherub head and wings above the windows of the St. James, Goose Creek Church.

Figure 3.4: A photograph shows the Pelican bas-relief above the front door of the St. James, Goose Creek Church.

Figure 3.5: A photograph shows Goose Creek.

CHAPTER 4: ST. JAMES, GOOSE CREEK CHURCH

CHAPTER 5: LITTLE PLACES

Figure 5.1: Steepbrook manor stands near Goose Creek.

Figure 5.2: A section of the Walker and Abernathy map describes Charleston.

Figure 5.3: The partial plat describes the boyhood home of Major General William Moultrie.

Figure 5.4: A detail of the Henry Mouzon Map shows the St. James, Goose Creek Chapel of Ease at Wassamasaw in 1775.

Figure 5.5: The image shows the title page of the *Bethlehem Baptist Church Sacred Book of the Covenant.*

Figure 5.6: This section of the Abernathie and Walker Map shows the main avenue to "Deas Junr. Esqr.

CHAPTER 6: THE BRIDGE IS TORN ASUNDER

Figure 6.1: The photograph shows Philip Porcher, Captain of the Goose Creek Militia.

Figure 6.2: The Photograph shows the main avenue to the Otranto Plantation settlement.

Figure 6.3: The Photograph shows the Otranto main house.

Figure 6.4: The map shows Berkeley County in the 1895 South Carolina Atlas.

Figure 6.5: The photograph shows persons approaching the entrance gate at the Oaks Plantation.

Figure 6.6: The image shows Medway House prior to twentieth century renovations.

Figure 6.7: The photograph shows David's House.

Figure 6.8: The image shows a South Carolina Railway Ticket.

CHAPTER 10: THE CITY AND THE SACRED PLACES

Michael J. Heitzler, Ed.D.

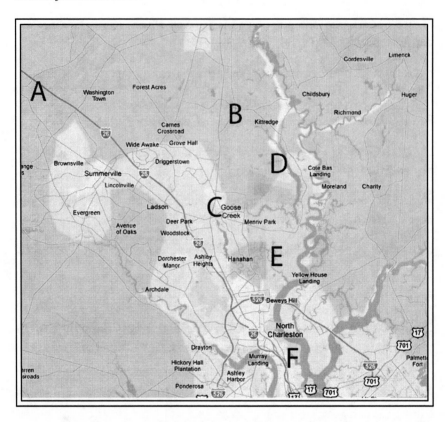

Figure 0.1: The map shows peninsular Charleston and its hinterland with contemporary labels. Manuscript letters indicate locations relevant to The Goose Creek Bridge, Gateway to Sacred Places. A- The battle site of Captain George Chicken's charge / B- Chicken's plantation / C- The Goose Creek Bridge, The Oaks Plantation and the St. James, Goose Creek Church / D-Back River / E- Goose Creek / F-Charleston. The map is courtesy of Yahoo.com.

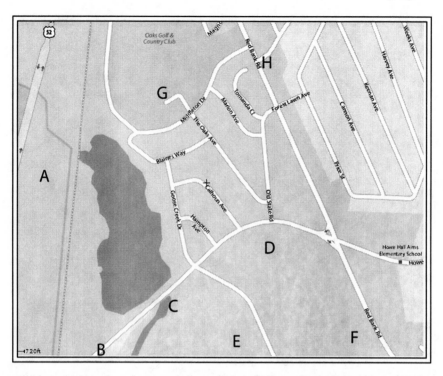

Figure 0.2: The image shows a road map of the Goose Creek Bridge and vicinity in 2010. The alpha symbols indicate the location of selected features during the colonial era. The features include A – The Elms Plantation, B- Otranto Plantation, C- the Goose Creek Bridge, D –The parsonage on Old State Road, E- The St. James, Goose Creek Church, F- The Church School, G- The Oaks Plantation House, H- The 17-Mile House Tavern. The map is courtesy of Yahoo.com.

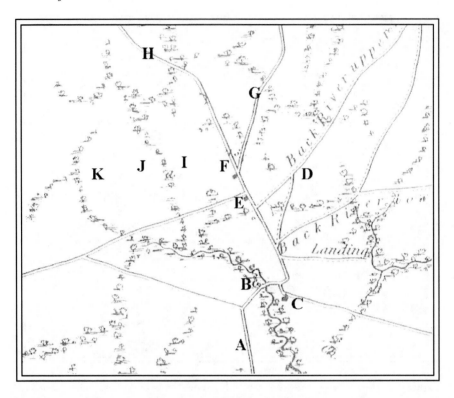

Figure 0.3: The image shows a section of Mills Atlas, 1825, Robert Mills, cartographer. The map is among the collections of the South Carolina Department of Archives and History, Columbia, South Carolina. The section indicates the routes of major roads in Goose Creek prior to the 20th century. Alpha letters added for this publication indicate principal features: A- The Road to Goose Creek, B – Goose Creek Causeway and Bridge, C – St. James, Goose Creek Church, D – Boochawee Manor, E – Eighteen-Mile House Tavern, F – 19- Mile House Tavern, G – Road to Moncks Corner, H – Road to Wassamassaw, I – Broom Hall Manor, J – Crowfield Manor, K – De La Plaine (Fleury's).

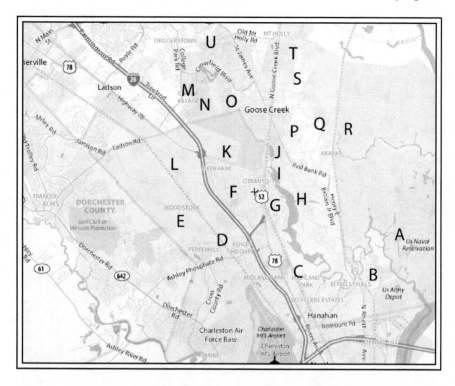

Fig 0.4: A contemporary road map with locations of plantations indicated with alpha letters. A- White House Plantation, B- Yeamans Hall Plantation, C- Steepbrook Plantation, D- The Hayes Plantation, E- Woodstock Plantation, F/G-Otranto Plantation, H-Schenckinghs Plantation, I- St. James, Goose Creek Church, J-The Oaks Plantation, K- The Elms Plantation, L- Keckley's / Spring Grove Plantation, M -De La Plaine's Plantation, N- Crowfield Plantation, O- Bloomfield Plantation (Bloom Hall), P- Button Hall Plantation, Q- Howe Hall Plantation, R – Liberty Hall, S- Spring Field Plantation, T- Mount Holly Plantation, U – Persimmon Hill Plantation. The map is courtesy of Yahoo.com.

CHAPTER 1

The Goose Creek Bridge

Moist sea breezes swept onto the south Atlantic shore and showered precipitation on the Carolina coastal plain, where Windsor Hill stood at the center of a peninsula formed by the Ashley and Cooper Rivers. Rain falling at Windsor Hill pooled into Goose Creek headwaters and began a slow twenty-five mile course toward Charleston and the sea. From Windsor Hill, the broad shallow flood flowed northerly for almost five miles before turning east against two miles of wetland forests and then bending south toward its outfall. Goose Creek drained more than fifty square miles of forests into wide wetlands before channeling into a navigable tributary. Where the creek bottom fell away and the tea-colored flood deepened to traversable depths, the creek commenced a winding eight-mile track to the Cooper River.[1] Along the way, the fresh water rinsed wide swathes of reeds, washed miles of clayey banks and diluted the briny three-foot pitch of undulating tides before it blended with the brackish Cooper River and emptied into Charleston Harbor, South Carolina.

For millennia, white-tailed deer and other animals skirted the banks of Goose Creek in pursuit of nourishing graze, and waded across the

---

1. Charles Edward Dutton, Captain, U.S. Ordnance Corps, *The Charleston Earthquake of August 31, 1886*, Ninth Annual Report, 1887-88, *U.S. Geological Survey*, (Washington D.C.: Printing Office, 1889). Captain Dutton shows an isoseismic map line crossing Goose Creek at the Goose Creek Bridge. An ancient fault at that place may explain the change in water depth. John B. Cook, P.E., *Goose Creek Reservoir, Berkeley County, South Carolina, Report of Findings and Recommendations*, (Goose Creek Task Force, Berkeley County Soil and Water Conservation District, June 1, 1995). A dam erected in the early 20th century, restricted the flow of the creek downstream of the Goose Creek Bridge.

shallows upstream of the deeper waters. Indigenous hunters followed the animal trace until it disappeared at the waters edge where they too crossed in pursuit. Later, European immigrants forded the creek with packhorses laden with frontier essentials in search of the bounties of the Charleston hinterland.[2] The fording place on the, "Broad Stately Creek… (Goose Creek) "[3] soon became a busy conveyance where long lines of burdened pack animals moving to and from the Carolina interior became common sights at all hours of the day. Packhorses trudged into the frontier with manufactured items imported from England, and back again with bundles of deerskins and peltry. Soon, equally long lines of enslaved Native Americans waded across the stream toward slave blocks in Charleston and sea captains bound for the sugar plantations of the Caribbean.

Predictably, some of the first European families settled near the convenient crossing and cleared the forests, tilled the land, watered and grazed free-ranged livestock, and drove herds through the shallows to the markets in Charleston, sixteen miles south-east of the ford. As more families depended upon the shallow crossing, some envisioned a sturdy bridge at that place to link their rising homes, farms, settlements and sacred places to Charleston – an important portal to the British Empire.

THE MIDDLETONS AND SCHENCKINGHS

Brothers Arthur and Edward Middleton arrived in Carolina with early immigrant families and acquired large tracts of land on both sides of the ford. In 1678, the Lord Proprietors granted land called "Yeshoe" to Arthur and Mary Middleton on the western approach (later named Otranto Plantation) and awarded acreage to Edward Middleton and his bride, Sarah on the eastern side that they called the Oaks Plantation. Barnard Schenckingh, his bride, Elizabeth, two sons and three daughters emigrated from Barbados to work the forests between Red Bank Road and Goose Creek, south of the Oaks Plantation. A successful herdsman, he free-grazed

---

2. Edward Middleton was the first owner of the Oaks. The warrant authorized Captain Maurice Matthews, Surveyor General, to apportion 1,780 acres of land for Edward Middleton and his wife, Sarah. Arthur and Edward Middleton received proprietary grants in 1678. Joseph and Jane Thorogood arrived in Goose Creek in 1680 and Abraham Fleury Sieur de la Plaine arrived in the province the same year.
3. John Culpeper, *Draught of Ashley River*, 1671, notes "A Broad Stately Creeke That Runs many miles into the Country," a map among the collections of the South Carolina Historical Society, Vol. 5. Charleston, South Carolina.

cattle and sheep on the rich sub-tropical fauna and watered the herds along a convenient freshwater stream that nearly bisected his property. He forced the fattened livestock across the shallows and drove them along the narrow packhorse trail to butchers in Charleston, making the sixteen-mile route wider, muddier and deeply pockmarked by innumerable hooves.

Barnard and Elizabeth Schenckingh claimed the last tract of land along passable depths of the creek, but later arrivals coveted the fertile soils on the banks of its non-navigable headwaters, and others sought the deep woods on nearby Foster Creek and Back River. Couples Joseph and Jane Thorogood, Abraham and Marianne Fleury, Robert and Sarah Howe and James and Margaret Moore enjoyed no deepwater frontage. They drained their fields into shallow headwaters and reached their properties by way of the convenient ford that the Schenckingh cattlemen used to drive their herds to market.

JANE AND JOSEPH THOROGOOD

The Thorogood family forded the waist-deep water in 1680, and probably purchased a bull and some milk cows from the Schenckingh cattlemen near the crossing. With cattle in tow, the newest frontier couple walked two miles northwesterly along the "High Roade [sic]"[4] to the nineteen-mile point, where they diverted due north along a gently ascending ridge two more miles to pastures above the headwaters of Back River. Joseph Thorogood resided on the land for two years before Governor Joseph West announced a proprietary award of 3,000 acres to him.[5] The governor described the land as "near the head of a branch of a creek which runneth [sic] into Medway River, and called by the Indian name of Oola-Coll."[6] To what the Native American title "Oola-Coll," specifically refers is unknown, but conceivably it referenced the freshwater swamp that emptied into Medway (Meadway) River, an early citation to Back River. Back River

---

4. John Herbert drew the plat from a survey conducted by him in 1716. Figure 2.2 in this publication renders the plat depicting the Goose Creek Bridge, the "High Roade [sic]," and the "Roade[sic] to Boochaw." The plat is courtesy of the South Carolina Museum, Charleston, South Carolina. S.C. Archives Series L10005, Reel 8, Plat 4254.

5. A warrant issues for 640 acres of property to Joseph Thorowgood [sic] in 1683, in anticipation of his arrival in Charleston. He may have been a son of Joseph, recipient of an earlier land grant, but the connection is unfounded. See South Carolina Historical and Genealogical Magazine (SCGHM), 18:5.

6. Henry A.M. Smith, Henry A.M. Smith Papers, Number 1102, p. 379 among the collections of the South Carolina Historical Society, Charleston, South Carolina, (SCHS).

flowed five miles east of the granted property and continued six more miles to blend with the Cooper River nine miles above Charleston Harbor.

Opportunity to own land was the enduring dream that lured European settlers to suffer the voyage to America and brave an uncertain future in the Carolina wilderness. Impatiently, Joseph and Jane Thorogood occupied their anticipated property before the distant proprietors formally granted the award. They walked along the unseemly cow path from Charleston with packhorses and a native hunter. They prepared their virgin fields for corn and cleared the highest knoll where they erected a sturdy frontier home.

At that time, the Thorogood family settled the most remote European homestead in Carolina. They felled pine trees from the higher dry ground, sawed and split the logs before notching and stacking them into interconnected walls higher than a man's head. They peeled away all of the sappy bark before laying heavy beams from wall to wall to strengthen the structure and secure a rigid base for rafters. The pine rafters supported split battens above, and finally shingles shaved from cypress log sections felled and pulled from nearby swamps provided a tight and dry roof. Clay sealed the walls and hearth.

The Thorogoods found clay in thick layers less than twelve inches below the topsoil. They scraped it up, kneaded and shaped it into fist-sized balls, and pushed each between the interconnected logs to dry, harden and seal. They similarly constructed a hearth and chimney with short, split pine battens crisscrossed stacked and plastered with moistened boles. The sun sufficiently stiffened the putty in the walls to provide a finished cabin, sturdy enough to withstand severe weather. The first fire baked and hardened the clay hearth and chimney where Jane hung pots of venison stew and pea and corn porridge.

Frontier life promised a bounty for those lucky and hardy enough to survive, but perils of illness and injury threatened them. Joseph Thorogood died merely two years after taking ownership of his Carolina estate, forcing his widow, Jane to flee to the relative safety of Charleston. There, she settled her debts that bought the necessities for the wilderness gamble and sold the land to James Moore in 1684. Soon after, Jane vanished into the annals of Carolina, but remarkably and notwithstanding their brief tenure, their "Thorogood," name remained attached to the 3000- acre tract for almost two hundred years.[7]

---

7. Susan Baldwin Bates and Harriot Cheves Leland, *Proprietary Records of South Carolina*, vol. I, *Abstract of the Records of the Secretary of the Province, 1675-1695* (Charleston, South Carolina: The History Press, 2005), 84, 90, 91. Also, see Charleston County Deed Book B, p. 39, August 10 & 11, 1720, among the records of the Charleston County Office

ABRAHAM FLEURY SIEUR DE LA PLAINE

Abraham Fleury arrived in Charleston with the first contingency of French Huguenot immigrants a decade after the earliest British families. The Lord Proprietors of England granted the most accessible and valuable properties along navigable reaches of Goose Creek to aspiring planters during the initial decade of British occupation (1670-1680). However, when discrimination against Protestants (Huguenots) worsened in France, Fleury and others sailed to Charleston where the Lord Proprietors tolerated religious dissent and offered less desirable, but extensive tracts along the shallow headwaters to enterprising families of most faiths.[8]

Abraham Fleury and his family sailed initially to England, but soon departed on the ship *Richmond* on December 17, 1679, passing first to Barbados and reaching Oyster Point on the Charleston peninsula three months later. He came ashore in April 1680 with his wife Marianne, stepdaughter Marianne, his brother Isaac and four servants. He counted his servants Lewis, Lucy, Sharto, and Gabriel Teboo as members of his family because he paid their passage to America, and contracted them to work eighteen months in his charge. The indentured servants provided Fleury with meager but immediate income from their labor, and counting them as family members qualified for a larger property grant in accordance with the head-right land distribution system of that day.[9]

In Charleston, Fluery applied to Governor Thomas Smith for land, but before the governor issued a warrant three years later for 350 acres to "Monsie[u]r de la Plane," the Frenchman explored and settled the tract nineteen miles from town where he slashed a clearing on the highest ground. The impatient frontiersman did not wait for the grant award, but led his family and packhorses laden with supplies beyond the walls

---

Building, Charleston, South Carolina. This James Moore was not directly related to the Moore family of nearby Boochawee Plantation.

8. Daniel Ravenel, 1789-1873, compiler of *Liste des Francois et Suisses. From an Old Manuscript List of French and Swiss Protestants Settled in Charleston . . . Probably About 1695-6* (New York: Knickerbocker Press, 1888) 929.31.S95 F74 1888, SCHS.

1888. Ravenel notes "Marianne Caroline Fleury" and "Abraham Fleury," husband and wife, living in the Carolina in 1695-6. He also records an Isaac Fleury, who was brother to Abraham. The Revocation of the Edict of Nantes enacted in 1685, but some foresaw the pending action and departed before the political discrimination commenced.

9. The Proprietors granted headrights to anyone transporting a laborer or indentured servant to the colony. These land grants consisted of 50 acres for a person arriving to the area and 100 acres for people previously living in Carolina.

of Charleston toward the tall trees spanning the northernmost shores of Goose Creek. By that time, the contract binding his indentured workers expired, and the servants remained behind in Charleston to pursue their own fortunes, but daughter Marianne, whose husband perished from illness, accompanied her parents and Uncle Isaac along the brutal trading path.[10]

The Fleury Sieur de la Plaine family followed the unseemly cow path all morning, sixteen miles inland to the fording point at Goose Creek where they eased into the chilled creek water. The women lifted their dresses while the men raised their muskets high as they urged the reluctant packhorses onto the solid bottom of the waist-deep creek. After sloshing across the hundred-yard expanse, the family ascended the gentle grade on the opposite side where herds of cattle grazed and watered. There, the sojourners met their newest neighbors and probably purchased cows from Benjamin Schenckingh, the second son of Bernard. When the cattlemen roped the beeves together in single file, the little troupe, with beasts in tow, vanished with the morning chill in pursuit of their last three-mile stretch along the ancient Indian path leading farther into the wilderness.

Although the hesitant cattle instinctively tried to slow the march, the family quickened its pace when they found a game trace eighteen miles from town leading west from the Indian path through tall grasses and hundred-foot tall trees. There, diverging from the trail, they commenced the final two-mile leg of their journey along a narrow, distinctive animal trace.

Small and large animals wrought that trace by skirting the higher ground above the northernmost reach of Goose Creek for thousands of years. The stream rose five miles distant flowing imperceptibly down a one percent or lesser grade until it bent east at Fleury's new homestead and soon turned lazily south toward its outfall in the Cooper River. All along the flow-way, the reliable irrigation produced abundant graze and mash in looming forests where regular rainfall and alluvial soils supported immense herds of deer and great numbers of birds, fowl and furbearing mammals. Native hunters pursued the trail stalking game for millenniums along the northernmost bend of the creek, and their suede footfalls braided the animal traces showing the way, exposing hardpan in places, and wearing

---

10. Agnes Leland Baldwin, *First Settlers of South Carolina 1670-1700* (Easley, South Carolina: Southern Historical Press, 1985), 268. Noted therein, James Dugue Jr. married Marianne, stepdaughter of Abraham Fleury De la Plaine. The estate settlement papers of Dugue's father document the son's death before 1696.

a narrow pathway that led the Huguenots home that early afternoon of an unusually bright Carolina day.

The Fleurys reached the forest that the brothers scouted many times in previous months. They rested briefly at a clearing near the center of their property where the women sparked a fire on familiar ground to dry their soaked dresses, chase the chill away and cook a hearty supper. The men improved the lean-to shelter thrown up on previous visits and together the family commenced a permanent settlement on the farthest western edge of Carolina.[11]

THE BRIDGE-A CONVEYANCE MADE OF EARTH AND WOOD

The fording point on Goose Creek lay between lands granted to brothers, Arthur and Edward Middleton.[12] After 1683, to accommodate the increasing volumes of land traffic at the crossing, the brothers committed their workers to build a bridge. They created a corduroy roadway that raised the low and soft approaches by laying logs side by side. Where the grade fell slightly away, they shoveled tons of clayey earth to shape a long causeway. They bridged the deepest water with sturdy hickory trunks, crossed beams, and split logs laid flat side up.

The structure presented no obstacle to boat travel because it spanned the highest navigable point on the creek, and at first, it was stout enough only for pedestrians and equestrians, but axmen shored-up the crossing to accommodate an ever increasing number of Europeans traveling the "Indian Trail," on bulky wagons with iron rimmed wheels, and beds of oak.

More families and tradesmen relied upon the rigid conveyance in pursuit of the frontier, or from the eastern and northern sections of the colony, to commence the final leg of their journey to Charleston. It became the most sought passage in Carolina. The indigenous Americans tagged

---

11. The Thorogoods arrived the same year as the Fleurys and resided two miles north of them. Their three thousand-acre plantation spanned between the Road to Moncks Corner and the Wassamassaw Road.

12. Edward Middleton was the first owner of the Oaks. The warrant authorized Captain Maurice Matthews, Surveyor General, to apportion 1,780 acres of land for Edward Middleton and his wife, Sarah. The grant specified that if the land was "upon any navigable river or river capable of being made navigable you are to allow only the fifth part of the depth thereof by the water side." Edward Middleton testified that the creek that bordered his land was "not capable of being made navigable."

the bridged stream "Adthau," a native word meaning, "Goose Creek," in reference to the abundant fowl that seasonally migrated to those waters. Subsequently, the Road to Charleston was conversely tagged the "Road to Goose Creek." That road and nearby Red Bank Road, which led to a high ocher bank of the Cooper River, converged near the crossing. These byways became important trade routes connecting to the Road to Moncks Corner leading to the wilderness. Soon, immigrants, such as James Moore and Robert Howe, with their families, guided packhorses across the squat wooden overpass to frontier settlements in the nearby land of "Boochawee."

BOOCHAWEE

Boochawee was wide wetlands with intermittent higher forests sprawling inland from the Goose Creek Bridge. Rain sheeting from the slightly higher elevations along Goose Creek and Back River washed into those flow-ways and eventually emptied into the Cooper River, but dense and imperceptibly higher woodlands encircled the broad Boochawee floodplain like the scalloped rim of a bowl. The natives called the enclosed wet land, "Boochawee," maybe in reference to the shallow freshwater swamps washing across it and the Europeans used that term for several decades. However, immigrants supplanted the native tag "Appeebee,"[13] for the principal creek that drained Boochawee when John Foster settled on its shore.

Foster Creek, named after the early settler, John Foster, meandered six miles through the nondescript forests, bogs and swamps collecting seepage from thousands of tiny pools until it deepened, became navigable and flowed three more miles to empty into Back River nine miles above Charleston Harbor. The innumerable streams that emptied into Foster Creek drained Boochawee sufficiently to expose its alluvial soil and enrich the thick hardwood forests where lush habitat supported abundant wildlife and a small clan of Native Americans.

The mild mannered Etiwan natives, in small groups of two dozen or more extended family members, wandered Boochawee, and camped in semi-permanent villages along low ridges that gradually ascended 45 feet above Foster Creek. The tidal creek produced sea life that supplemented venison and other foods wrought from the forests and the abundant native

---

13. The labels "Boochawee" and "Appeebee" feature an "ee" ending that typically referenced water in the Etiwan native tongue.

corn, beans, squash and other garden produce. The waterway was not salty enough to support oysters, but it yielded a bounty of crab, shrimp and fish. The natives usually speared, smoked and dried the fish with salt and woodland spices but occasionally, a hungry pod of dolphins herded sea life into roiling shallows and unknowingly drove bountiful schools into woven traps set by the natives. Boochawee was rich, and beckoned the land-hungry Europeans, who chanced the voyage to America, longing for the security and independence that only property ownership brought.

Robert Howe and his bride, Sarah crossed the bridge in 1682 and received the land grant the following year. He approached his property via a shaded avenue through mixed forests that conveniently intersected the Goose Creek Road near the wooden crossing. His avenue gradually ascended more than a mile to a small clay knoll before descending to the banks of navigable Foster Creek. He built his home "… after the rustic order…"[14] to stand for more than fifty years beneath looming shade trees, above three freshwater springs, and overlooking the shallow and fertile swamps of Boochawee.

James Moore and his bride, Lady Margaret Berringer acquired a 2,400-acre land grant named, "Boochawee" in 1683. Their one-half mile avenue diverged from the main highroad at the seventeen-mile marker near the bridge to pursue a slight rise at the intersection of two paths later named, "Back River Lower Road" and "Back River Upper Road."[15] At that intersection, James Moore raised shelters for his family, slaves and livestock, and began slashing and clearing the dense forest.[16]

MEDWAY PLANTATION

Shaded avenues near the bridge, soon led to rising settlements of some of the most successful planter/merchants in provincial South Carolina. The Indian trail to Moncks Corner and beyond, the footpaths to settlements on the headwaters of Goose Creek, Back River and Foster Creek and the avenues to Boochawee converged near the Goose Creek Bridge, creating a confluence of commerce and a nexus for herdsmen, traders, planters, and politicians.

14. Sales advertisement for Howe Hall property, *South Carolina Gazette,* 3-25-1732.
15. Some cartographers label these roads, "Lower Road to Back River," and "Upper Road to Back River."
16. Boochawee Manor was located in today's Greenview/Liberty Hall Road section of the City of Goose Creek.

Figure 1.1: Above is a section of a map entitled *New and Exact Map of the Dominions of the King of Great Britain...*, 1732, London. The cartographer indicated selected settlements including those occupied by "Thorowgood, [Thorogood]," "Dee Plaine, [Abraham Fleury Sieur de la Plaine]" "Moor, [James Moore]" "Middleton, [Edward Middleton]" "Stherneking [Schenckingh]," as well as the St. James, Goose Creek Church. Foster Creek and Back River are not labeled but indicated in the upper right quadrant. The Indian Trail traversed the waterway at the Goose Creek Bridge, near the church, and continued toward the frontier. The map is courtesy of the North Carolina Collection, University of North Carolina at Chapel Hill.

Consequently, as the 18th century dawned, the bridge became the threshold to the most important commercial and political neighborhood in the Charleston hinterland and a pathway to vast new-world opportunities untapped and awaiting the strong young men and women of Europe. Consequently, adventurers such as Edward Hyrne, the first of second-generation settlers, learned of Goose Creek before departing from England and immediately after debarking in Charleston he purchased land in that locale. Edward Hyrne, an English merchant, did not seek a proprietary award but agreed to an £800 mortgage from Governor Thomas Smith (son of the earlier governor), in exchange for the sprawling Medway Plantation on Back River.[17]

Sometime near 1687, John Signeur D'Arssens arrived in Charleston from Holland. He erected the original Medway House. His widow married Thomas Smith, father of Thomas Smith, the sitting governor when Edward Hyrne arrived. Medway featured dense forests, broad lowlands, livestock, farming accoutrements and a neat brick house and in its pursuit, Hyrne and one young Native American slave, "almost a man,"[18] led several laded packhorses over the bridge in 1700 to commence the most direct and well-used land route to Medway. They followed the narrow woodland trace past James Moore's maturing Boochawee settlement to a thin ridge that traced the Back River Upper Road and circumvented the sprawling, thick and seemingly impenetrable Boochawee wetlands. As they walked inland along the western ridge of the swamp, the emerging lands worked by David Davis (later, Springfield Plantation), came to view as the land lifted imperceptibly into a dry forest. Then the trail fell, as gently as it rose, into the Back River watershed at the southernmost boundary of the fertile 2,250-acre Medway tract. That day he delivered valuable horses to his new home before sending for Elizabeth, his bride in England.

Elizabeth Massingbred Hyrne arrived by boat via the Cooper and Back River to join her husband, Edward Hyrne the following year. She disembarked within sight of the Medway Manor, a large, "80 Foot long, 26 broad, cellar'd [sic] throughout,"[19] brick home overlooking Back River.

---

17. The second Thomas Smith mortgaged the property to Edward Hyrne. Hyrne's finances, as well as some questions of character, figured into his emigration. Officials accused him of misappropriating more than £1,300 sterling, while a port collector in England. Nevertheless, Smith granted Hyrne credit to purchase Medway.

18. Virginia Christian Beach, *Medway* (Charleston: Wyrick and Company, 1996), 10.

19. Beach, 10.

Hyrne described his "brave plantation," in a letter to his brother-in-law, boasting of cattle, hogs, horses and the "best brick house in all the country."[20]

Sadly, within three years, the young couple lost their slave to a rattlesnake bite. Soon after, their home burned to the joists, causing Elizabeth to rue, "we was [were] burn[ed]... out of all, our house taking fire I know not how in the night and burned so fiercely that we had much to do to save the life of poor burry [Burrell, their son]..."[21] Their little boy perished from fever three years later, and although the couple rebuilt a smaller version of the original home upon the charred foundation, more bleak seasons followed until Thomas Smith reclaimed the plantation due to the defaulted mortgage. Consequently, the overwhelmed couple departed in search of opportunities elsewhere and eventually returned to England.

CABIN CHURCHES NEAR THE BRIDGE

The avenues to the nearby plantation settlements intersected the main road near the bridge. Although Schenckingh's noxious cow path also originated near the bridge, the proximate convergence of the byways, paths and avenues consigned that busy place as the preferred center of the community. There, the dynamic and durable institutions of the emerging British Empire in North America appeared when energetic families erected a log church, cemetery, parsonage and school.

The same year Edward Hyrne embarked upon his tragic epic at Medway, the first minister to Goose Creek, Reverend William Corben arrived at the cabin church. By the time Reverend Samuel Thomas replaced Corben two years hence (1702), Goose Creek was a dynamic Anglican center and the largest and most populated Carolina community after Charleston.[22] Reverend Thomas met his rugged and "ignorant but well inclined," souls in his small log prayer house across the road from Middleton's avenue of stripling oaks. From that perspective, the learned minister watched herds of cattle, packhorse- peddlers, burden men and native slaves stream daily within his vista. Already a human bouillabaisse; multiple European,

---

20. Beach, 10.

21. Beach, 13.

22. *Letters of the Society for the Propagation of the Gospel in Foreign Parts* (SPGFP) *to the Ministers of St. James Church, Goose Creek, 1702-1765* (SPGFP) among the Society for the Propagation of the Gospel in Foreign Parts (Great Britain), letter books, 1702-1786. The letters are on microfilm, number 45-296, SCHS.

African and Native ethnicities characterized the people, and a palette of accents from every European and Caribbean city with a seaport, painted the countryside, creating a unique demography that surprised the minister from London, who was stunned by the "…heathen slaves in this parish… [who] come constantly to Church."[23]

Anglican missionary Francis LeJau arrived in 1706 amidst provincial turmoil as the Goose Creek Men political faction wrested control of the Commons House of Assembly and forged the "Church Act," establishing the Church of England parish system in Carolina. With guidance from the missionary and the support of the colonial government, the burgeoning congregation collected materials to build a larger wooden church and a parsonage upon 100 acres of glebe-land donated by Benjamin Schenckingh, the son of Barnard.[24] The parsonage rose upon Schenckingh's gift, but Benjamin Godin awarded a gratuity of sixteen contiguous acres more convenient to the bridge and there the second, larger, log church ascended.[25]

A dozen French families followed the Fleurys to nearby Ladson during the closing years of the seventeenth century. The Huguenot Protestants refused to comply with the hierarchical structure of the Catholic Church in France, and transplanted their anti-establishment religious philosophy on the headwaters of Goose Creek. They first worshipped together in their personal cabins as they had in their European homes, but began to assemble in a tiny log sanctuary erected on land owned by Abraham and Marianne Fleury four miles west of the Goose Creek Bridge. James Francis Gignilliat briefly served as minister for the French Assembly.[26] Titled "clark [clerk]," Gignilliat kept church records, such as burials, marriages and baptisms; but the members, albeit reluctantly, assimilated into the English dominated colony and within two decades, they joined the St. James, Goose Creek Parish congregation led by a fellow Frenchman, Francis LeJau.[27]

---

23. Arthur Henry Hirsch, *Huguenots of Colonial South Carolina* (London: Archon Books, 1962), 68.

24. Joseph Ioor Waring, *St. James' Church, Goose Creek, South Carolina: A Sketch of the Parish from 1706-1896* (Charleston: Lucas & Richardson Co. Printers and Engravers, 1897), 7.

25. Ralph Izard, George Canty, Captain James Moore, Arthur Middleton, Captain John Canty, William Williams, and Captain David Deas served as vestry in 1706-1707. Robert Stevens and John Sanders served as wardens. Benjamin Godin, Arthur Middleton, Benjamin Schenkingh, Captain James Moore, Robert Howe, Major Thomas Smith, Anne Davies, Benjamin Gibbes, John Gibbes received granted pews.

26. *The Jean Boyd Map and Letters, Charles Towne*, Transactions of the Huguenot Society of South Carolina, Supplement number 110, (Charleston, 2006).

27. Hirsch, 68.

The enthusiastic French and English parishioners subscribed £60 annual allowance for Reverend Francis LeJau in addition to his regular missionary salary. By his careful stewarding, church attendance increased steadily and he welcomed many slaves into the fold. He reported, "… slaves are sincerely desirous to do well, for they come constantly all of them near and about the windows of our church…and behave themselves very devoutly." However, the persistent reverend complained of "some few atheistical [sic] persons, and scoffers at all revelation."[28] Notwithstanding those disappointments, the French minister, who trained in the British Isles, glorified in his vast New World responsibilities and dreamed of converting the wilderness to Christianity. He convinced his missionary society to send Benjamin Dennis, the first schoolmaster to South Carolina, to instruct European, African and Native American children. Benjamin Dennis opened a tiny school and began a long tradition of formal education that attached to the church into the modern era.

Eight years after the parishioners opened the second wooden church and within sight of it, Reverend LeJau watched stacks of brick rise as shallow draft barges and wobbly wagons delivered heavy loads from local kilns on both sides of the waterway. John Gibbes sent bricks from nearby Crowfield Plantation, where his workers scrapped out sticky clay from beneath the top soil, chopped and molded it into blocks, dried it in barns, baked it in long kilns, and stacked the heavy loaves on barge bottoms for delivery.[29] Soon, workers excavated a 40 x 50 foot foundation for the new sanctuary, and English brick masons with African helpers constructed a simple room to receive the first assemblage in the fall of 1714. The rising house of prayer marked the slow transition from the "starving times," of the frontier era to a more bountiful period, but five more years and the Yamassee War intervened before the artisans completed the St. James, Goose Creek Church, a stout little building with a jerkin roof and sturdy brick walls.

---

28. LeJau to SPG, July 14, 1710, SPGFP, and Elizabeth A. Poyas, *Olden Times of South Carolina* (Charleston: S. G. Courtenay & Company, No. 3 Broad Street, 1855), 188.

29. Most planters baked brick for on-site use, such as the construction of footings, hearths, chimneys and fireplaces. Some constructed their homes entirely of brick, and a few early Goose Creek dairies featured brick floors. At first, there was no standard for bricks, and the colors, sizes, densities and weights varied widely. Later (early 19th century) masons plastered the walls of the St. James, Goose Creek Church with stucco. That application protected inferior clay bricks from deterioration, as well as provided a uniform and attractive finish that hid discordant layers of blocks, shaped in varying molds, and baked to differing hues, textures and densities.

THE GATEWAY BRIDGE

During the frontier era, the Goose Creek Bridge connected the St. James, Goose Creek Church, and its geographically sprawling parish to Charleston, forging iconic frontier institutions of England with far corners of its empire. A century later, when revolution dissolved the partnership between Britain and Carolina, the bridge remained the busiest land conduit from the Charleston hinterland to the economic and political centers of the emerging State of South Carolina. The wooden conveyance tied the rural people to the wider world until steam locomotives arrived in the 19th century. When railroads pierced the countryside, the greatest burdens of land commerce shifted from the Goose Creek Bridge to squat loading platforms at depots strung every few miles along the railway. Nevertheless, the bridge remained the most sought-after road passage in South Carolina well into the 20th century.[30]

Figures 1.2 and 1.3: The photographs show the Goose Creek Bridge circa 1904 (above) and the bridge in 2008 (below). By the turn of the 20th century, a raised causeway and road traversed all but a narrow channel of the waterway. The 1904 image is courtesy of the South Carolina Historical Society, Charleston, South Carolina. The 2008 image is among the collections of the author.

---

30. The State Road began at the Goose Creek Bridge and terminated at Greenville, South Carolina. It was one of the earliest public projects engaged by the State of South Carolina.

The common appearance of the Goose Creek Bridge belied its function as an important conveyor of communication and commerce for three centuries. The overpass carried official couriers, law enforcing militias and national armies across the convenient ford. British infantry crossed in search of wily patriots during the Revolutionary War and decades later, Union soldiers marched over, bent on transforming the slave-based society. However, no army, militia or messenger brought more traumas to the people of Goose Creek than the alarm riders galloping along the earthen causeway and across the wooden bridge on Easter Sunday, 1715. That morning, exhausted couriers brought news of painted natives on the paths of war, murdering every non-indigenous man, woman and child within their reach, and endeavoring to vanquish the British reign from Carolina.

CHAPTER 2

The Yamassee War at Goose Creek

Reverend Francis LeJau, Doctor of Divinity and Rector of the St. James, Goose Creek Church, greeted each parishioner at the front door of his new house of worship on Sunday morning, April 17, 1715. He eagerly prepared the first Easter celebration in the newest and finest country chapel in Carolina and he barely contained his excitement. The church was unfinished, and although the priest believed, "A trifle would do it..." the artisans did not complete their work for five more years. Nonetheless, masons laid most of the bricks, the shingled roof was tight, the flag stone floor was set, and the tall windows and doors admitted mild breezes with scents of spring. Standing against the thick budding forest his "House of God" presented an elegant appearance befitting the new-world aristocracy emerging with it from the Goose Creek wilderness. Thus, as the missionary priest beheld his new sanctuary within sight of the, "quite open[e]d and ruin[e]d"[31] log and chinked structure that it replaced, there were many reasons for the fifty-year-old missionary to celebrate. However, he nervously tensed his aging frame beneath his chasuble each time horsemen galloped across the nearby Goose Creek Bridge shouting reports of barbarity erupting on the southern frontier. Packhorse traders and militia leaders branded the

31. Frank J. Klingberg, *The Carolina Chronicle of Reverend Francis LeJau, 1707-1717* (Los Angeles: University of California Press, 1956), 139 and 192. Francis LeJau to John Chamberlain, 4-20-1714 and Lejau to the Secretary, 1-3-17. Workers completed the project in 1719. He described the old log church the following year as "too little and not solid..." The letters of Francis Lejau are an important source of information about South Carolina and more specifically, Goose Creek from 1706 to 1717.

two-day-old conflagration the "Yamassee War" in reference to the tribe that committed the initial assault, but most native clans impulsively joined as the violence spread widely and intensified.[32]

MASSACRE AT POCOTALIGO

Before sunrise on "Good Friday," Yamassee Natives,[33] leapt upon sleeping English emissaries in Pocotaligo, South Carolina. The natives instantly murdered most, killed a few by slow torture and hurried to dispatch others within their reach.[34] As the horrific news traveled eighty-eight miles to Goose Creek, Yamassee warriors and hostiles from other tribes swept southeastern South Carolina with a series of brutal assaults that threw the young colony into war. Within days of the assault in Pocotaligo, painted natives killed ninety English traders "in the field," and nearly one hundred colonists near Port Royal. During the following week, a great swath of destruction spread across the southern coastal plain from North Carolina to Florida with almost all of the indigenous tribes participating in the widening war. The gravest perils concentrated in the Charleston hinterland, between the Savannah and Santee Rivers, where the St. James, Goose Creek Parish lay at the vortex of the fury.

---

32. Cecil Headlam , ed., *Calendar of State Papers, Colonial Series, American and the West Indies, 1714-1715* (London, 1922), 166-169, Charles Rodd to his Employer in London, May 8, 1715, (hereinafter CSP, AWI). Poyas, 111. A native reported to John Fraser that "... now the Spanish Governor was their King and not Craven anymore." The tribes engaged in the conflict included the Alabama, Apalache, Catawba, Choctaw, Coweta, Creek, Cherokee, Edisto, Santee, Sara, Savannah, Talapoosa, Waccamaw, Wateree and Yamassee. The Yamassee nestled in small towns near tidal creeks at the southern extreme of Carolina.
33. Herbert Ravenel Sass, *The Story of the South Carolina Lowcountry* (West Columbia, South Carolina: J.F. Hyer Publishing Company), 63. Sass interpreted the reports of the natives during the "Good Friday" attack as "demons risen from hell."
34. Verner W. Crane, *The Southern Frontier,* 1670-1732 (Ann Arbor: Ann Arbor Books, The University of Michigan Press, 1956), 168 and David Duncan Wallace, *The History of South Carolina* (New York: American Historical Society, 1934), 206. A hidden trader reported that two men were slowly tortured *a petit feu.* Wallace states two women captives were tortured in "unspeakable ways." "The Indians mocked them by repeating their cries, 'O Lord! O, my God!'" Klingberg, 159, Francis LeJau to the Secretary 5-21-1715.

Figure 2.1: The Reverend Doctor Francis LeJau was a Protestant Huguenot from Angers, France, who escaped with his family when the King's Council revoked the law that protected Protestants in 1685. After studying in Dublin's Trinity College and mastering six languages, he ascended as canon of St. Paul's Cathedral in London. He did not remain in that exalted position, but chose the mission field and arrived in Goose Creek in 1706, the year the Assembly established the St. James, Goose Creek Parish.

CALL TO ARMS

As alarm riders carried orders to mobilize and calls to arms resounded across British North America, able-bodied men in Goose Creek reported to militia captains. Best prepared for a fight, the Goose Creek frontiersmen were familiar with the ways of indigenous Americans, because many discovered long before that one way to wealth was through business with the tribes.[35] The Goose Creek community straddled the busy trading path northwest of the provincial capital and by 1715 long established trade with the Native Americans. Thus, as many Goose Creek planters successfully raised cattle, processed naval stores or harvested inland rice, most remained engaged in native trade to some extent, augmenting their coffers and enhancing their reputations as bold and cagy backwoodsmen.[36]

Some Goose Creekers used indigenous trade to acquire comfortable countryseats and some designed abodes to ward off native assaults. The basement at Yeaman's Hall featured loopholes for muskets and a fresh water well for long sieges. The Palmetto House featured musket ports and John Parker hung exceedingly heavy doors "against Indians," on his Hayes Plantation home. Moreover, many Goose Creekers built their homes with profits from native trade. John Berringer, a retired Charleston merchant, used money from native trade to develop a countryseat (later named Crowfield) in Goose Creek. He died in 1703 on a foray against the Apalachee Natives. Thomas Broughton purchased 1,000 acres (later named Broom Hall) on the headwaters of Goose Creek with wealth amassed from deerskin exports.

The James Moore family was notorious for buying and selling pack trains by the dozens and native slaves by the hundreds. The Moore celebrity spun to mythical proportions in some circles, and conveyed to his son, who true to his name, engaged numerous native clans. James Moore II expanded the deerskin export business and the thirty-year-old mounted as a military commander in 1712, leading white and native volunteers to North Carolina. He rescued European families from rampaging Tuscarora in North Carolina where he captured native slaves and returned to greater wealth and wider renown.[37]

---

35. Steven J. Oatis, *A Colonial Complex, South Carolina's Frontier in the Era of the Yamassee War 1680-1730* (Lincoln and London: University of Nebraska Press, 2004), 35. South Carolina Historical Magazine (SCHS:1920), 19: 68, 69, (SCHM and SCHGM).
36. Goose Creek Traders purchased imported items to exchange for deerskins and peltries from bear, beaver, cat, elk, fox, martin, mink, raccoon, wolf and more. Some planters, such as Abraham Fleury expressed little or no interest in native trade.
37. James Moore claimed he captured 1000 natives. He sold many into slavery.

Arthur Middleton of the Oaks Plantation, and Andrew Allen of Thorogood were also famous Goose Creek traders who maneuvered among the wealthiest merchants of the era. They reigned from the finest country and town homes, while others like John Fraser,[38] John Wright,[39] and Thomas Rose[40] were packhorse peddlers who lived in the Indian towns, much of the year. Thus, when the Governor declared martial law, he required Goose Creek men to muster, and expected them to lead.

COLLECTIVE CULPABILITY

As the able-bodied men galloped to their assigned stations, few were surprised the interior tribes rebelled. The overseers of the British mercantile system and greedy traders trumped human morality in Carolina decades before and many of them long expected violence to result. When the initial settlers pushed beyond their enclave on the Charleston peninsula, they encountered opposition from the Westos natives near the Savannah River. The settlers overcame that obstacle by using the resources of the British Empire to arm with muskets, ball and powder, a wandering tribe called the "Savannah." The better-equipped Savannahs easily overran their rivals in the Westos War of 1680, drove them from the territory and consigned the Savannah River trade to the English accomplices.

The victorious colonists soon propagated that effective tactic of conquest in subsequent native conflicts, perpetuating a low- key, yet persistent proxy war between native allies of the Spanish in Florida, the French on the Mississippi River and the English in Carolina. Consequently, as each of the great European empire builders vied for control of the southern wilderness, they strived to dominate the native trade by sending dependent tribes against enemies of their realm. Additionally, as a bonus for engaging in a growing number of skirmishes across a widening battlefield at the farthest reaches of three empires, the victors sold the defeated captives into slavery and divided the handsome royalties among the confederate natives and the consorting mercenaries, insuring an eager cadre of warriors for the next foray.

---

38. *Fraser Family*, SCHM, 5:56. A native warned John Fraser of the impending slaughter, allowing him to retire safely to his home in Goose Creek.
39. Henry A.M. Smith, *Goose Creek*, ed. Mabel Louise Webber (Charleston: SCHM, SCHS, January 1928), 29:277. John Wright, one of the emissaries murdered at Pocotaligo, resided in Goose Creek.
40. Thomas Rose had the dubious distinction as the only man to survive a scalping.

In addition to proxy wars that underpinned institutional greed of the empires, personal avarice rapidly expanded the sinful deerskin and native slave trade. At first, long lines of burden-men toted indigenous goods to town, but incisive traders hired hostlers to manage five or six horses each in lieu of employing a dozen laborers. They usually joined their small drove of horses with longer teams before departing together into the dangerous wilderness. Their objectives were to return alive from each venture with as much profit as possible. Thus, traders preferred beasts of laden in lieu of human porters because animals carried heavier loads, seldom ran away and never slashed their employer's throats. A surviving trader usually returned each packhorse with one hundred fully dressed doeskins, seventy-five buckskins, or an equally weighty collection of various cuts of peltry, all coveted by wealthy shoppers in Europe. The fashionable classes in Europe sought leathers and furs for the finest coats, vests, jackets, shoes, boots, purses, valises and more and paid high prices for the imported luxuries. Greed permeated the motivation of the trader, the merchant and the shopper, making many on both sides of the Atlantic culpable on a personal level.

The ill-will propagated by proxy wars and personal greed convinced most people in South Carolina, some residents of other colonies and a few of the Proprietors in London to fear a catastrophe. From time to time, the Lord Proprietors attempted to temper the native trade and they established an Indian Commission years before to regulate it and prevent abuses. However, the secretary for the commission lodged complaints repeatedly without resultant reform prompting the proprietors to upbraid the colonists for allowing, "…all these horrid wicked things to get slaves." When the secretary entered two-dozen complaints against traders in the years and days leading to the outbreak at Pocotaligo,[41] the Lord Proprietors, in frustration, declared the commission null and void. They astutely concluded, "[the colonists] obtained the [Indian] Commission for the oppression rather than the protection of ye Indians…"[42]

In addition to the proprietors in London, observers in other North American colonies criticized the Carolinians. For example, William Andrews, an Anglican missionary to the Mohawks in New York explained to his superiors in London that the South Carolinians brought horrors upon

---

41. Douglas Summers Brown, *The Catawba Indians, People of the River* (Columbia: University of South Carolina Press, 1966), 135.
42. Chapman J. Milling, *Red Carolinians* (Chapel Hill: The University of North Carolina Press, 1940), 144.

themselves by cheating native families and kidnapping their children.[43] Finally, from the perspective of his parsonage near the Goose Creek Bridge, Reverend Francis LeJau chronicled the impending chaos as early as 1708, when he complained that some dealers encouraged cruelty among the natives.[44] Three years later, he wrote, "I hear that our Confederate Indians are now sent to war by our traders to get slaves." He gravely regretted "the Bloody Wars" and once watched a trading party march "100 of these poor souls," across the Goose Creek Bridge.[45] That day the astute minister cited personal greed as the cause of the horrid transgression and failed to fault the inept colonial policies that covertly shored-up the collective turpitude.[46]

Driven by greed on multiple levels, increasing numbers of peddlers of varying pedigrees and moralities slouched deeper into the wilderness in pursuit of larger and better organized tribes with more hunters, more skins and more potential profit. The resulting confluence of a multitude of personal, institutional and global sins curdled the moralities of generations of immigrants and smirched the values of their new-world estates. Ultimately, the rising tide of immorality weighed down upon the Native Americans until the whole wilderness imploded, sending violent winds of war from the high villages of the Cherokee to the brackish littoral of the Yamassee.

MOBILIZATION

The Yamassee uprising at Pocotaligo prompted Governor Charles Craven to mobilize all available troops including Thomas Smith of Yeamans Hall Plantation on Goose Creek. Thomas Smith sent his family to Charleston and mustered his band of experienced woodsmen, including William Bull, James Alford, William June, William Scott, John Woorams, John Dickson, Charles Hasting, John Herbert, George Chicken and John and Maurice Moore, younger brothers of James Moore, the new commander.[47] Although the assembly did not authorize a "standing army" until months later, the governor improvised to cope with the rapidly expanding emergency. He ordered a contingency of paid soldiers to assemble under the command

---

43. Brown, 135.
44. Klingberg, 39.
45. Klingberg, 94.
46. Klingberg, 109.
47. Poyas, 111.

of Colonel James Moore II (promoted to Lieutenant General in July) and directed him to "follow after, take and destroy all our Indian enemies."[48] The governor called up all white males, black males and some Native Americans between the ages of sixteen and sixty years of age to serve in one of sixteen militia companies and he sought armaments and supplies for all.

The South Carolina colonial government supplied each white militiaman with a musket, a gunlock cover, twenty powder and ball cartridges, wads of wax to polish and protect the metal parts of the musket, a steel worm to dislodge misfired balls from the barrel, and four spare flints. Militiamen typically carried a hatchet, officers sported swords or short pikes and the black slave militia members carried whatever was available ranging from muskets to handcrafted lances. The men wore regular work clothes and wide brimmed hats, but a few officers donned red coats to distinguish themselves on the battlefield.

Governor Craven organized the militia companies into three groups: a garrison force to erect and staff breastworks and palisades at strategic passes, a waterborne contingency to raid the tributaries near Beaufort, and a mobile cavalry to strike where needed. The governor assigned Thomas Smith's and Thomas Barker's Goose Creek cavalry to Captain George Chicken's mobile force and sent Chicken to patrol the rising stockades stretching from the Santee River, south of the Wassamassaw and Cypress Waterways to Colleton County.

As the natives tightened a cordon of fear around the coastal parishes, the volunteer militia and the new colonial army garrisoned a thirty-mile-deep perimeter arching across the Charleston hinterland, erected small fortresses at strategic crossings, and assigned alarm riders to picket between the stockades. The militia erected one stockade to store powder and munitions on the headwaters of the Edisto River at Jackson Bridge near a place called "Edisto Bluff," (sometimes Pon Pon). They also "threw up" one at a watering and pasture site called "the Ponds" on the upper reaches of the Ashley River. Cattlemen fortified "Izard's Cowpens," a corral owned by Walter Izard at a fording pass through the Wassamassaw Swamp. Resourceful families shored up Wantoot Plantation already sturdy with heavy cypress boards on the headwaters of the western branch of the Cooper River. The Common House authorized John Pight, a Goose Creek

---

48. South Carolina Colonial House Journal (SCCHJ), May 6, 1715, 388, 389, May 8, 1715, 399 and May 10, 1715, 406.

trader, to contract four hundred slaves into a private "negro company."[49] Dr. Nathaniel Snow assembled families at an "improvised garrison" at his Red Bank Plantation,[50] and cattlemen re-enforced a sturdy barn and corral called "Schenckingh's Cowpen" on the Santee River. Volunteers mounted these stockades while panicked families retreated within the wide perimeter, passing near the St. James, Goose Creek Church and parsonage, streaming across the Goose Creek Bridge and rushing along the Road to Charleston.

PRIEST, PRAYER AND POWDER

Reverend LeJau was responsible for the spiritual welfare of more than five hundred white and one thousand black souls. Four of these mortals were his own wife and children who followed him to the Carolina frontier eight years before and now depended upon his wisdom for their lives. "Several Plantations are Deserted our planting hindrid [hindered] so yt [yet] we may also fear a Famine," observed the priest, but tugged by obligations to his congregation, he did not flee immediately.[51] His house lay within sight of the Goose Creek Bridge, over which he could rapidly escape with his family if necessary. Furthermore, because the bridge concentrated all of the land travel and information to and from the eastern part of the colony, he gathered updates from those passing his parsonage, assessed the progress of the war at all hours of the day and night, and relayed the news as needed.

Good news arrived near the end of April when the fury of the Yamassee

---

49. The Common House, by a special act of assembly, authorized John Pight to command a company of African- Americans. The Assembly paid the owners for each slave in service. The will of John Pight, dated July 20, 1726, is with Bundle KK, number 16, Works Project Administration Will Book, V.61-A, 1726-1727: 72. John Pight appears on the Poyas list of 1684, He owned 700 acres of planting land on the south side of Goose Creek contiguous to the "Path to Charleston." See Smith, SCHM, 29:11. He was a registered native trader. See Journals of the Commissioners of the Indian Trade, *September 20, 1710~August 29, 1718, pp.14-16,* ed. W. L. Mc Dowell (Columbia, South Carolina).
50. Klingberg, 153, 159, Francis LeJau to the Secretatry, 5-10-1715 and Francis LeJau to John Chamberlain, 8-22-1715. Volunteers erected a fort on the Elms Plantation for defense against Native Americans. The adobe walls rose ten feet and featured loopholes on all sides for aiming and firing muskets. The ruins were discernible as late as the early 20th century.
51. Langdon Cheves, *A Letter from Carolina in 1715,* Year Book – *1894,* (Charleston: Walker, Evans & Cogswell Co., Printers, 3 Broad Street, Charleston, 1894), 315-317.

warriors withered before the musket fire of the South Carolina militia led by Governor Charles Craven. The volunteers chased the hostiles across the Savannah River into the Georgia wilderness. Disappointingly, the encouraging gazettes dissipated near the end of the month with rumors of war parties approaching the northern defensive perimeter, and by the first day of May, tales of atrocities relayed from the Santee Hills.

Earlier in the conflict, some suggested that the Carolinians might keep alliances with some tribes, but that optimism waned when hostiles summarily murdered the traders among most of the native groups, as did the Yamassee. Adding to the desperation, large bands of warriors systematically vandalized vacated frontier households, dashing hope for reconciliation. Soon small war parties probed farther south along the Santee River toward the western branch of the Cooper River, forcing most of the frightened families to flee into Goose Creek, the last bastion before Charleston.[52]

To reduce the numbers crowding Charleston, the Common House on May 7, ordered supplies sent to the volunteers at Red Bank Plantation. They ordered "...one fortification [to] be made at...Dr. Snow's...for the reception of the women and children...and others in distress...."[53] As the first days of May faded, more families joined the traumatized evacuation, and Francis LeJau watched and feared for them as they streamed past his glebe. He also worried about his only son, Francis, and his church-school master, Benjamin Dennis. Both men garrisoned under the command of James Moore II, at a stockade near the Wassamassaw/Cypress Swamp, twenty- two miles west of the bridge.

From couriers crossing the bridge each day, the missionary sought updates from the front, as well as news of his son and teacher. On May 8, he carried the latest information, as well as the Sunday service to a patch of forest six miles north of the parsonage, which he called the "camp." There, a group of volunteers, " ...the greatest Part of their Women & Children are

52. Theresa M. Hicks, ed., *South Carolina Indians, Indian Traders and Other Ethnic Connections, Beginning in 1670* (Spartanberg, South Carolina: Peppercorn Publications Inc. 1998), 43. Claudius Philipe de Richebourg wrote to his superiors in 1716 that the families fled the North Santee Region May 6, 1715, but returned to "secure that frontier..." Richebourg fortified his house a week later to withstand assaults. Anne Baker Leland Bridges, and Roy Williams, *St. James Santee, Plantation Parish History and Records* (Spartanburg, South Carolina: Reprint Company, 1997), 33.
53. SCCHJ, Assembly no. 12, September 22, 1713-November 8, 1715, Saturday, May 7, 1715, Microfilm, 392. "Dr. Snow's" was a plantation near the confluence of Goose Creek with the Cooper River.

in Town," camped near the entrance to "Capt. Chicken's Plantacon [sic]," where a reliable spring guaranteed ample water during the most severe droughts. They were "thrown [throwing] up a breastwork," above a creek between the 22nd and 23rd road mile markers on the Moncks Corner Road, near George Chicken's main avenue.

"THE CAMP"

Before riding to his assigned bivouac, Militia Captain George Chicken organized a defensive bulwark at his plantation boundary to protect the northern threshold into Goose Creek. An experienced militia leader, Chicken learned fortification and defensive battle proficiency while protecting Charleston from a Spanish invasion during the Queen Anne War in 1706, when he stood garrison watch over Charleston Harbor. Eleven years after, he garnered offensive skills supporting Colonel James Moore II assaulting the Tuscarawas in North Carolina. Additionally, while assigned to a six-man committee charged with the "Repairing and finishing fortificac'ons [sic] ...and appointing lookouts..." he learned battle logistics and defensive technical knowledge as a member of the Common House of Assembly. With experience in garrison construction and intimate knowledge of the topography of his sprawling plantation, he was best suited to arrange a redoubt at the strategically located camp. Thus, before he departed to his assigned station, he introduced his overseers, servants and some brave neighbors to a carefully placed footprint of a fortress spanning the road and shoring the wetland that skirted the northern boundary of his plantation.[54]

At Chicken's front door, young black and white men removed the wetland trees to clear an open firing zone, cut logs from the forest on both sides of the Indian path, and posted timbers in entrenchments across the gateway. Finally, the volunteers erected a formidable bulwark rising above the killing ground, from which they aimed upon the sprawling wetland below. Nonetheless, the priest, Francis LeJau, remained unconvinced by these efforts. Two days later on May 10, he lamented, "...the province is in danger of being lost & our lives are

---

54. The governor sent no garrison to the fort on George Chicken's property. That place was a private fortification defended by Chicken's workers, neighbors and volunteers. Chicken did not name his plantation. The name "Cedar Grove" appears on plats and deeds after 1787. See transfer of land to Isaac Dubose, CCDBY5:252, June 1787.

threatened…by the General Conspiracy of the Indians that Surround us-from the Borders of St. Augustin [sic] to Cape fear…"[55]

Most families passed through Goose Creek without stopping, but dozens of exhausted travelers slept on the pasture near the Eighteen-Mile Stone, and some fleeing families cooked and slept in a mixed forest along the main road near the Seventeen-Mile House corrals. Others camped upon the glebe within sight of the parsonage, resting and grazing their horses, pursuing the last leg of their journey at sunrise. As days vanished, Reverend LeJau saw fewer refugees traverse the bridge until the last of the local women and children hurried to the safety of the fortified port city and the remaining able-bodied men mustered. Within thirty days of Pocotaligo, overseers, workers and strong young sons of the evacuated families remained on some isolated plantations. They prepared for the worse, and the priest reported that a "few dozen" of the most stubborn white parishioners with a "body of negroes," remained. They slept at the camp at Chicken's Plantation and as the tempo of war quickened, LeJau rode there more frequently to see the remainder of his flock and bring encouragement and news from the bridge. He prayed with the men and offered communion to the baptized black and white Christians huddled among the defenders.

MURDER IN THE HILLS OF SANTEE

By the end of the first month of conflict, circumstances were disturbing to all warring parties. The situations were daunting for the colonials. As the theatre of war widened, more refugees crowded into Charleston, and supplies of provisions rapidly dwindled. When couriers reported fewer victories, rumors swirled, public confidence in the military leaders shrank and signs of panic descended. Conflicts also perplexed the natives and shook morale because they too wrested with logistical complications. The tribes suffered from shortages of munitions and division in their ranks. The most intractable Cherokee remained determined to murder as many English settlers as possible, as were the most resolute Catawba. However, all of them depended upon European metal and weapons

---

55. Klingberg, 153, LeJau to the Secretary of the Society of the Propagation of the Gospel… 5-10-1715. Interview with Eugene Bryant at his residence at mile marker 23 on Old Highway 52 (Old Moncks Corner Road) on February 23, 2008. Mr. Bryant testified that he used the spring at the camp as a reliable livestock watering hole for much of the 20th century.

trade and that reality tempered native zeal in some indigenous circles. By 1715, imported metal provided knives, hatchets and almost all arrow tips, and the trade muskets, though shorter and shoddier than the ones commonly used by Europeans, were more deadly than bows and preferred by indigenous hunters and warriors. The natives needed gunsmiths to keep the muskets operable, and depended upon traders to re-supply powder, ball and shot. Notwithstanding the nagging problems with logistics and re-supply, Catawba warriors on May 14, employing a defensive tactic to counter approaching militias, killed a family near the northwest corner of the St. James, Goose Creek Parish, fueling the war in that sector.[56]

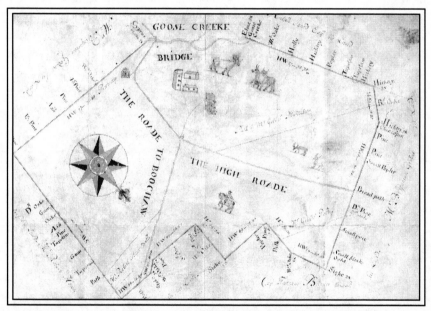

Figure 2.2: A survey conducted on 11-10-1716, during the tenure of Reverend Francis LeJau, produced this drawing. The drawing shows the Goose Creek Bridge, "The High Roade [sic]," into Goose Creek, "The Roade [sic] to Boochaw," the house and out buildings of the Oaks Plantation and a two-story parsonage that defies the description Reverend LeJau gave it. The church stands west of the parsonage and is not included in this drawing. The image is courtesy of the South Carolina Historical Society, Charleston, South Carolina.

On a Saturday morning in May, a Catawba war party approached the log home of John Herne and murdered him and most of his family. John Herne, his wife and children built a log cabin in the Hills of Santee to

56. Crane, 172.

take advantage of the famously rich soil and the abundant fresh water in the many creeks and streams that fed the river. Their home near the Santee River, and forty-five miles north of Charleston, lay within an easy reach of hostile tribes and well beyond the thirty-mile radius of protective forts hurriedly erected by order of the governor. Nevertheless, John Herne declined to evacuate his large family, preferring to trust his well-honed instincts and bile.

For decades, John Herne relied upon his trading experiences to keep good stead with natives of most tribes and he usually avoided disaster. He traveled among many Native Americans clans, lived in Indian towns, and refined keen awareness of indigenous subtleties, nuances and motivations. Consequently, when the Catawbas approached his home in a friendly manner, showing their hands, and touching their mouths, he assayed them honorably and admitted the leaders into his small, dim cabin to sit, eat, and maybe smoke, unaware that a trusted associate betrayed him the day before.

Figure 2.3: The map entitled *Carolina* by H. Moll Geographer 1729 shows "I. Hearn's" between the Santee River and the headwaters of the Cooper River. The map is among the collections of the United States Library of Congress.

Wateree Jack, a native spy betrayed John Herne. Wateree Jack, who lived at Boochawee Plantation in Goose Creek, dispatched a runner the previous morning to alert native allies of an assault strategy that the governor divined. The new colonial tactic centered upon the Herne family farm and Jack's secret knowledge prompted the natives to attack the frontier family. Thus, in the cabin, after a moment of cordial exchange and a burst of feigned anger for some faux pas at the table, the natives rose up, bludgeoned the Hernes unconscious and whooped to spring their compatriots upon all humans within their reach. They struck quickly, furiously, lethally, and vanished silently without vandalizing the farm, disturbing the animals or putting the cabin to blaze, as was common practice in recent weeks. Through stealth, the natives intended to screen their violence, deter rising smoke from broadcasting their position, and abate any alarm that might arouse the skittish population. However, miraculously, two terrorized victims escaped into the forest and rushed the news along the riverbank.[57]

The report resonated rapidly, racing thirty-seven miles down the Santee and Cooper Rivers, and farther south alerting the people in Goose Creek late that evening,[58] but not before, as Jack predicted, Captain Thomas Barker called-up his Goose Creek Company. True to the message that Jack whispered to his native brothers, Governor Charles Craven ordered Captain Barker to mobilize.

THOMAS BARKER, "BRAVE YOUNG GENTLEMAN"

The Governor feared that 1,200 colonial militia could not survive a defensive war against a tide of more than 10,000 native musketeers and bowmen. Thus, the governor arranged a northward offensive to attack tribes one at a time, to overpower each and prevent large coordinated native maneuvers. Additionally, the governor hoped that an overwhelming show of force would convince some clans, such as the Congaree, to remain loyal to the English and reject the warpath in return for trade and mutual defense. The governor concluded that the rapidly

---

57. Klingberg, 158, Francis LeJau letter to the Secretary, 5-21-1715, states "Northern Indians came a Week ago [May 14] to Settlemt [sic] belonging to one John Herne..." also see B.R. Carroll, *Historical Collections of South Carolina* (New York: Harper & Brothers, 1836), v. I, 196. See A.S. Salley and R. Nicholas Olsberg, ed., *Warrants for Land in South Carolina 1672-1711* (Columbia, South Carolina: University of South Carolina Press, 1973), 145. Peter Hern, Jr., Mary Hern, Bridget Hern and Richard Hern received a warrant for 280 acres of land in 1677. "I. Hernes" is indicated near the Santee River on the Map entitled *Carolina nebst einem Theil von Florida*, 1737, among the collections of the North Carolina State Archives.

58. A courier notified Francis LeJau shortly before midnight on May 17, the day the natives ambushed Thomas Barker and his men.

deteriorating circumstances required a concerted response with definitive and offensive action.

Captain Thomas Barker sent Rebecca, his wife of six years, and their little son, Charles to her familial home at nearby Boochawee Hall and dispatched alarm riders to muster able-bodied men to the Eighteen-Mile Stone near the entrance to his Button Hall Plantation Avenue. For decades, a stone by the side of the road, eighteen miles from Charleston denoted the divergence of an ancient passage west. The old trail commenced near the stone at a narrow tupelo floodplain where the topography broke imperceptibly, but sufficiently to separate two drainage fields. Wetlands on the south seeped into Goose Creek, and the other meandered north, then east into the headwaters of Foster Creek. The land separation and slight grade relieved the ground sufficiently to allow dry passage west through the lowland strip. Across the decades, the trace improved until it became the Road to Dorchester, creating a busy intersection with the Road to Charleston, conveniently connecting with the avenues of several affluent planter/merchant homes.

The tupelo swamps and drainage fields provided water and pasture for livestock and as the Road to Dorchester and the Road to Charleston became busier byways, more travelers favored the intersection as a campsite. Eventually, entrepreneurs cobbled together a way station featuring an open-air shelter, grazing fields, ponds, and corrals. Later still, an energetic proprietor built a cabin with a hearth. He hung pots of corn mush, or peas and sometimes onions and beans over coals; and served full bowls with flat biscuits to hungry men in exchange for a penny or two. During most times of the year, young horsemen loitered there, some sitting near campfires, others milling about or sleeping in the tall grasses and scrub. They waited days or longer with their ponies for packhorse trains to assemble into longer and safer lines. The departing convoys sometimes counted more than one hundred laded beasts trudging single-file along the narrow wagon Road to Moncks Corner, where a horse trail of three-foot breadth led west into the dangerous backcountry.

Barker's alarm riders fanned out along the diverging roads and avenues calling all able-bodied men to assemble on the pasture near the stone. The murders in the Hills of Santee stunned and puzzled Barker. He knew Herne and his family and deplored their passing, and the native descent upon the militia rendezvous within a day of his orders caused worrisome introspection. Nonetheless, he received orders and departed as directed at sunrise the next morning, Sunday, May 15, believing that the success of the mission depended upon his timely arrival at the crime scene.[59]

James Moore II, Barker's neighbor and brother in law, led the army and George Chicken commanded the Goose Creek militia. The Governor stationed these commanders on the defensive perimeter south and west of Goose Creek, and he could not spare both from that theatre.[60] Thus, the Governor commanded Barker to lead his militia to Herne's Plantation and lodge there until one company from the perimeter, under the command of General James Moore II could join him. He ordered Barker to proceed along the trading path through Moncks Corner, and Moore set out upon a route north from the head of the Ashley River.[61] The well-conceived tactic allowed the converging routes to screen Goose Creek from invasion until the separate militias combined into a formidable force sufficiently large to meet individual war parties. Both militias departed within hours of each other to affect the strategy, "compel the allegiance of the Congarees," and turn the tide in that sector, unaware that hundreds of hostiles lay in wait.[62]

Captain Barker, a "brave young gentleman," with ninety white "men on Horseback and 12 Negroes,"[63] trotted north with out-riders galloping ahead. Most of Barker's scouts were local natives, long familiar with the Europeans who settled among them forty years earlier. However, by 1715, the Etiwan was the sole tribe in Goose Creek and it consisted of only two hundred and forty souls, and all eighty of the Etiwan men were, "bad souldiers [soldiers]." Nonetheless, most Goose Creek households, "kept an Indian," who came and went at will, sometimes disappearing for days or longer, to hunt and supply the planter's table with turkey, deer flesh and other wild game. Wateree Jack hunted for the Moore families for many years, and many knew him as a skilled woodsman, interpreter, and warrior. Barker expected Wateree Jack to muster with the others at the stone and to lead them into the wilderness as he did many times before.

59. Klingberg, 159. Francis LeJau wrote on May 21 that Barker departed on May 15, and did not know of Herne's fate at the time of his departure. See Klingberg, 159.
60. Poyas, 111, Klingberg, 160. Francis LeJau wrote that his "Onely [sic] Son is in our Camp 22 Miles from this Town."
61. Francis LeJau, son of the minister served as Moore's aide-de-camp, and participated in Chicken's pivotal charge. The path used by Moore was later improved and named *Gaillard Road*.
62. Crane, 172. The colonial policy was "playing one Indian tribe off against another..."
63. Crane, 172.

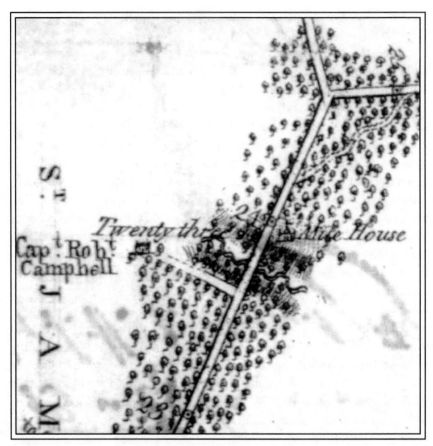

Figures 2.4 and 2.5: The author acquired this image and the one that follows from the Abernathie Map, drawn in 1785. The upper image shows the Road to Moncks Corner crossing Chapel Creek between the 23 and 24-mile stones, before branching from the Road to Strawberry Ferry. The lower image shows the Road to Charleston from the parsonage house to the Road to Strawberry Ferry. Not shown is the chapel of ease, erected at the camp by the road and creek. It may have been in ruins by time the map was drawn. Later named "Strawberry," and "Strawberry Chapel," it should not be confused with Strawberry Plantation nor the chapel, located overlooking the north bank of the western branch of the Cooper River.

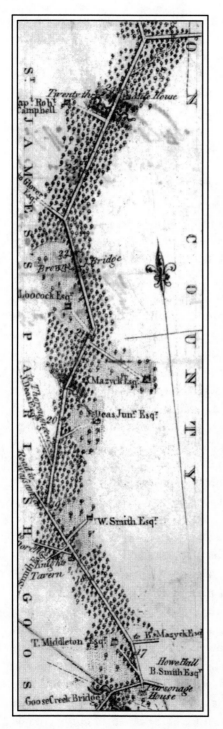

Little more than an hour after departing the Eighteen-Mile Stone, Barker and his men passed the twenty-two-mile marker near usually busy crossroads with converging plantation avenues, noisy tavern traffic, and stock corrals. Barker found it deserted except for defiant men raising the breastwork.[64] As news of the murders resonated, more volunteers rushed to prepare for the worst, and Barker edged his mount past the imposing stockade, and departed the tense neighborhood through its vulnerable gateway.

64. Francis Le Jau wrote on May 10, 1715 that Goose Creek plantations were deserted, but he met with his parishioners at "our camp 6 miles of me Noward [sic], the greatest part of their women and children are in town."The 23-mile road marker on the Road to Moncks Corner is six miles north of the parsonage.

After fording a creek and intersecting the Road to Strawberry Ferry, the cavalry entered St. John's Parish. From there the Road to Moncks Corner generally paralleled the western branch of the Cooper River until reaching its destination ten miles distant, where the path turned west. By early afternoon of May 16, Barker's men were trotting single file along the narrow packhorse trail, toward St. Stephens where more riders, including Edward Thomas and David Palmer joined the expedition and Wateree Jack cantered alone, miles ahead, rapidly closing onto his tryst.

WATEREE JACK

Wateree Jack was on the mission of his lifetime, and success depended upon his stealth and knowledge of the British strategy. That the natives murdered the Herne family at Barker's destination was not a morbid coincidence. Instead, the governor's plan put the family in peril, when Jack divulged the secret to his Wateree confederates who were on the warpath with Catawba allies. With the knowledge of the planned assault and its destination, the war party murdered the frontier family to eliminate all who may divulge their presence and prepared an ambush of each militia as it arrived at the crime scene, twisting the Governor's "divide and conquer" strategy to the advantage of the natives. Jack understood a successful ambush must commence early on Tuesday, and end quickly, ahead of Colonel Moore's timely convergence from the south and he knew both militia commanders well and expected them to arrive as ordered.

Two decades before, Colonel James Moore II was a boy and Captain Thomas Barker was a baby when someone plucked Jack from a skirmish field in North Carolina and sent him to Boochawee as a slave. Jack served James Moore I as a translator and hostler during many trading forays into the wilderness. At first, he walked and ran alongside the pack train, assessing the land with each of his footsteps and later counted the miles from his own pony that his master awarded. During those years, Jack watched young Moore grow into a man at Boochawee Hall and later inspected Thomas Barker after he married Rebecca, his master's youngest daughter. Jack accompanied both men through the Hills of Santee many times, as he had John Herne, who now lay bludgeoned and dead.

Eighteen years before in 1697, Jack accompanied John Herne and Robert Stevens from Boochawee in pursuit of horses in Virginia. The rapidly expanding packhorse business in South Carolina employed more animals than bred. Consequently, the price of the beasts of burden soared and James Moore I entrusted the traders and Jack with "one hundred pound Sterling in money," to ride to Virginia and return to Goose Creek with ponies.[65] "They travelled [sic] safe by the assistance of Indian Jack their Guide and Interpreter..." until hostile natives assaulted them while they slept one night in North Carolina. One native shot Robert Stephens and another bludgeoned him to death, "...his head bruised all to pieces." Another shot Jack, while Herne roused, ran and swam across a river to safety leaving Jack and the money behind.[66]

Wateree Jack, though severely wounded, managed to slip into the dark wearing nothing but a "blew [blue] shirt" and while the distracted natives were "rifling of Stephens," Jack stumbled through the night with a bullet in his thigh, throbbing and bleeding with every step. Without a weapon or provisions of any kind, Jack's chances of survival dimmed by the minute, but he persisted in weakness and pain for eleven days, consuming "what he could find on the bushes..." and sleeping fitfully when overcome with exhaustion. Moving always north, he eventually reached an outer Virginia settlement where a merciful family sheltered him.

A few days after the attack, John Herne convinced some deerskin traders to return with him to the camp to investigate the crime scene and perhaps recover the money. At the vandalized bivouac, he retrieved three of his horses grazing in the forest, some of the strewn currency, and Steven's mutilated "Corps [sic]." He dutifully sank the body in the river and with no sign of Jack, and fathoming no way the native survived the overwhelming odds, John Herne and his acquaintances turned again toward Carolina.

Within days, Jack strengthened sufficiently to move to a trading post where a surgeon extracted the shot from his muscle and he convalesced for several months. Finally, "perfectly cured," and restless for home, he accompanied eleven traders in need of a guide to South Carolina where he wished to "acquire his master."[67] "Indian Jack," led the troupe west through numerous native lands, translating as needed and assisting mightily with his own dangerous Wateree clan. The sojourners persisted to fording points near the shallower headwaters of the major rivers and moved ever south for more than a month, hunting and fishing every day for nourishment. They accomplished the 941-mile journey in thirty-seven days, resting each

65. Richard Traunter, *Travels of Richard Traunter of the Main Continent of America from Appomattox River in Virginia to Charles Town in South Carolina, Two Journals 1698, 1699* (Richmond, Virginia: Virginia Historical Society), 4, Alexander Moore produced typeset pages.
66. Traunter, 5.
67. Traunter

Sunday and rising to walk twenty to thirty miles daily until crossing the Santee River and turning east into familiar terrain. They acquired the more frequented trails leading from the Hills of Santee, through Moncks Corner and arrived at "Capt. Ja: Moor's" Boochawee Plantation on Monday, September 15, 1697. Now, almost two decades later, on a pleasant May morning in 1715, Jack trotted along the familiar path through the well-known "Sandy ground with Pine Trees..." onto the hills and upon the scene of murder.

Although most of Jack's life lay behind him, some of his years remained obscured. The trauma of battle when he was a boy, his capture on that skirmish field, his enslavement and painful discipline at Boochawee, and weeks of deprivation until his spirit fled, dulled his recall and muddled the memory and duration of his first years in Goose Creek. Nonetheless, he accepted his bondage long ago, his master thoroughly trusted him and he earned the title "Indian Warr [sic] Captain,"[68] after Moore manumitted him. Now a free man for twelve years, respected by white and red warriors, and intuitive of two worlds, Jack was skilled at the hands of wily and pugnacious James Moore I. However, recent lucidity brought conflicted convictions and recall of boyhood promises, and tribal allegiances haunted him as he lay in wait to murder James Moore II, the eldest son and Thomas Barker, the son-in-law of his deceased master.

JAMES MOORE I

James Moore I, the one time master of Wateree Jack died nine years earlier. Moore was an educated and ambitious young man who emigrated from Ireland by way of Barbados to serve as plantation manager for Lady Margaret Yeamans, wife of the governor of Carolina. He wed Margaret Berringer, the governor's stepdaughter[69] and acquired the 2400-acre Boochawee Plantation.[70] From Boochawee, Moore traveled the convenient

---

68. Klingberg, 152, Frances LeJau to the Secretary May 10, 1715. The Etiwan remained loyal to the colonists and received "3£ reward for enemy scalps." "Crowley," an Etiwan received a match coat after the war and "Robin, King of the Ittuan," received a coat, as well as native women and children slaves. George Chicken became an official trader after the war. William Treadwell Bull to the Secretary, 9-2-1715, states that Wateree Jack was an "Indian Warr[sic] Captain," SPGFP Letter Books, Series A, 1702-1737, V. 8-11, 95869/4 among the collections of SCHS.
69. Crane, 119.
70. Boochawee Manor was located in today's Greenview section of Goose Creek.

half-day horseback ride to Charleston where he kept quarters, but one mile from his avenue in the opposite direction, the road branched. One leg, the Road to Wassamassaw, extended ten miles to a swamp of the same title where Moore obtained a second land grant. The other leg of the road branched into the frontier. Thus, the principal trading route passed Moore's front door and predictably, he engaged in that lucrative business by first dealing directly with the natives, and later underwriting peddlers who foraged deep into the interior. He expanded his business by purchasing entire pack trains and chartering sea captains to rush the skins and peltries to European markets. He profited handsomely from those transactions, but he also branched into the nefarious native slave trade, which garnered greater returns, but cast him into bitter political disputes.

During his tenure at Boochawee, James Moore and his family flourished until there were four girls and six boys.[71] A grand manor replaced the small frontier settlement when a substantial two story brick home flanked by pleasure gardens featuring ponds, terraces, walkways, and ornamental plantings emerged.[72] A carefully tended orchard, a stand-alone kitchen, as well as barns, sheds, shops, stables, pens and coops supported the growing family, including more than 60 African and native slaves.[73] Stately Boochawee Hall and its demesne bespoke wealth, with hundreds of cattle and horses grazing freely, dozens of sheep and hogs fattening in pens, and wide fields of corn and rice, but native trade more than husbandry returned the immense fortune. Jack soon shone as a loyal translator and essential asset to Moore's lucrative enterprises and as Jack's frame fleshed into manhood, he emerged a skilled musketeer, accompanying Moore on each wilderness journey including one in search of precious metals in the distant mountains.

James Moore I accompanied Colonel Maurice Matthews on a trek to the Appalachian Mountains in pursuit of gold and silver. Ostensibly, Moore sought trade opportunities with the hill and mountain tribes, and although he returned empty-handed, he remained a "gentleman of good estate" in the Grand Council. He kept key alliances with Mathews and

71. Mabel L. Webber, contributor, "The First Governor Moore and His Children," SCHGM, 37: 5.
72. Cheves Papers, Land papers of Langdon Cheves, 1735-1932, 2/182/9, among the collections of SCHS. Langdon Cheves recorded, "extensive ruins of terraces, walks, ponds and signs of gardens," on the Boochaweee Tract.
73. Webber, 4. The Charleston County Inventory Book categorized the slaves, Works Project Administration (WPA).

nurtured support of the rising political party known as the "Goose Creek Men," composed of many of his neighbors.

James Moore I skillfully mixed politics and business by consistently opposing any law that slowed his quest for fortune and his avarice sullied and besmirched the Colonial government and defamed any feeble attempts to rectify unethical treatment of the Native Americans. Opponents questioned his unethical motives, some challenging his loyalty to England and claiming that he descended from Roger Moore, the hated leader of the Irish Rebellion. During one roaring debate, opponents derided him as "the heating Moore" and "the next Jehu of the party."[74] Undaunted, Moore grew wealthier, more influential, more determined, and never repentant. He named one son, "Maurice," the first name of his political ally, Maurice Matthews. He named another son, "Roger," and proudly titled a third son, "Jehu," all names with which some chided.

By the time the Goose Creek Men tightened their political grip on the colonial government and successfully maneuvered the ascent of Moore to the governor's chair in 1700, Wateree Jack was a free man, earning his liberty through years of loyalty, culminating with extreme bravery against Combahee Natives. As a free man, he shared the bounty returned with captives from each foray and Jack became wealthy in his own right. Consequently, when Governor Moore I enhanced his pugnacious reputation by leading 600 white and the same number of native mercenaries in an unsuccessful siege of the Spanish in St. Augustine in 1700, he returned with Jack and a fortune in captives. Despite the failure to dislodge their European enemies, the town people cheered him as a hero. Undaunted, he led another expedition the following year against the same foe in Guale (Georgia),[75] and again in 1703, against Apalachee Natives. Each time he returned with Jack and a fortune in bound souls.

James Moore I remained unapologetically in public service until he succumbed to fever in Charleston in 1706, at the age of 56.[76] He lived longer than most, and wisely prepared a last will and testament in which he characteristically violated traditional practices by refusing the time-honored principals of entail and primogeniture by ordering the division of

---

74. J. G. Stewart, "Letters from John Stewart to William Dunlop," SCHGM, 32: 24-28. Also see, Eugene M. Sirmans, *Colonial South Carolina: A Political History 1663-1763* (Chapel Hill, North Carolina: University of North Carolina Press, 1966), 41.

75. Webber, 2.

76. Webber, 4.

Boochawee among his ten children.[77] Margaret Moore, his wife received the plantation at Wassamassaw, as well as some slaves and two "Indian men," while the oldest son, James Moore II acquired two-ninths of Boochawee, amounting to less than 500 acres. Rebecca Moore, the youngest daughter, received Button Hall, which she brought to her union with Thomas Barker and the other sons and daughters acquired the remaining shares. Then, on May 17, 1715 James Moore II, son of a former governor and almost as tested as Jack, rode north ahead of one hundred cavalrymen, and Thomas Barker warily approached from the east.

AMBUSCADE

As the sun rose on Tuesday, May 17, Jack lay with his native brethren beneath felled and tousled trees, south of Herne's cabin near Eutaw Springs, later named "Barker's Savanna." Prior to that day, Barker never saw the twisted and uprooted forest looming before him because a "great Hurricane," felled the trees merely twenty months before. Reverend LeJau reported that the countryside was "thick" with felled "large trees," but Barker did not know the extent and depth of the destruction.[78] As a result, he blindly led his riders deep into the tangled thicket until concealed natives, hiding among the turned-up roots and twisted trunks and branches, encircled the riders. At a moment, Jack discharged his musket, knocking Barker from his mount and sparking an aimed volley.[79] The initial report killed the captain and shocked the others awake; but instantly more riders fell by trained musket fire, including Thomas and Palmer[80] and a moment again, stunned horsemen lay pierced by arrows, knives, and hatchets from all directions and bludgeoned with war clubs until twenty-seven "very pretty young men,"[81] lay crumbled and writhing on the ground. The stunned survivors dismounted in confusion to discharge their heavy muskets, but

---

77. Webber, 4.

78. Walter J. Fraser, *Lowcountry Hurricanes* (Athens, Georgia, The University of Georgia Press, 2006), 11. A hurricane felled trees across the trail in September 1713, twenty months before the ambush. Natives ambushed Barker on Tuesday, May 17, Klingberg, 159, Francis LeJau to Secretary, 5-21-1715.

79. William Treadwell Bull letter sited in, *"The Mystery of the Lost Prince,"* SCHM, 63: 25. Klingberg, 137, 163, Francis LeJau to the Secretary, 1-22-1714. A hurricane lasting twelve hours struck the South Carolina coast on September 5, 1713.

80. Hicks, 42. Natives wounded Edward Thomas and killed David Palmer.

81. Klingberg, 161, Francis Le Jau to John Chamberlain, 8-22-1715.

without leadership and more than one third of their comrades dead, dying, or moaning in pain, they quickly remounted into a retreat.[82]

Most blamed Catawbas for the ambuscade at Barker's Savannah, but before the sun reached its zenith that day, the natives disappeared with Jack into the twisted forest, leaving little evidence of the identification, size or destination of the party. When Colonel James Moore returned to garrison, the Catawba and other tribes moved unopposed within the northern defensive perimeter causing immense anxiety that sent frightening tales of real and imagined evils throughout St. Johns, St. Stephens and St. James, Goose Creek Parishes.

Francis LeJau remained steadfast at his duties after the attack at Pocotaligo, thirty-three days before. During the first weeks of May, he traveled between the camp and his parsonage but when an exhausted courier woke him near midnight on May 17 to report the death of Barker and his men, the aging priest quickly gathered his wife and daughters. Under a clear sky and by the light of a waning quarter moon, the minister and his family embarked upon a five-hour walk to Charleston. There he found refuge at the home of Commissary Gideon Johnson, a fellow priest and classmate from Trinity College, Dublin.

As Wednesday morning broke, the LeJau family was safer, but all of British South Carolina was in peril. That day, reports flew of "savages" probing Mulberry Plantation on the western branch of the Cooper River,[83] and the next day, reports swirled of war parties, eight miles southwest of Mulberry. Others saw natives stalking even closer to Goose Creek, until on May 20, three days after the ambush, colonials spotted "spies" near the breastwork at the camp.[84] No one identified Jack during these harrowing days, but most assumed that he was near, eager to lead his compatriots to fat larders, livestock and other coveted Goose Creek riches with which he was intimately familiar. Furthermore, as the month of June commenced, sightings became more frequent until a group of hostiles "batterd [battered] one of our small p[f]orts..." at Schenckingh's Cowpens.[85]

82. Klingberg, 159, Francis Le Jau to Secretary 5-21-1715. Francis LeJau received word of Barker's death at mid-night on Tuesday May 17, the same day of the attack. He departed immediately with wife and two daughters for Charleston. Post-war testimony contended that Wateree Jack was an abused slave who resented the English and LeJau reported 8-23-1715, that Captain Chicken defeated the war party that included Wateree natives on 6-13-1715.
83. Klingberg, 159. Francis LeJau letter to the Secretary, May 21, 1715
84. Klingberg
85. Klingberg. Francis LeJau letter to the Secretary, 5- 21- 1715 and 8-23-1715.

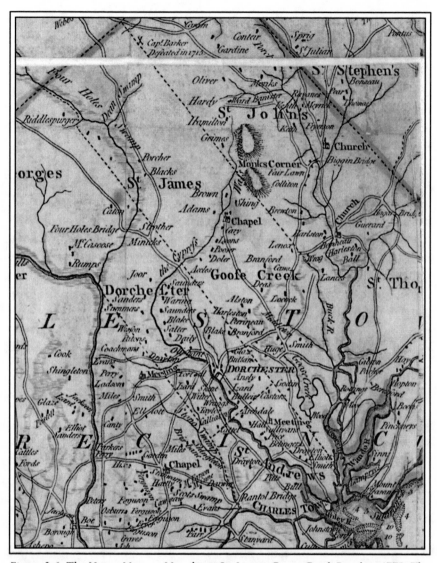

Figure 2.6: The Henry Mouzon Map shows St. James, Goose Creek Parish in 1775. The map shows Black Tom Bay, Wassamassaw Swamp and Cypress Swamp transecting the center of the parish. It shows *The Road to Moncks Corner* as well as the *Road to Strawberry Ferry*. It shows Chapel Creek flowing into Back River. It also shows a crossed-sword symbol above the white map defect line and left of upper center noting, "Capt. Barker Defeated in 1715."

SCHENCKINGH'S COWPEN

On June 5, four hundred and seventy warriors overwhelmed a little stockade, called Schenckingh's Cowpens merely thirty miles north of the camp at Chicken's Plantation.[86] Benjamin Schenckingh, the successful herdsman on Goose Creek, acquired additional properties on the Santee River where he developed a cattle range. At a wide and shallow section of the central Santee River, where the sandy bottom was sufficiently firm to ford cattle, he constructed holding corrals, fodder barns and quarters, and then reinforced the outpost against attack.[87]

On Saturday evening of June 4, Catawba, Cherokee, Wateree and possibly warriors of other tribes, surrounded Schenckingh's make-shift fort, defended by thirty black and white cattlemen and volunteers under the command of Captain James Reedwood.[88] The bulwarks were sturdy, made of heavy timber, and the stockade well supplied, and although startled by the sudden presence of natives, the wary defenders knew of the savagery at Herne's farm and the debacle at Barker's Savannah. Nonetheless, the natives outnumbered the cattlemen more than fifteen to one, and the captain searched for a way out of certain disaster. Captain Reedwood ended the stalemate when he disarmed his men and granted a parlay to a cadre of native leaders ostensibly to discuss peace.

The wily natives convinced the hopelessly out-matched captain to simply push open the heavy gate and admit them. According to an eyewitness, Reedwood complied, chanced an encounter to prevent the slaughter and, "suffered the Indians to come amongst them." Once in,

---

86. Oatis, "...another Cherokee-Catawba war party surrounded a make-shift South Carolinian fort on Benjamin Schenckingh's Plantation," 138. Klingberg, 161, Francis LeJau to John Chamberlain, 8-22-1715, writes that the same body of natives that attacked Barker overcame the defenders at Schenckingh's on June 5.

87. *The Mystery of the Lost Yamassee Prince*, 1962, SCHM, v. 63: 24. Here it is stated that "a small garrison of ours of about 20 men, one of them only escaping to tell the news." Reverend Francis LeJau believed that Wateree and "Saraws" accompanied this war party.

88. Susan Baldwin Bates, and Harriot Cheves Leland, ed., *Proprietary Records of South Carolina, V. III, Abstracts of the Records of the Surveyor General of the Province 1678-1698* (Charleston, South Carolina: The History Press, 2007), 72, 81, 84, 87, 88, 90, 95, 125, 163. The "Captain," was probably James Redwood, son of Isaac Redwood (sometimes Reedwood), who owned property near Schenckingh's Square in Charleston. "Sheniningh Ft." is indicated on the Santee River on *A New and Accurate Map of North and South Carolina...1747*. The map is among the collections of the North Carolina State Archives. Poyas lists James Redwood as overseer, 36.

the natives "...drew out their knives and tomahawks from under their Cloaths...."[89] When the trap sprung, war whoops alerted the forest to come alive with painted men wearing raven feathers in their hair. Warriors rushed from the forest to scale the walls while those within slaughtered all living things and the evening air filled with the blasts of muskets, choking gun smoke and the sickening thud of war clubs. The hostiles "knocked 22 of our men on the head, burnt and plundered the Garrison...."[90] During the melee, the natives took four "young lads"[91] including "Steven Ford's son"[92] prisoner, but not before "Wallace," a resourceful "Negro man," jumped the ramparts, dove into the river and escaped down stream. Wallace, born and reared at Benjamin Godin's Plantation on Goose Creek swam on many summer days in cool waters near the Goose Creek Bridge and now employed his swimming skill to evade capture. Once across the wide slow waterway he ran for his life toward the Cooper River plantations where he alerted the barricaded families of the invading horde.[93]

Prior to the assault, most families residing between the Santee River and Goose Creek departed by road or river to Charleston. However, some garrisoned at Wantoot Plantation on the upper reaches of the Cooper, a few hunkered with their Anglican missionary, Reverend Robert Maule and others found refuge at Mulberry "Castle," further down-stream. Daniel Donavan put his faith in his stout cabin and cowpen where he kept a large pack of fierce dogs "trained to kill and eat Indians."[94] However, no one expected the little garrisons to stop the warriors who easily tricked Herne's frontier family, humbled Barker's well-armed cavalry, and outwitted the cattlemen at Schenckingh's.

---

89. British Public Records Office (BPRO), V. 10: 266 Charleston 7-19-1715, George Rodd to Joseph Boone and Richard Beresford agents of the Province of London. The records are on microfilm among the collections of SCHS.

90. BPRO, Rodds to Proprietors, Charleston, 7-19-1715 states that 22 men were slain and other accounts state that as many as thirty men died.

91. Klingberg, 160, Francis LeJau to John Chamberlain, 8-22-1715.

92. BPRO, Rodds to Proprietors, Charleston, 7-19-1715, claims that "Steven Fords Son," was taken by the Cherokee from Schenckingh's and then removed to their village after departing the Catawbas.

93. BPRO, 7-19-1715, and *SCCHJ*, 8-16-1715, 442. The South Carolina Government rewarded "Wallace" with a "new hat and a shirt," for his "service to the Publick [sic]," because he escaped from Schenckingh's cowpens and spread the alarm.

94. David Ramsey, *The History of South Carolina from the First Settlements in 1670 to the Year 1808* (Charleston: Walker, Evans and Company, 1858), 90, 91. Also see Stoney, 21, Hicks, 31. The SCCHJ Wednesday, 11-21-1716, noted "...some of those white men who were in the late engagement at Daniel Donnovan's Cowpen..."

At Schenckingh's, native victors feasted on roasted beeves, took what they coveted, fired the stockade and departed with five captured porters. However, after the easy victory at the cowpen, the plunder, and arms stolen "from our poor People whom they had massacreed [sic] in all parts of the Province from the beginning," slowed their movements. Additionally, a group of indigenous women and children somehow attached to the hostiles, followed the camp and further slowed its passage.[95] Thirty miles north of Goose Creek, the war party laboriously traveled south, arriving at the camp three days later and three weeks behind Barker's defeated riders.

CONFRONTATION AT THE CAMP

Predictably, Thomas Barker's men returned home via the familiar route that carried them west, re-entering the parish through the breastwork where most of the company, humbled by defeat, joined the white defenders and the "Body of Negroes waiting for orders."[96] At the camp, the church minister believed "...our Chief Fort & best Body of Men lay...but 6 miles of my parsonage."[97] With Barker's re-enforcements, the number of men mounting the walls increased to more than one hundred, and as the summer heat intensified, they lay in the shade on high ground above the spring and wetlands waiting for the natives to assault from the north.

The defensive position was formidable. The little creek washing through the thick subtropical forest was no more than seventy feet wide and because of the drought was less than a foot deep, but wide soggy ground bordered it and the little flow-way connected two broader swamps that reached for miles. Moreover, the sturdy breastwork featured an elevated musket line aiming down upon the open expanse. Nonetheless, many temptations lay beyond the gateway fortification beckoning the natives onward.

95. Klingberg, 163, 164, LeJau to SPG Secretary 8-23-1715.

96. Klingberg, 153, Francis LeJau to the Secretary, " I continue with my family at my Parsonage endeavoring to do wt [sic] I can to Encourage my Parishioners whom I meet in our Camp 6 Miles of me Noward." Klingberg, p. 159 Francis LeJau to the Secretary 5-21-1715. Edward McCrady, *History of South Carolina Under Proprietary Rule, 1670-1719* (New York: Mcmillan, 1897), 536, Ramsey, 91 "After this advantage, a party of four hundred Indians came down as far as Goose creek [sic]. Every family there had fled to town, except in one place where seventy men and forty negroes [sic] had erected a breastwork and re-solved to remain and defend themselves." Klingberg, LeJau to SPG Secretary 8-16-1715.

97. Klingberg.

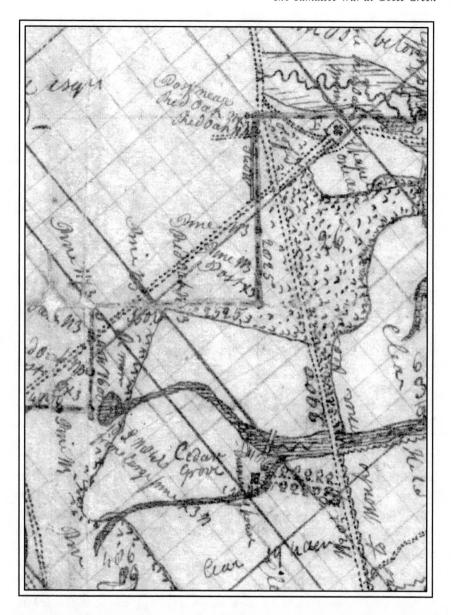

Figure 2.7: The plat detail describes a section of Chicken's Plantation (later called Cedar Grove Plantation). The Road to Moncks Corner divides the image north to south. The 23 Mile House is describes near the road at the top of the plat. Indicated at upper center is a creek, wetlands and a road bridge. The bridge shows the location of the breastwork. The tree-lined avenue leads from the road to the main house at lower center. The McCrady Plat number B-435/1335 is among the collections of the Register of Mesne Conveyance Office at the Charleston County Office Building, Charleston, South Carolina.

Figure 2.8: A New & Accurate Map of the Provinces of North & South Carolina, Georgia &c. Drawn from late surveys and regulated by astronl. Observants [sic]. By Emannuel Bowen, 1747, shows "Sheniningh Ft." (Schenckingh's Cowpens) on the "Congaree or Santee River," and Wantoot on the headwaters of the Cooper River.

Six hundred yards behind the musket-line commenced an avenue leading ¼ mile to George Chicken's home-site and four hundred yards farther commenced the eastern route to wealthy Thorogood Plantation. More plunder opportunities lay beyond those two avenues where paths to houses, barns and pastures intersected the road almost every ¼ mile through the eastern parish to the bridge and beyond. The breastwork was everyone's best hope for survival because it was stout and well positioned on the shallow waterway.

The creek connected two wide swamps sprawling east to the Cote Bas Peninsula and west through Thorogood. The eastern detour skirted north of the wetlands and terminated ten miles distant at the confluence of the deep Back and Cooper Rivers. The western choice avoided the floodplain by arching above the Thorogood wetlands before rising to dry ground nine miles away, and less than ten miles west of Wassamassaw Swamp. Consequently, the warriors could invade frontally, across a wet and open killing field and into the barrels of muskets, divert across soft muddy and wide wetlands around the obstacle, or walk on dry ground above Thorogood to spoils unknown. A series of recent events forced a decision.

The war party consisting of Catawba, Cherokee, Wateree and other warriors was flushed with easy victories, and encouraged further when runaway slaves reported that the English were despaired and retreated. However, a series of setbacks dampened the native enthusiasm as they neared the camp. First, Colonel Edward Hyrne, commanding the garrison at Wantoot Plantation on the western branch of the Cooper River,[98] surprised and killed a group of natives who stayed behind feasting at Schenckingh's corral. He did not kill many, but his action quashed the conviction that the English would no longer fight. Secondly, though nourished with plenty of stolen beef, the natives needed gunsmiths to "mend their Arms [arms]."[99] Such logistical problems kept them from assaulting the well fortified Wantoot Plantation and Mulberry Castle, and hastened their descent to Goose Creek. At the St. James, Goose Creek Parish line, another setback appeared in the form of runners from the interior. Native couriers brought word that Cherokee tribal leaders reached a peace agreement with the colonists, and called their warriors home.[100] Consequently, seventy experienced bowmen departed within three miles of the little fortress, decreasing the party to less than four hundred warriors.[101] Additionally, after traveling one more hour, the scouts came upon the biggest setback of all, when they assayed the looming fortress at the camp.

Spies reported defensive walls rising weeks before, but only when they approached the bulwark did the hostiles see the armed men at the walls and assay their resolve. The mounted defenders dispelled the lies whispered by spies and dashed all expectations of an easy passage to the livestock and other plantation treasures. The English were not despaired or in retreat but emboldened by Barker's cavalrymen and re-enforced by determined Africans.

---

98. Edward and Elizabeth Hyrne lost their Medway home in 1711 for failing to pay the mortgage and relocated to land on the western branch of the Cooper River.
99. Klingberg, 162, Francis LeJau to John Chamberlain, 8-23-1715. BPRO V 30: 478 Charleston, 11-30-1715, S. Molyneuse to William Popple Esq. He writes that the natives needed nothing because, "a little parched corn and puddle water is good victuals for them and fattens them like hogs."
100. Milling, 270, Oatis, 138. Oatis contends that the Cherokee departed for their villages from the "outskirts of the Goose Creek Parish."
101. The records estimate the party to consist of 470 warriors when they attacked Schenckingh's. Colonel Hyrne killed some at the cow pens when they remained behind, seventy Cherokee departed near the parish line, and an unknown number of noncombatant women and children accompanied. Thus, the band invading Goose Creek consisted of less than four hundred warriors. The Cherokee warriors took one captive with them when they returned to their villages.

Hurried legislation allowed the arming of trusties against native attacks, and in Goose Creek, there were many trusted Africans. Some of the old Goose Creek homesteads were hearths of multi-generational slaves, who, as members of extended frontier families, defied the "savages."[102] Consequently, "Every family had fled to town, except in one place," at the camp, where reinforced with Barker's survivors, "... seventy white men and forty Negroes had surrounded themselves [sic] with a breast-work, and resolved to remain and defend themselves in the best manner they could."[103]

The black and white sharpshooters proffered a stubborn defense with musketeers atop the firing line aiming down upon the wide wetland from protected positions and near supplies of gun powder, while the sprawling swamp water slowed attack movements and spoiled the natives' dry powder until the incursion was "... fortunately checked."[104] Oddly, some accounts of that frightful day tell of "savages," overrunning the redoubt, and other reports contend that the defenders were "barbarously slaughtered." These stories sprang from the Schenckingh assault five days earlier, and some incorrectly associated the accounts with the encounter at the camp.

The duration and extent of the attack and the number of casualties are unknown, but no natives penetrated into Goose Creek, or vandalized any property. Instead, the accumulating setbacks weighed heavily upon the native warriors and forced them to retreat on June 11.[105] The natives rested above Thorogood Plantation Saturday night and proceeded Sunday morning, on June 12 in a wide sweep to avoid the Thorogood Swamps, from where they eventually turned southwest toward the Cypress/Wassamassaw waterway.[106] All day Sunday, as the natives labored beneath the considerable weight of plunder, Captain George Chicken's rangers reconnoitered the diaspora as it unwittingly closed within range of the main body of his militia.

---

102. Carroll, 197. Also see Ramsey, 91. Ramsey states, "this whole garrison was barbarously butchered."

103. McCrady, v.1, 536-537, "When the Indians attacked them, they were discouraged and rashly agreed to terms of peace; and having admitted the enemy within their works, this poor garrison were [sic] barbarously butchered, after which the Indians advanced still nigher to town..."

104. It is difficult to swab, load and ram a single shot musket without standing upright and placing the wooden stock on dry ground. Thus, the sprawling swamps were a formidable deterrent to musketeers.

105. Jasper and Susanna Ashworth probably evacuated Thorogood ahead of the native invasion by way of their avenue intersecting the main road two miles above the bridge. A second allee connected their settlement with the Road to Moncks Corner near the camp. They raised livestock and began rice culture by the time of the Yamassee War.

106. Henry AM Smith, "The Town of Dorchester, South Carolina, A Sketch of its History," SCHM, 6: 62-95.

Figure 2.9: The photograph shows Chapel Swamp in the spring of 2004. Shallow swamps reached in both directions from the Road to Moncks Corner at the camp. The image is among the collections of the author.

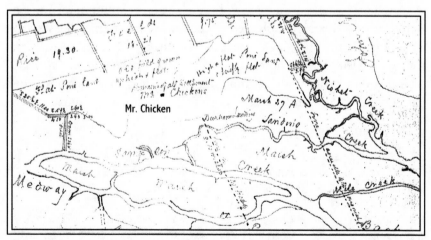

Figure 2.10: A survey conducted in 1784 produced the drawing showing the "Remains of Old Settlement Mr. Chicken [']s," east of the breastwork at the camp, as well as the wetlands and creeks that prevented native advances beyond the breastworks. George Chicken Jr. owned the settlement indicated here. Henry A.M. Smith copied the plat and it is among the collections of the South Carolina Historical Society.

CAPTAIN GEORGE CHICKEN, "BRAVE AND BOLD"

Captain George Chicken acquired the location of the invaders as they approached from the north and he improved the position of the militia by riding toward them from the Edisto to a place called "The Ponds."[107] At "The Ponds," three small lakes on Edward Percival's Plantation remained flooded even in dry weather, and here his formidable cavalry force, with five carriage cannons and caissons, watered, grazed and rested their large herd of warhorses for two days in preparation for battle. Two companies of Goose Creek Militia, one under the command of Captain Paul Lebas and the other led by Richard Harris, withdrew from the garrison at John Woodward's Plantation at the head of the Ashepoo River in Colleton County days before to shore-up Captain George Chicken at the Ponds.[108]

The natives approached through a deserted section of the central St. James, Goose Creek Parish, below the Wassamassaw homesteads. During peaceful times, few resided in that section, and now it was empty, but the large invasion force presented an imminent threat to distant settlers in several directions. The gritty defense at the camp halted penetration from the north, but no such defensive obstacles stood on the western front to keep warriors from debauching to the heart of Goose Creek. The Road to Wassamassaw conversely led to Goose Creek and the Road to Dorchester accessed the center of the planting community of Ladson. Both paths, although poorly kept, accessed many frontier homesteads including Abraham Fleury's vineyards less than two hours away. From Fleury's settlement, the hostiles could intrude further to vandalize the emerging estates of John and Ann Gibbes, and neighbors Benjamin and Jane Gibbes,[109] or continue to the central settlements of Button Hall,

107. Yearbook, 315, note 2, 324; Francis LeJau to the Secretary, 8-22-1715, Bull to the Secretary, 8-10-1715, SCHM, *Mystery of the Lost Prince*, 1962, v. 63: 24. SCCHJ, 8-16-1715.

108. Yearbook of the City of Charleston, ed. Langdon Cheves, (Charleston, South Carolina, 1894), 315, note 2, 324. Lejau to the Secretary, August 22, 1715. Rodd to Boone and Beresford, July 19, 1715. Also see the Post and Courier Newspaper (Charleston, South Carolina) February 10, 2003. An inventory of items stored at the fortifications at the Ponds conducted in 1732 listed 30 old muskets and 5 carriage guns.

109. Benjamin Schenckingh owned the Goose Creek cattle plantation, as well as the cow pens on the Santee River.

Boochawee, Howe Hall, Schenckingh's[110] and the Oaks. However, Captain George Chicken hurried his militias into position.

As his scouts shadowed the invaders, the captain finalized a plan to screen the homes, while delivering a deadly blow. He deployed his one hundred and twenty horsemen into three columns, and led them four miles north of Percival's to a mixed forest east of the Cypress/Wassamassaw wetlands.[111] He sent the eastern column to screen any movements toward the Goose Creek plantations, and directed the western column to prevent retreats into the swamps.[112] With companies moving parallel to the enemy, he "brave and bold,"[113] intended to lead personally the central column into the middle of the envelopment with canon and musketry ablaze.[114]

Captain Chicken was a quiet and patient man, honed by lonely months in the wilderness, and he observed as keenly as the best native scouts did. Indeed, some chastened the Christian Chicken for his heathen habits and his apparel afore the line of battle was no exception. As did his militiamen, he wore work clothing, but unlike most of them, he donned leggings tied to a hip cinch, and preferred moccasins for walking rather than shoes or boots for riding. That hot day he wore a simple blouse with a sash tie and unlike some Captains, who donned red coats, he brandished his leadership via a scarf tightly wrapped around the brim of his wide felt hat.

As he "lay in ambuscade,"[115] flushed with anticipation and the

110. BPRO, V10: 266, 7-19-1715, Letter to Proprietors. Some Native Americans assisted Chicken as scouts. Black and white cavalrymen participated. The location of the battle is near today's New Hope Community.
111. BPRO, V10: 266, 7-19-1715, Letter to Proprietors. Some Native Americans assisted Chicken as scouts. Black and white cavalrymen participated. The location of the battle is near today's New Hope Community.
112. Ibid. and see Letter from a Gentleman in Charles Town to the Carolina Agents in London, 319.
113. William Treadwell Bull to the Secretary, SPGFP Letter Books, Series A, 1702-1737, v. 8-11, 95869/4 among the collections of the South Carolina Historical Society, Charleston, South Carolina, July, 1715, and *Mystery of the Lost Yamassee Prince*, 24.
114. Klingberg, 163, Francis LeJau letter to Secretary of SPG, 5-21-1715. Francis LeJau relayed that the Diaspora numbered between 300 and 400 souls. With that estimate and discounting women and children, the number of battle- ready warriors may have decreased to less than 300 by the time of Chicken's assault.
115. Douglas Summers Brown, *The Catawba Indians: The People of the River* (Columbia,: University of South Carolina Press, 1966), 21, Klingberg, 162-163, Francis LeJau to SPG Secretary, 8-22-1715.

oppressive, sticky heat of the June 13 afternoon, the plan conceived by the accomplished Indian fighter unraveled when two native scouts approached within yards of Chicken's position. As the native scouts trotted closer, bent low and leaning forward to balance their muskets, shots rang, killing both and divulging the position of the central militia line. Chicken instinctively mounted, signaled his riders, turned and prodded his horse to a steady trot to close within seventy yards of the enemy, before the thirty-year-old Scotsman drew his saber, kicked his heels into his steed and leaned into a furious gallop toward the center of the enemy.

The natives were excellent guerrilla fighters, but Chicken surprised them with his rapid assault and the approaching warriors wilted from repeated volleys of canon grapeshot and disciplined muskets that railed from four o'clock that afternoon until late evening. Chicken commanded the field throughout the engagement. He ordered dismounted musket volleys and remounted his men to charge into the fray where his cavalrymen saber-slashed the wounded and the stunned. He ordered retreat behind his canons and drilled back again into dismounted musket lines before he stormed anew into the uncoordinated resistance. When the smoke of the powder and the haze of adrenaline cleared, the enemy was hiding among the cypress and tupelo trees, the battlefield lay littered with stolid, still and wreathing bodies and the day belonged to Chicken.[116]

The militia chased the warriors through the wetland, taking some prisoners, but withdrew as the dense forest darkened after nine o'clock that evening. The next morning they counted the remains of more than forty indigenous souls,[117] including several women and children. There were only a few militia casualties including John Carmichael who convalesced six months with severe wounds.[118] Also, among the survivors were four exceedingly grateful Euro-American prisoners who the natives captured at Schenckingh's Cowpen and kept alive for some unfathomable reason.[119]

116. George Chicken, *A Journal from Carolina 1715*, in the Charleston Yearbook, 1893, 325, foot note: Colonel Chicken charged the natives near the place where "…Wassamas-saw Road crosses the heads of Cypress Swamp…"
117. Various sources reported a 40 to 60 body count.
118. Francis LeJau reported sixty native deaths and wrote, "…we lost one white man & a Negro." See Frank J. Klingberg, 161, Francis LeJau letter 8-22-1715. Also see, SC-CHJ, Assembly no. 13, 2-28-1715, 2-16-1716/17, microfilm, 5-11-1716, 103, "…John Carmichael was about four months incapable of getting his living, by means of wounds he received in Col. Chicken[']s fight"
119. It is likely that the natives kept the captives alive to use as porters and later for ransom.

The captain executed the stunned native prisoners[120] and collected from the littered battlefield "...all of their ammunition & baggage & a considerable number of their Arms, which through Haste in flight they threw from them."[121]

Figure 2.11: The photograph shows a section of Wassamassaw Swamp in March 2002. The image is among the collections of the author.

The Yamassee War continued, but Chicken's charge proved to be the coup-de-grace of the struggle. At its apogee, the confrontation pitted the greatest native alliance in colonial history against a world empire, creating wide fissures in the foundation of the colony until the British reign in South Carolina almost collapsed. At the time, the English blamed their archenemies, Spain and France for instigating the bloody attacks, but prevailing wisdom assigned the fault to unscrupulous English traders and greedy settlers who cheated and

120. SCCHJ, Assembly no. 12, 9-22-1713-11-8-1715. Saturday, 8-20-1715, 441, 442.
"That Mr. Benj. Waring for the use of his Indian slave be allowed 30 [?]...in consideration of taking a Catawba Indian alive, who was afterwards killed by order of Captain George Chicken."
121. William Treadwell Bull letter cited in, *The Mystery of the Lost Prince*, SCHM, 1962, v. 63: 24.

abused the natives, and encroached upon the promised native lands until the tribes despaired and conspired to push the intruders into the sea.[122] Mercifully, the crescendo of the violence that took approximately three hundred colonial lives and a greater number of natives fell off precipitously that summer.

The Catawbas retreated through the wetlands and followed trails west to their villages. They soon asked for terms, and although a perilous attack by other tribes the next month in the southern sector countered their defeat at Wassamassaw, the natives never re-acquired the psychological edge that propelled their earlier victories, and bonded their heterogeneous families.

Dispatch riders galloped across the Goose Creek Bridge with news of the outbreak of the dreadful war on Sunday morning April 17, 1715. Eight weeks hence, Captain George Chicken halted the native advance when, at four o'clock in the afternoon on June 13, 1715, he charged ahead of the Goose Creek Militia into the center of the Catawba war party and drove the interlopers into retreat. Now the bridge conveyed the conscripted militias home from the frontier in pursuit of their unkempt forests and fields.

A CALENDAR OF EVENTS FOR SPRING 1715:

April 15: Friday, Natives assault the emissaries at Pocotaligo

May 1: Sunday, Rumors spread about war parties in the Santee Region

May 10: Tuesday, Reverend LeJau laments the threat to his parish

May 14: Saturday, Natives attack the Herne family at their frontier home

May 15: Sunday, Captain Thomas Barker departs for the Herne settlement

May 17: Tuesday, Natives ambush Thomas Barker

May 18: Wednesday, Francis LeJau takes his family to Charleston

May 20: Friday, Defenders spot native scouts near the breastwork at the camp

June 5: Sunday, Natives overrun Schenckingh's Cowpens

---

122. The Yamassee War was another in a series of proxy wars in which Spain, France and England used Native-Americans to vie for the control of the natural resources of North America.

June 6-10: Hostiles travel from the Santee River toward the camp near the northern edge of the St. James, Goose Creek Parish

June 10: Friday, Seventy Cherokee warriors depart near the St. James, Goose Creek Parish line

June 11: Saturday, The war party diverts from the breastwork at the camp

June 13: Monday, Goose Creek Militia defeats the Catawba war party near the Cypress/Wassamassaw wetlands

CHAPTER 3

Gateway to Sacred Places

Although George Chicken's charge in June of 1715 was the prelude to normalcy, neither the Native Americans nor anyone else perceived it as such, and fear and pessimism pervaded the typically hot and humid July and August. As the summer waned, Goose Creek plantations remained deserted with unplanted fields and doomsayers portended famine. However, the frontier remained silent through August and soon signs of confidence shone in displaced individuals and families re-crossing the Goose Creek Bridge in search of their disrupted lives.

During the last week of August, General James Moore released Benjamin Dennis from garrison duty to reopen his tiny church-school near the bridge. Tired and frail, the young schoolmaster found the deserted parsonage and academy undisturbed allowing him to stow his heavy musket, pull his saddle and paltry possessions off his battle steed and turn the mount out to graze upon knee-high pasture grasses. His horse contented, Dennis carried a familiar straw mattress from his stifling cabin and lay beneath a spreading oak. There, in familiar shade, he slept more soundly than he had for months, briefly ignoring the nagging ache in his thigh that tortured his every move at Wassamassaw.[123]

Within days of his return to the evacuated neighborhood, the exhausted teacher requested reassignment, complaining of few students

---

123. Benjamin Dennis fractured his thigh soon after arriving in "Boochaw [sic]," Goose Creek. The injury left him with a painful and chronic limp. On August 25, General Moore discharged Dennis from the garrison to continue teaching 10 students. Benjamin Dennis informed the SPG June 20, 1716, that his school increased to 15 pupils with "one half Cherokee boy." See SPGFP series A, volume XI, 163 and series B, volume IV, 138.

in the desolate land and explaining, "I have suffered enough for the service of this place, being quite worn out w[i]th misfortunes, Disappointments and sickness."[124] However, no reply was forthcoming and by early fall more families crossed over the bridge, including Reverend LeJau, his wife and daughters arriving on October 28. Soon, small groups of citizen-soldiers, released from stockade and patrol duties, escorted their loved ones from Charleston to their Goose Creek homes where they exhausted every hour of the dwindling autumn sun reordering their fences, coops, sheds and barns, and gleaning the cluttered forests and weedy fields.

Captain George Chicken garrisoned at Wassamassaw, picketing the frontier until Colonel Maurice Moore joined him. Maurice, brother of James Moore, arrived from North Carolina in July with one hundred colonials and a company of Tuscarora.[125] During his tenure at the Wassamassaw garrison, Maurice Moore depended greatly upon Captain John Herbert and recently promoted Colonel George Chicken, both accomplished Indian fighters. That winter, those three officers led three hundred men into the backcountry on a daring mission to show force, and parlay an alliance with the Cherokee.[126]

During that exceedingly cold season, Colonel Moore, and Chicken, Herbert and John Pight with his "negro" company and his "Indens [Indians],"[127] successfully shored up native alliances in western South Carolina. By the end of March, they were home and cautiously optimistic about the frontier that remained uneventful, except for excessive rain forcing the hillsides into early bloom.[128]

124. "Mr. Benjamin Dennis to the Secretary, Boochaw near Goose Creek, South Carolina, September 2, 1715," SPGFP Letter Book, Series A, 1702-1737, v. 8-11, 95869/4 at the South Carolina Historical Society, Charleston, South Carolina. Schoolmaster, Benjamin Dennis returned from garrison duty in August 1715.
125. Born and reared at Boochawee Hall, Maurice Moore was well versed in the habits of South Carolina natives.
126. George Chicken, Chicken Journal, *A Letter from Carolina in 1715*, see George Chicken notes entered in his journal on November 27, December 25, December 30, 1715 and January 31, 1716. The parties reached a mutual defense agreement on January 31, 1716 and Chicken returned to Goose Creek during the following weeks.
127. Chicken Journal, Friday January 13, 1716. The winter of 1716 was so abnormally cold that the River Thames in England froze.
128. Chicken Journal, George Chicken Journal, Yearbook 1894. 128. Chicken Journal, George Chicken Journal, Yearbook 1894. 127. Chicken Journal, George Chicken Journal, Yearbook 1894.

Michael J. Heitzler, Ed.D.

REVEREND DOCTOR FRANCIS LEJAU

Reverend Doctor Francis LeJau rose early, on Easter Sunday, April 12, 1716 to greet the day from his kitchen garden. He typically enjoyed a solitary walk through the glebe in the early hours, and though his buried seeds showed no signs of life, ferns sent tender asparagus shoots overnight above the temperate earth, as if defying chances of late frosts. That morning he felt his own confidence surge as his world gradually returned to normal. Spring rains scented his fields where Arthur Middleton sent two stout Africans the previous week to spread manure, and tomorrow he expected them to return to mound the corn rows, as they did each spring of his nine-year tenure. The humble priest accredited that type of charity and the mercy of God for seeing his family through the perils of war, the memories of which were fading into a terrible dream. A year ago, from where he stood, he watched frightened families noisily flee across the Goose Creek Bridge on creaking, overloaded wagons. Now, he listened as his beloved wife, his only son and two daughters, stirred from their sleep, and Mr. Dennis, the clumsy schoolmaster rustled next door.

The Reverend grew more hopeful as he unlocked the great double front church door, threw open the two on the sides, donned his cassock, collected his vestments from the small robbing closet under the balcony stairway, and prepared the chancel for the second Easter mass. The previous spring, dreadful news from Pocotaligo sullied that celebration, but now he felt renewed. He expected a thankful congregation in greater numbers than ever, and he trusted that some of the newly famous wartime personalities, such as his churchwarden, Lieutenant General James Moore, Colonel George Chicken and Captains Thomas Smith, and Arthur Middleton would attend. He hoped they stayed after the service to visit before departing for lunch at the Oaks, as was their recent custom.[129] Food was dear,[130] but it was

129. George Chicken, *A Journal from Carolina*, Sunday, 11-27-1715, Chicken noted in his journal, "This day I left my own house and came to Boochawee to Colonel Moore's [house]...From there we [Chicken, Moore and Thomas Smith] went to church and after church was done we went to Captain Middleton's and dined with him. After dinner we set out for the Ponds." James Moore resided at Boochawee Hall, Thomas Smith resided near the head of Foster Creek at Howe Hall, Arthur Middleton resided at the Oaks Plantation near the parsonage and George Chicken lived between the 22 and 23-mile markers on the Road to Moncks Corner. The men successfully shored-up relations with the Cherokee and returned to Goose Creek by Easter 1716.
130. "We are ready to eat each other up for want of provisions," wrote Richard Beresford 4- 27- 1716. House Journal 11-14-1716. That spring, Abraham Dupont wrote to a rela-

the habit of the parishioners to bring something for a noon meal and share it in the shade of the budding hickory trees. The minister depended upon the generous support of the congregation and bemoaned the loss of John Gibbes, a devoted benefactor who died four years before. LeJau lamented, "I must arm myself with patience and for want of a potent friend must submit to see neither my church nor house finish'd [sic]."[131] Unyielding, he optimistically expected the children to run and play as usual, while the adults laughed and gossiped. It was a beautiful day, a holy day, the busiest day of his canonical year, and revolution was in the air.

REVOLUTION

Benjamin Schenckingh tried to avoid politics, especially talk of "revolution," but the war fractured his confidence in the hapless Proprietors. He rebuilt his cattle herd on the Santee River and increased his Goose Creek property when he married Margaret Moore, oldest daughter of James and Elizabeth, and added her inherited lands to his.[132] The couple remained on their creek-side range near the church until retiring to Charleston eighteen years later,[133] but not until he rallied with his neighbors to oust the incompetent Lord Proprietors.[134]

Colonel George Chicken seldom harbored thoughts of revolution, but on that crisp morning, he felt invigorated. He departed his plantation astride a spirited mount leading a wagon piloted by his nine-year old son George Jr. Aboard the wagon rode his wife Catharine with their children, Catharine, William, Thomas and Frances. Another wagon followed with Edward Keating and his bride Mary who resided near the twenty-three

tive in France that, "Indians made war, laying waste to ½ country…we had to abandon planting."
131. John Gibbes Sr. died in 1711 before the sanctuary received its first congregation and his son John Gibbes Jr. took up his father's work. However, eight more years and a war intervened before artisans completed the sanctuary in 1719. Nelson, 269, Waring 9, Poyas, 190.
132. South Carolina Department of Archives and History (SCDAH), Columbia, South Carolina, Series S213019, volume 0038, p. 0423, item 04.
133. Benjamin and Margaret Schenckingh purchased the original Boochawee house in 1712. General Moore resided next door at his "Boochawee Manor" on 900 acres south of Mount Holly Plantation.
134. Michael Heitzler, *Boochawee Plantation Land and Legacy in Goose Creek* , SCHM, January-April 2010, v. 111, numbers 1-2: 40. South Carolina Gazette, Feb. 24, 1733, on microfilm, Charleston County Library, Charleston, South Carolina.

mile road marker. The two families often traveled together for safety and convenience and near the end of their two-hour trek, James Moore II and his loved ones joined the procession at their avenue near the seventeen-mile marker. From there, George Jr. surrendered the reigns to his mother and walked the remaining mile with the Moore boys, James III, John and little Jehu, who were too proud to accompany the women and girls atop the bumpy wagons.

When James Moore II arrived at church that Sunday, he was the most influential celebrity in Carolina. He was a war hero, Common House member, and son of a governor, but above all, he personified revolution. The assembly voted the August before, to create and pay an armed force consisting of one lieutenant general (James Moore II), and one colonel (George Chicken)[135] along with lieutenant colonels, majors and captains. Furthermore, the assembly organized six hundred white soldiers under ten captains and four hundred "negroes" with a captain for each cadre of sixty men, all of who were successful in wresting a peace treaty with the powerful Cherokee. Consequently, Lieutenant General Moore and Colonel Chicken led the long-established "Goose Creek Men" political faction as well as the provincial army. They undoubtedly reigned as the most dynamic pair in Carolina and within that formidable context, Moore, Chicken and their allies conspired to affect a revolution to oust the Proprietary Governor from Carolina and secure a royal replacement from the King of England.[136]

The distant Lord Proprietors grew increasingly unpopular as talk of rebellion swirled beneath the shade trees, and the Easter morning warmed, portending another hot and humid summer. Now the emboldened citizenry expected Moore to guide them in peace as he so ably lead in war. The Lord Proprietors failed to come to the aid of the stricken colonials during their darkest hours and,[137] and three years later, James Moore II ascended to the

135. SCCHJ, Assembly no. 12, 9- 22-1713-11- 8-1715, Microfilm, p. 441. The record referred to "Col [Colonel] George Chicken ..." on Saturday, 8-20-1715. The Common House Journal the previous day referred to him as Captain George Chicken.

136. Poyas, 36. The "Goose Creek Men," in addition to Moore and Chicken included Thomas Smith, Peter St. Julien, Thomas Smith, Jr., Benjamin Schenckingh, John Newe, Benjamin Godin, Henroyda Inglish, Major Robert Daniel, Arthur Middleton, Ralph Izard, Robert Gibbes , Edward Hyrne, and Benjamin Mazyck. Nathaniel Johnson later joined the group and became one of the most influential leaders.

137. BPRO, 2-3-1719/20, Letter to the King enumerates grievances against the Lord Proprietors and asks for relief.

governor's office and held it until the first royal administrator arrived the following spring.[138]

Prior to riding back to North Carolina, Maurice, the younger Moore, flooded his Boochawee boyhood home with outrageous laughter and bravado, desperately needed by his sister, Rebecca who still reeled from the murder of her husband. She returned to Button Hall and remarried seven years later. There, she helped her son, Charles, and her new husband, William Dry, build a showcase rice plantation. The successful couple retired to Cape Fear, North Carolina, in 1734 to be near her brothers, Maurice and Roger.

Rebecca never forgot her handsome Captain Thomas Barker or Wateree Jack, the man who murdered him, but no reliable news told of the spy after the awful ambush in the twisted forest. The Colonial Assembly confirmed that Wateree Jack was the "...author of most of ye mischief they have done us,"[139] and although no one ever identified the body of the native mole, most hoped that Colonel Chicken settled the score with his decisive charge.

A SACRED PLACE

When Colonel Chicken returned from the frontier during the winter of 1716, and the governor relieved him of emissary duty, he undertook numerous chores at his neglected plantation. Chicken rounded-up his horses, cattle, sheep and other livestock that free-ranged all winter. He sought the colts and calves to acquaint them with barns, corrals, and branding irons, but he also found the breastwork on high ground above the creek, spanning both sides of the Road to Moncks Corner near the avenue to his house.

A year before, as war fever pitched, Reverend LeJau rode to the fortress at the camp on Chicken's Plantation[140] to bring news and sacraments to the determined souls who remained after sending their loved ones to town.[141] After Colonel George Chicken reported to his Wassamassaw

---

138. In 1719, the Assembly removed the Proprietary Government and invited the King to send a Royal Governor. James Moore II served as Governor of South Carolina during the transition.

139. Cecil Headlam, ed. *Calendar of State Papers, Colonial Series, American and the West Indies, 1716-1717* (London, 1922), 221. Committee of the Common House of Assembly, report to Boone and Beresford, 8- 6-1716.

140. Klingberg, 159, Francis LeJau to Secretary, 5-21-1715.

141. Klingberg.

assignment and Captain Thomas Barker departed toward his fate, black and white volunteers transformed the forests at Chicken's camp into a sturdy stronghold, from where they repelled the native assault on Saturday, June 11. The details of that day remain obscure, but Reverend LeJau lamented that among the deaths in his parish that year were "20 Left in the fields of Battle and buryd [sic] there…" Undoubtedly, survivors interred the bodies of fallen defenders at the camp, where LeJau prayed ten days before it erupted as a battlefield.[142]

Understandably, the colonel awarded the hallowed ground at his plantation for a sacred place of worship,[143] and there, Doctor Francis LeJau, the academic missionary with a French accent,[144] and Colonel George Chicken, the highland warrior with a Scottish brogue,[145] promised to raise a chapel on the high ground beneath the tall shade trees to memorialize their fallen kinsmen and bondsmen.

Back home at the parsonage, Reverend LeJau greeted bedraggled families every day throughout that year as they crossed over the long causeway and bridge. For many, the little wooden passage was a welcomed portal to normalcy, but a dreadful uncertainty and rumors of danger persisted. Within weeks of the dedication of the site for the chapel of ease and a year after the gallant charge at Wassamassaw, Reverend LeJau complained of, "…barbarous Ennemy [sic] in Small partyes [sic] of 3 or 5 or 6 [who] make incursions every week…".[146] LeJau reported that he and his family, "…expect[ed] every hour to be alarmed out of our [their] houses and forced to fly away…" As the transition to peace evolved, Reverend LeJau remained on duty at his parsonage near the gateway bridge, until he weakened and died in the early evening of September 10, 1717.

---

142. The assault probably occurred two days before Captain Chicken's charge 27 miles distant on June 13, but one account written in July of 1715 states that the Cherokee departed the day before the Catawbas encountered Chicken's militia. See BPRO v. 10:266, Charleston 11-19-1715. Also in Klingberg, 173, LeJau letter to Secretary, 3-19-1715/16, LeJau reports 20 bodies buried in the battlefield during the war year, but on 5- 21-1715 he reported that he lost "10 very brisk Parishioners with the Captain…" at Barker's ambush. The number buried at the camp is unknown but LeJau's letters hint that the number may be 9, 10 or 20.

143. Ministers typically conducted services at chapels of ease four or five times a year as a convenience to the parishioners.

144. Reverend Doctor Francis LeJau was a Frenchman trained at Trinity College in England and employed by the Society for the Propagation of the Gospel in Foreign Parts.

145. Chicken's handwritten journal illuminates his Scottish brogue. He wrote phonetically, divulging his vocal interpretation of phonemes and words.

146. Klingberg, 188, LeJau to the Secretary, 11-16-1716

Figure 3.1: The image shows the eastern avenue to George Chicken's plantation. The avenue is contiguous to the site of the breastwork at "the camp." The author produced the photograph in 2005.

When he foretold his fast approaching demise, he bemoaned "...the I[i] mpenitence of too many of us..." but he continued to assess the passing road traffic with the same cautious optimism that marked all of his ten years in the Carolina wilderness. Persistently, he endeavored to save souls at his sanctuaries until he declined beyond the ability to move or talk and finally expired after suffering long days in bed. His widow, daughters and only son laid him to rest at the foot of the chancel of his unfinished, St. James, Goose Creek Church, and later sealed his grave with a marble tablet.

ST. JAMES, GOOSE CREEK CHURCH

Francis LeJau's beloved St. James, Goose Creek Church reflects the Caribbean origin of the families that emigrated from the British colony of Barbados and dominated the Carolina colony for fifty years. The brick walls, laid in the sophisticated Flemish bond pattern, formed the

35 by 43 foot rectangular sanctuary. Structural elements, such as the hipped roof and the tall, airy windows are common in the tropics, and if somehow the building transported to a Caribbean island, it would not seem architecturally out of place. Intriguing features include cherub's faces and wings made of stucco on the keystones above the windows, five bas-relief hearts gracing the entrance mantle, and a plaster model of a pelican feeding hatchlings atop the tall, double front doorway. The pelican icon is the symbol of the "Society for the Propagation of the Gospel in Foreign Parts" (SPG), the organization that sent missionaries to the wilderness. The bas-relief pelican appears to feed chicks by tearing meat from its own breast, thereby symbolizing the sacrificial acts of the missionary society.

Figure 3.2: Photographs 3.2, 3.3, and 3.4, among the collections of the author, show the St. James, Goose Creek Church on March 4, 2004. On July 14, 1719, the vestry agreed, that the church was to be "set apart from all Temporal Uses, and wholly appropriated to and for the uses aforesaid [Divine Worship] forever." See Nelson, 48.

Figure 3.3: Stucco Cherub head and wings grace the apex of each window. Reverend Richard Ludlam described the sanctuary in 1723 as "built of brick cornered with plaister [sic] work in imitation of Hewed Stone, as are 3 Door cases Wst [west] No [north] & So [south] and 9 handsome arched Windows are plaistered [sic] answerably." See Nelson, 66.

Figure 3.4: The photograph shows five bas-relief flaming hearts symbolizing missionary fervor and the image of a pelican sacrificially feeding three hatchlings above the double entrance doors.

REVEREND RICHARD LUDLAM

The Society for the Propagation of the Gospel in Foreign Parts (SPG) sent Reverend Francis Merry to Goose Creek in 1720 to fill the vacancy after Francis LeJau's demise, but the vestry reported that his "behavior is so indiscreet that the parish can not elect him." Thus, the SPG recalled Merry immediately and sent Reverend Richard Ludlam, A.M, three years later. The new minister reported to work among a newly affluent class of inland rice planters reaping great returns from the wetlands and importing as many Africans as affordable.

During Ludlam's tenure, the affluence reflected in the sanctuary when cabinetmakers installed a tall elaborate pulpit in the right front corner, with winding stairs. A large sounding board above the pulpit employed the latest amplification technology. The vestry placed a small reading desk, and communion table within the chancel rail and Ralph Izard bequeathed £10 "to buy a convenient piece of plate for the use of the congregation at Goose Creek forever as they celebrate the holy sacrament of the Lord's Supper."[147] Optimism shone when the vestry improved the glebe by clearing the forest away from the buildings, expanding the cornfields, advancing work on the parsonage, and building a tiny school cabin. Moreover, within a short walk of the parsonage lay agricultural miracles new to Carolina.

Manmade ponds, strategically dammed and shaped, reserved water supplies along the clay banks. The released pond water irrigated the tall grassy rice plants as needed, and flooded the fields at appropriate intervals to drown weeds, reducing time-consuming hoe and handwork. Upstream from the bridge, tall forests rose sharply upon banks rising twenty-five feet above the waterline and from that perspective, Reverend Ludlam enjoyed a wide vista spanning more than two miles west toward the distant headwaters of Goose Creek, and the same distance downstream to the navigable flow-way below the gateway bridge.

---

147. Louis P. Nelson, *The Beauty of Holiness, Anglicanism and Architecture in Colonial South Carolina* (Chapel Hill: University of North Carolina Press, 2008), 76. The vestry originally placed the pulpit in the front southern corner of the church where it did not block the view of the altar and Eucharist. A ceiling hook and remains of a posthole indicate its original position. A small robbing room once opened under the gallery stairs and painted pews, walled in the traditional square-box pattern. The pew panels are approximately four inches shorter than the original heights because workers cut off the water damaged bottoms of the wooden boxes during a renovation.

Figure 3.5: The photograph shows Goose Creek from the bank above the bend of the waterway. Rice fields spanned both sides of Goose Creek, above and below the bridge. The July 10, 2008 photograph is among the collections of the author.

The creek flowed from the west onto Henry Middleton's Oaks Plantation and then washed south, bisecting the tract and creating an ideal setting for rice culture. During Ludlam's tenure, the wide fields steadily expanded until they fringed both sides of the entire course of the stream, showing brilliant green blades of new sprouts in the spring, deep gold panicles in the fall, and every shade of both colors according to the season, angle of the sun, and shimmers from a Carolina breeze.

Reverend Ludlam witnessed significant improvement in water and road transportation wrought from the exponentially expanding rice exports. The navigable creeks afforded the most efficient transport of the precious grain because roads were usually soft and unreliable. Consequently, the bridge-side landing remained busy most of the year but activity increased significantly during September and October when teams of Middleton slaves rolled rice barrels along inclined planks onto bateaus, and laborers from other inland rice plantations incessantly arrived to do the same. The busy landing continually expanded downstream to accommodate more bateaus and work crews until the loading area stretched a hundred yards along the clayey bank. There, workers stacked heavy rice barrels evenly and securely in bateaus, and six oar men each embarked the eight-mile ebbing tide to the docks on Charleston Harbor where merchants consigned the export to British bottoms bound for distant lands.

Most Goose Creek rice plantations, including Boochawee, Springfield, Button Hall, Thorogood, and Fleury's, lay beyond navigable waterways. Thus, in some instances, planters relied on shallow draft barges and narrow canals to access navigable streams. In addition, some sent drivers atop wagons behind two or more horses to transfer points at the nearest landing on Goose Creek, Foster Creek or Back River although the heavy and bulky wagons often bogged on the soft roads.

TAVERNS
—

Understandably, prosperity garnered from rice exports reflected in improved byways, convenient and accommodating taverns, as well as better-refined homes and gardens. The wherewithal of contiguous landowners guaranteed maintenance of these roads because the public treasury accepted no byway for up keep. Consequently, planters assigned expensive slaves and costly overseers to keep the roads passable for most traffic including heavy transport wagons and light chaises. The slower wagons carried increasingly heavy loads and the fastest carriages with large circumference and thinner width wheels, glided faster above the mire, along the hardpan, corduroy surfaces, raised causeways and bridges. Understandably, the improved conveyances concentrated locals and travelers to accommodations at several Goose Creek stopovers, each less than a one-day walk to Charleston.

During the first half of the eighteenth century, successive owners of the Seventeen-Mile House Tavern, near the parsonage, modified it to accommodate an increasing number of travelers to and from navigable Foster Creek and Back River. Back River Upper Road emerged as a busy connector tying the Goose Creek Bridge and landing traffic to vast inland fields and the navigable Back River. Back River Lower Road accessed traversable Foster Creek. There man and beasts pulled various types of shallow craft as far as four miles aside the winding banks of the waterway to its outlet on Back River.

Owners of the Eighteen- Mile House Tavern near the Eighteen-Mile

Marker and the Nineteen-Mile House Tavern, another half-mile distant, facilitated access to the Road to Dorchester, the Wassamassaw Road and the Road to Moncks Corner. These intersections became the busiest in the Charleston hinterland.[148] The proprietors of both taverns expanded and fenced the pastures to graze large herds of cattle where young boys from nearby farms typically delivered one or two cows at the end of a lead rope. When the proprietor at one of the cowpens collected a sufficient number of beeves, he paid wranglers to drive them from the taverns along Schenckingh's old trail to slaughter barns relocated more conveniently from the wharfs to the peninsular neck of Charleston. The new destination kept the herds off the crowded town squares and streets.

The taverns accommodated cattlemen as well as other pedestrians and riders of all descriptions, some astride thoroughbred horses, some atop large heavy-duty transport wagons and others in fine carriages. No one traveled as stylish as did William Middleton, the oldest son of Arthur of the Oaks Plantation. He rode behind four thoroughbred steeds and atop a four-wheeled chaise, "neatly carved and gilt, lined with crimson coffroy [?] [and] iron axletrees,"[149] He typically by-passed the roadhouse, preferring his personal cooks and dining room, but sometimes a Middleton servant arrived to retrieve a letter or package deposited there from some distant place.

Many other travelers stopped to eat, drink, water horses, repair harnesses and re-shoe their beasts. A blacksmith in an open barn adjacent to the Eighteen-Mile House Tavern worked a hammer, anvil and bellows fashioning horse and mule shoes, buckles, hinges, rivets, wheel rims, doubletrees, coal tongs, hearth hooks, grids, plowshares, barrel bands and more. Eventually the owner accumulated a small assortment of hardware and converted the three-sided shed into one of the first general stores in South Carolina. Additionally, several small cottages appeared at that convenient intersection, where the owner of Button Hall Plantation housed his overseer and sometimes sheltered guests.

---

148. The Goose Creek Bridge, one mile south of the Eighteen-Mile-House-Tavern was the only bridge crossing between the eastern half of South Carolina and Charleston. Thus, the crossing concentrated the greatest number of land travelers. The intersection at the Eighteen-Mile Stone was the busiest crossroads in South Carolina.

149. Harriot Horry Ravenel, Charleston, the Place and the People, (The McMillan Company, New York, 1906), 393.

ST. JAMES, GOOSE CREEK CHAPEL OF EASE

During those heady times, the public treasury agreed to pay a yearly salary of £100 in Carolina currency to Reverend Richard Ludlam, and erect a handsome brick parsonage for the energetic minister. During one of his daylong excursions to see parishioners residing near the St. John Parish border, he visited the Twenty-Three Mile House Tavern, but not before pausing at the camp cemetery where the bodies of the volunteer defenders of the native war lay interred. By then, the sturdy breastwork was fallen and a sanctuary rising in its place above "Chapel Creek."

To accommodate the chapel, builders excavated to a base below the black organic earth, and leveled the ground where they laid an eight-brick wide foundation upon which English masons, with African helpers, set the first brick in 1720. Within weeks, workers tapped in clay blocks, alternating a Flemish pattern to anchor the footings upon which the heavy walls depended. However, congregants released the necessary labor sparingly and work progressed slowly during the brief winter months. As a result, years faded before masons capped and sealed the tall cruciform walls.

Laborers lifted great cypress beams high to span from wall to wall, tying the thick sides together in a solid frame. Cypress rafters further anchored the beams upon which split heart-pine battens and cypress shingles repelled the hardest summer downpours. Finally, carpenters fashioned a tall door, taller arched windows and an altar.

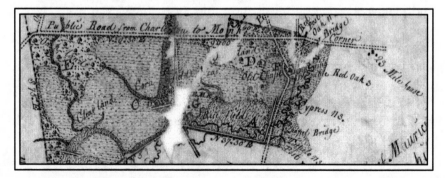

Figure 3.6: The partial plat describes the "Old Chapel [St. James, Goose Creek Chapel of Ease]," the "23 Mile house," and surrounding land. The drawing depicts the chapel right of center in the drawing. A creek borders to the north and east of the structure. This McCrady Plat number B-475/1336 is among the collections of the Register of Mesne Conveyance Office at the Charleston County Office Building, Charleston, South Carolina.

Colonel George Chicken visited infrequently at first and then more often as the walls rose during the winter months. The chapel ascended in the center of the knoll across the busy road and five hundred yards from his main avenue, within sight and sound of his busy native trading center. The large chapel stood firmly upon the hallowed ground of the ancient camp as a plaintive reminder of that terrible spring when men fell in defense of British Carolina.

Figure 3.7: Ann Yarborough drew the conceptualized image of the St. James, Goose Creek Chapel of Ease June 18, 2011. The image is among her collections.

Finally, on a spring morning in 1725, Reverend Richard Ludlam led the initiation service and began the tradition of bi-monthly services practiced by him and several of his successors. The busy church minister described the chapel in a letter to his missionary society, as "seventy feet long by thirty feet wide, in shape cruciform." He worked converting the African-born slaves and leading his "sober, [and] well-disposed...," parishioners in that neighborhood.[150] He brought holy sacraments as needed, including marriage, anointing of the sick, and funeral services to the expanding cemetery, and he frequently brought "Communion" to those professing the fundamental beliefs of the Church of England.

---

150. Nelson, 76 and 153. Nelson states, "Begun in 1727 the chapel ...was one of the largest constructed in the colony, measuring sixty feet long by twenty-two feet wide, with a chancel approximately ten feet deep. Also see Hirsch, 71 and McCrady, 1719-1776, 435. The contemporary footprint of the chapel indicates a forty by thirty feet cruciform dimension.

WASSAMASSAW CHAPEL OF EASE

In addition to visits to the chapel at the camp, Reverend Richard Ludlam more frequently found his way to the rising village of Wassamassaw, where he prayed with Christians in their rustic homes. The hey-day of rice culture in South Carolina facilitated the passage of legislation that promised teachers for the wilderness. Ludlam and others lobbied the Assembly to employ a judge for the busy Wassamassaw neighborhood, ten miles beyond the 19-mile stone, in the central section of the parish. They prompted the Assembly to authorize the judge to qualify schoolmasters, pay instructional salaries and select students for tuition-free instruction. The act also assigned one school to Wassamassaw and another at the church, but allocated no money to build either until a year later when another act authorized the justices to assess land and slaves for that purpose.

Reverend Ludlam encouraged public instruction, but accomplished little until seven years after his arrival when Thomas Smith of Yeamans Hall granted forty acres at Wassamassaw for a free academy. He named nearby French Huguenot landowners, Isaac Porcher, Cornelius Dupre, Francis Cordes and Abraham Dupont as trustees.[151] Sadly, the good reverend never witnessed any school openings, but died twelve days after the demise of his wife in 1728.[152] He and his spouse probably lay buried side-by-side on the grounds of the St. James, Goose Creek Church, and although no markers denotes the place, they are remembered by bequeaths of nearly £2,000 to establish schools for the poor.[153]

REVEREND TIMOTHY MILLECHAMPE

The new minister, Reverend Timothy Millechampe, A.M. did not arrive until 1732 after a four-year evangelistic lull. His belated appearance delayed the application of "Ludlam money" for the education of impoverished youth, but moreover the greater needs of the neglected parish diverted the new minister from giving any attention to instruction for several years. Instead,

---

151. Henry A.M. Smith, Henry A.M. Smith Papers, 1744-1922. The papers are among the collections of SCHS, 11/404/9.
152. Register of St. Andrew's Parish, 1728-1897. The register is among the collections of SCHS. Someone stamped a brick at the Chapel of Ease with the number 1721, probably indicating the year of construction.
153. Klingberg, 50. £2,000 is an impressive amount of money, considering that John Harvard's gift to Harvard College was approximately £800.

Reverend Millechampe lamented the spiritual disarray of the congregation of 2,160 non-baptized African slaves and "20 Indians." He failed to bring them quickly within the fold and meekly admitted that he baptized only one "Negro" during his first four months in the field. Not dissuaded, the energetic man of God reached vigorously to his far-flung congregation, bringing regular services to the chapel of ease at the camp and seeking prayerful families wherever he could find them. He regularly drove his wagon fourteen miles from the parsonage to Wassamassaw carrying news from the bridge and the gospel of the Christian God to the passage, through which Catawba and their allied warriors escaped two decades before.

At Wassamassaw, Reverend Timothy Millechampe met clusters of families at their farms and by his encouragement; the men erected a meetinghouse at the intersection of the north-south wagon road with the old western trail. Near that intersection, higher ground fell sharply away into a dense floodplain where a deep, clear spring flowed under a thick forest canopy. The reliable water supply at the rural crossroads marked an ideal location for a second chapel of ease. When completed, the parish touted two chapels and the energetic minister ventured to each, conveying service to the Wassamassaw Chapel one month, and sharing the gospel at the camp the next, all the remaining years of his tenure.

When venturing into the field miles from the parish church, Reverend Millechampe usually remained overnight or longer near the chapels. There he performed marriages, baptisms and burials and always departed his grateful congregations with a wagonload of gifts. His cache sometimes included folded quilts, bundled fat lighter, myrtle wax in tiny clay jars and small wooden kegs caulked with tarred hemp and filled with turpentine. Products of each season typically accompanied his departure. The gift larder included vegetables and other first fruits of summer, peaches, pears, corn, and nuts in the fall, smoked hams during the cold months, and young hens and lambs in the spring.

EASTER SUNDAY 1732

Spring arrived early in 1732, encouraging more families to remain for Easter Service, celebrated on March 25 that year. The unusually crowded sanctuary hushed to greet the newest family into its fold when Reverend Timothy Millechampe, A.M. recognized Dr. John Moultrie, his bride, Lucretia Cooper, their eldest son John Jr. and a fat two-year old red-headed boy named William, asleep on his mother's lap.

Doctor Moultrie, patriarch of the famous family, arrived in Carolina months before. He converted a derelict settlement to one suitable for his growing family, and shaped a 400-acre Goose Creek rice plantation to supplement his medical practice. His home lay near the twelve-mile stone on the Road to Goose Creek where new businesses such as cabinet and rope makers, tar and turpentine dealers, and coopers and carpenters were appearing.[154] That Sunday, more artisans than planters attended service and five weeks later John Lloyd advertised in the newspaper:

> "Leases of 64 Acres of Land, viz. 8 Lotts, consisting of 8 Acres each Lott, all fronting the Broad Path.... four [miles from the] Goose Creek Bridge; and the Trade thought most proper to settle on it are a Smith, Carpenter, Wheel-wright [sic], Bricklayer, Butcher, Taylor, Shoemaker and a Tanner."[155]

The Easter service hailed a chilly and exceedingly dry spring worrying most planters, but allowing them to show-off new carriages along the drier and faster roads. Dr. John Moultrie drove a work wagon to carry his family, but some congregants departed on elegant conveyance. Some rode behind thoroughbred steeds cantering ahead polished carriages hurrying to the homes of Carolina's wealthiest rice planters. Imported wines spiced the evenings at some of the elegant halls where wives and servants arranged house parties after special events such as weddings and baptisms. The women decorated elaborate "pleasure gardens" at Paul Mazyck's and Henry Izard's plantations,[156] and men at Medway retired to the back parlor overlooking grand lawns falling away to Back River while they enjoyed brandy and a "sly chew" (tobacco), but no place in Carolina compared to Crowfield Plantation ascending near the Eighteen-Mile Stone.

CROWFIELD

The Honorable Arthur Middleton of the Oaks Plantation applied his immense wealth to reconstitute most of the forested tracts that the proprietors originally granted to John Berringer in 1701. Arthur Middleton served as President of the Council and Commander and Chief of the

---

154. SCDAH, S213019, V. 38: p. 157, Item 1.
155. *South Carolina Gazette*, 5-20-1732, on microfilm at the Charleston County Library. Also, Henriette Kershaw Leiding, *Historic Houses of South Carolina* (Philadelphia: J.P. Lippencott, 1921), 22. Edward Ball, *Slaves in the Family* (New York: Farrar, Straus and Giroux, 1998), 107. Near this time, Elias Ball of Comingtee Plantation on the Cooper River ordered shoes from a Goose Creek cobbler for his son and a selected slave.
156. Paul Mazyck owned Springfield Plantation and Henry Izard owned The Elms Plantation.

Province before he transferred the reconstituted 1,543- acre estate to his nineteen-year-old son, William in 1729.[157] William, the oldest Middleton of his generation, enthusiastically took up the Herculean task of transferring a dense forest into a "Capital Mansion," and converting a practical farmland into a showcase of gardens, lawns and luxuriant fields. William[158] tagged the "Crowfield" moniker to his grand estate because he wished to replicate the status and ambience of Crowfield Hall, owned by his great-aunt in County Suffolk, England. Thus, he and his family relocated to the old cypress settlement, built by a previous owner on the highest ground. They commenced construction of a grand messuage in Carolina, exalted by some as the most "elaborately beautiful place in the province."[159]

William Middleton put his laborers to work moving tens of thousands of yards of top soil, clay and fill to create a masterpiece retreat. They shaped ponds, raised lawns, rolled pathways, leveled malls, and appropriately placed ditches, drains and dikes to irrigate the orchards, groves, lawns, gardens and parterres and to sustain preferred levels in the decorative water features.

The centerpiece brick edifice stood upon a raised basement, with windows on both levels, looming imposingly above the manor lands.[160] Thick white masonry blocks studded the four edges of the edifice. The stucco blocks appeared as heavy imported chiseled stones that framed the three-dimensional structure and enhanced its commanding impression.[161] A tall brick wall tied the main house to two flanking buildings, presenting a long, solid and massive form rising from the forests.[162]

When William Middleton converted the cypress village to slave use, he diverted the entrance avenue toward his new showplace manor on the lower land near the rice fields. He planted small oak trees every twenty yards along both sides of the avenue, keeping the imposing brick manor framed by the trees and in the view of anyone approaching along its mile-

---

157. Mesne Conveyance Office (MCO), Book E, 280 and Memo Book, v. 7: 98 and v. 1: 275.

158. William was the older brother of Henry Middleton of Middleton Place on the Ashley River.

159. St. Julien Ravenel, *Charleston: The Place and the People* (New York: The Macmillan Co., 1929), 125.

160. Contemporary testimony purports that the main house stood two-stories upon an elevated basement. However, documentary and archaeological evidence indicates that the structure stood as a single story upon a raised basement.

161. Similar stucco application created the appearance of stacked "hewed stone" framing the edges of the St. James, Goose Creek Church.

162. "Drayton Hall Painting, A Little Less Mysterious," *The Post and Courier*, Newspaper, 9-7- 2009, Charleston, South Carolina. A painting depicts Drayton Hall on the Ashley River with a screening wall connecting the main house with two flanking structures similar to the Crowfield layout.

long length. In 1740, a visitor noted that the house stood in sight from the Road to Dorchester, presenting "a very handsome appearance."[163] Furthermore, within one hundred yards of its terminus, the grand avenue separated to trace circumfluent routes along the shallow "moon pond," meeting at the front door. Gravity-flow waters replenished the pool that was round as the moon and reflected the house and lunar glow together like a watery mirror at appropriate times of the month and year.

Carriage lanes approached the front door of the main house where equestrians dismounted and lashed their mounts to a carved stanchion, and two bollards demarcated the parking place for carriages.[164] Orange trees lined the entire partition wall, absorbed the southern sun, scented the spring breezes, and delighted unsuspecting visitors with tropical blossoms and fruit. The imposing brick bulwark protected the citrus trees from northern winds during all hours except the bitter nights when slaves lit smoky fires and tented the vulnerable roots to thwart damaging frosts. Sheep grazed near the citrus screen shearing the lawn and workers tended the grasses incessantly, irrigating, weeding and spreading dried manures.

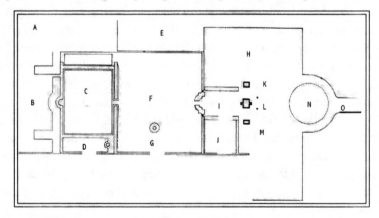

Figure 3.8: The image is adapted from Samuel Gaillard Stoney, *Plantations of the Carolina Low Country*, New York, Dover Publications Inc. 1938, 119. The alpha letters indicate significant features: A-Rectangular shaped retention ponds / B- Shaped pond/ C-Rice fields / D – Ornamental rectangular pond/ E- Lake / F- Lake gazebo/ G-Ornamental rectangular pond/ H- Court yard / I- Mount / J –Forest and Lawn/ K- Court foyer/ L - Bowling green / M- Western flanking guest house / N- Main house with carriage bollards / O- Eastern flanking guest house/ P - Moon pond (250 feet south of the front door, 816 feet in circumference, 130 feet in diameter) / Q – One-mile avenue to the Road to Dorchester.

163. Elise Pinckney, ed. *The Letterbook of Eliza Lucas Pinckney 1732-1762* (Columbia: University of South Carolina Press, 1972), 61 and Henriette Kershaw Leiding, *Historic Houses of South Carolina*, (Philadelphia: J.B. Lippencott, 1921), 24, 25.
164. Pinckney, 12.

Middleton described his home as "My Capital Mansion on Goose Creek... with twelve good rooms ... fire places in each, besides four in the basement with fire places."[165] The house stood before an impressive backdrop approachable along a wide central mall, with parterres of gardenias and other flowering shrubs to the west and a shady forested wood to the east. A wide walk parted the inner court reaching from the back door of the elegantly furnished house onto wide expanses of lawn and live oaks.

Immediately behind the rear portico, visitors passed along a mall through a funneled threshold created by two high brick bulwarks that channeled pedestrians into a whimsical and artful display of water and earth sculptures unsurpassed in North America. Visitors marveled at the massive brick pediments that lined the elaborate gardens and a large pond "situated in the midst of a spacious green..."[166] Middleton punctuated the visitors' experience with a striking Greek temple, a grotto and finally three large rectangular reflection ponds, replete with fish, fowls and other wildlife.

William Middleton lived a life unsurpassed in British North America. He worked 100 slaves at Crowfield, keeping a grand appearance and gleaning an impressive income from the sale of rice, indigo, and cattle; but his family fortune in Charleston and England supplemented his lifestyle and the hard wrought returns from the woodland rice plantation never substantiated his grand experiment. The laborious process delivering rice barrels to the distant markets required expensive maintenance of the road and bridges, and each labor hour dedicated to road upkeep deducted from agricultural profits.

EIGHTEEN-MILE HOUSE TAVERN

Many Goose Creek Plantations transformed to renowned countryseats and by mid-century, the taverns, like noisy foyers, welcomed travelers to some of the grandest places in North America. Broom Hall Plantation (later Bloomfield) loomed on the northern side of the road west of the Eighteen-Mile House . Tavern, after which Crowfield and Fleury's Plantations came into view. Travelers easily accessed the Oaks and the Elms Plantations south of that road, and the intersection at the stone conveniently connected by way of Gibbes Path

---

165. *South Carolina Gazette*, 9-23-1783. William Middleton reported that the structure contained "twelve good rooms..." His comment probably included rooms in the two flanking structures, therefore counting four rooms in each of the three structures.
166. Leiding, 24, 25.

to Back River Upper and Back River Lower Roads and the extraordinarily well developed Button Hall, Springfield and Parnassus Estates to the east.

Near mid-century, the Eighteen-Mile-House Tavern shone at the epicenter of the most technologically advanced inland rice cultivation zone in South Carolina. Inventors Peter Villeponteaux of Back River Plantation[167] and Samuel Knight, who resided in a cottage next to the busy tavern,[168] frequented it to sell their ideas and inventions. They built competing animal powered thrashing machines, consistently improved the efficiency of their creations and advertised for sales in the *South Carolina Gazette,* published in Charleston. Thus, Goose Creek planters were well-positioned at their premiere inland rice plantations to take advantage of the newest labor saving devices such as winnowing barns, trunk gates, and various types of horse-drawn thrashers.

However, as the years vanished, elaborate townhouses with uniformed servants, and imported furniture appeared more commonly in Charleston and fewer of the wealthiest landowners remained in the countryside during the warmer months. More planters employed permanent overseers to supervise laborers, while they enjoyed the social amenities of the port city and the pleasant harbor airs, thus causing the number of celebrants at the St. James, Goose Creek Sunday service to steadily decline when hot weather arrived soon after Easter service.

In addition to the seasonal exodus to townhouses, soil exhaustion and disease further reduced the congregation. Estates with wetlands continued to produce bountiful rice crops as the organic-rich waters nourished the soils, but without crop rotations and the general application of dried manure or other fertilizers, many plantations and smaller farms on higher ground declined due to leached soils. Some families continued to clear and plant fresh acreage, allowing more "old fields" to lay barren. Applying expensive slave labor to clear and convert thick mixed forests into plowed fields was not an option for most, and some families departed in search of richer virgin soils to the west. Additionally, the success of rice culture brought malaria epidemics that drove many from wet Goose Creek and prompted more of the wealthier families to flee to sea breezes away from the sacred little prayer halls near the "bad air" of the inland swamps.

---

167. Hirsch, 212.

168. Charleston County Register Mesne Conveyance (RMC) Book M-5, 330, 331. The Button Hall overseer usually lived in the cottage, but Samuel Knight rented the abode for a time.

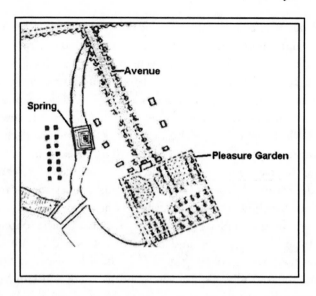

Figure 3.9: The partial plat shows the capital messuage of Springfield Plantation in 1791. The drawing describes four large ornamental gardens with walkways and a central axis behind the main house. This was the principal country home of the Mazyck family and the seat of Paul Mazyck in 1745, the year he made a generous contribution to the St. James, Goose Creek Church school construction fund. Source: Microfilm number L10005, Reel 0009, Plat 05025 and L 10005, Reel 0002, Plat 01329, South Carolina Department of Archives and History, Columbia, South Carolina.

Some loyal parishioners, such as Henry Smith and his family, attended services regularly during all seasons. On Sunday mornings, the Smith family floated a carriage and horse on a flat boat across Goose Creek from their Yeamans Hall home while they paddled alongside in a canoe. The postillion harnessed the horse to the wagon on the far side and all rode the final six and one half miles to the sanctuary. With the support of a few loyal members, such as the Smiths, the minister vigorously undertook extraordinary projects to renovate the church,[169] parsonage and grounds.[170] Reverend Timothy Millechampe also planned a new school and continued reaching out to the distant parishioners at both of the chapels of ease. Discouragingly, the congregation shrank steadily until merely twenty white and two black

---

169. SCCHJ, 12-15-1732. The Commons House of Assembly granted £100 in 1735 for structural improvements and more for groundwork. In addition, the Common House allocated £500 toward the purchase of a piece of land for a glebe and free school, and £375 to repair the parsonage house.
170. SCCHJ, 2-27-1742.

communicants attended Christmas service in 1742.[171] Notwithstanding the shrinking congregation, the energetic minister initiated one more project.

Before his departure, Reverend Millechampe organized a solicitation drive to build a school. Fifty-six church members, including the most successful planters participated.[172] Collectively, they pledged £2,220 to acquire property and erect an institution of learning, committing varying amounts over a three-year period. Most kept their promise, but neither Reverend Millechampe nor his next two successors advanced the project. Nonetheless, the vestry wisely invested the sizeable sum of £5,927. The money included all of the Ludlam education dollars and the subscription schoolhouse money and it earned 10% annually until they built a school twenty years later.[173]

William Middleton pledged monetary support for the school project, although by mid-century, he and his family spent less time in Goose Creek, relegating the management of Crowfield to overseers and multi-generational slave families. As additional years faded, William Middleton moved more of his experienced workers to productive fields fronting the Cooper, Ashley and other coastal rivers, until in 1750, merely twenty-one years after his father awarded the property to him, he abandoned Crowfield entirely, leaving neither caretaker nor watchman.

After the workers departed, the subtropical elements that nurtured the elegant gardens and groves rapidly brought the resurgence of a thick unkempt forest. Consequently, the carefully cultured land reverted to a deer park, replete with game, tranquil waters, wide pastures and shady woodlands favored by Native American hunters. Late in the spring of 1753, a large band of "Northern Indians" camped at the long abandoned domicile, greatly alarming the skittish neighbors who recalled the deadly native invasion almost forty years before. However, after feasting on the bounty from the plentiful land, the natives moved to an undisclosed destination and normalcy returned.[174]

---

171. Klingberg, 92. Reverend Timothy Millechampe reported in 1736 that he administered the sacraments at the Wassamassaw Chapel because the village was too distant for the people to attend the St. James, Goose Creek Church.
172. Paul Mazyck of Springfield Plantation, William Middleton of Crowfield, Peter Taylor of Bloomfield, Zachariah Villeponteaux of Parnassus, Benjamin Mazyck of Howe Hall, John Parker of the Hayes, Henry Izard of the Elms, Richard Singleton of Foxbank, and John Mackenzie of Button Hall contributed the greatest amounts.
173. The vestry erected no schoolhouse until Reverend James Harrison urged the society to build one. In 1765, the Society consented to the vestry plan for supervising the teacher, the curriculum and assessing the effectiveness of the program. A church school opened that year with the support of a £100 bequest from Peter Taylor for the erection and maintenance of a place of instruction.
174. *South Carolina Gazette*, 6-3-1753 reported "… 17 northern natives were seen on Mr.

Figure 3.10: The 1922 photograph shows some of the stucco masonry that smoothed and protected the interior walls at Crowfield. The image also shows a tall airy window opening designed to capture breezes. William Henry Johnson (1871-1934) produced the photograph. The image is in the William Henry Johnson Scrapbook, circa 1920-1923, from the photographic collections of the South Carolina Historical Society (34/293), Charleston, South Carolina.

Later that summer, William Middleton announced plans to sail with his family to England and advertised the sale of 1,800 Crowfield acres in the *South Carolina Gazette.* He touted the place as suitable for rice production and claimed that corn and indigo flourished in the cultured fields. A subsequent advertisement described the large brick house with many convenient outbuildings and a "neat regular garden."[175] Another advertisement appeared early the following year touting the 150 acres of rice lands and furniture, china, plate, and between 200 and 300 books.[176] That year William Walter and his wife, Mary Cattell purchased "furniture, china, plate and 300 books," as well as the house and outbuildings. They soon relocated to the country manor as the newest congregants to the old St. James, Goose Creek Church.

Middleton's place on Goose Creek."
175. *South Carolina Gazette,* 8-8-1753.
176. *South Carolina Gazette,* 1-15-1754.

REVEREND ROBERT STONE

As Reverend Millechampe aged, he ventured to England for long rests, "[and] to cure palsy at the waters of Bath."[177] Each time he departed, he remained for longer periods as his condition worsened until Reverend Robert Stone arrived to assume the parochial duties. Immediately, Reverend Stone found a raging malaria epidemic forcing families to flee.[178] Some simply packed as many possessions as they could carry and drove away from the "bad air," before they sickened, but others survived the fever, weakened and died later from related ailments. Despondently, the minister buried eight people in the first nine weeks in Goose Creek, and reported, "Forty-five was the common age of man." Nonetheless, he persevered and grew optimistic when, the scourge abated and the numbers at Sunday service reflectively improved. Remarkably, after two years in the field, attendance increased to such a level that the minister set aside Sunday afternoons to teach and serve the "Negroes," whose "numbers crowded the Church," and were very "off [ensive] to the whites." The minister confidently believed that both the Africans and their masters appreciated the segregated assemblies that he dutifully led until his death in 1751.[179]

REVEREND JAMES HARRISON,

One year after Reverend Stone died, the vestry elected Reverend James Harrison, A.M. as his successor, allocating an extra £340 to "purchase a Negro for the use of the Parsonage." The parish was rebounding from the epidemics and more people attended church and socialized with confidence. Some parents brought babies from as far away as 280 miles

177. SCCHJ, 6-6-1746. Also, see Wallace, 8, 12.
178. Frederick A. Dalcho, *A Historic Account of the Protestant Episcopal Church in South Carolina* (Charleston: A.E. Miller, 1820, reprinted 1969), 258. Memorials displayed on the walls include a testimonial to Colonel John and Mrs. Jane Gibbes, as well as to Ralph Izard and Peter Taylor. Located over the main entrance is the gallery, which provided seating for church members who did not own a pew. A diamond shaped, wooden symbol of the Izard family, known as the family hatchment, is displayed on the face of the gallery. In accordance with English tradition, family members carried the hatchment in front of the coffin during the burial procession of the head of the family. After the mourning period, the sexton re-hung the hatchment inside the church. The Izard hatchment is one of two in America.
179. Klingberg, 93-94.

for baptism, and young common-law husbands appeared at the parsonage door with pregnant partners seeking matrimony. The minister proudly and enthusiastically administered Holy Communion to "30 white and 17 Negro" in 1757, and further reflecting the economic rebound that year, William Middleton presented the Decalogue, Apostles' Creed and Lord's Prayer on large marble plaques, for placement on each interior side of the last window of the church.

The maturing colony demanded reliable highways, and insisted that all male slaves from sixteen to sixty years of age perform road duty, forcing reluctant planters under legal penalties to release their valuable laborers from the fields. A new bridge spanned Goose Creek after mid-century, but discouragingly the structure deteriorated rapidly beneath the destructive weight of increasingly sturdy wagons, with heavier loads on wider wheels and four or more horses at the fore. Consequently, the wooden crossing that typically needed repair every five or six years required extensive work twice annually and the new schedule severely burdened the landowners contiguous to the roadways. Notwithstanding loud protests in the colonial house, the government did not relent and the largest and sturdiest bridge yet conceived emerged in 1757 with all of the necessary timber and labor supplied by increasingly disgruntled planters.[180]

The increased volume of traffic brought commerce to the countryside and business to artisans who converted the wayside taverns into livery, blacksmith, and leather works. At first, the increasing activity invigorated Reverend Harrison as he enthusiastically welcomed more families to his diversifying congregation and soon he baptized and married more souls than he buried but that progress halted when the war with the Cherokee Nation erupted.[181]

Within a year of the frightful sighting of "northern Indians" at Crowfield, the French and Indian War erupted in North America and two years hence, the "Seven Year War" spread to Europe. As weeks and months faded, incessant rumors of painted warriors incited a surge of families to flee across the bridge in pursuit of the relative safety of Charleston, similarly to the evacuation that followed the riders from Pocotaligo, thirty-five years before.[182]

---

180. SCCHJ, 3-1-1757, 4-1 2-1757, 364.

181. Klingberg, 96. George Chicken Jr. was a renowned "Indian Fighter," like his famous father, and led Carolina troops against the Cherokee in western North Carolina.

182. The French and Indian War erupted in North America in 1754 and ended in 1763. It commenced in Europe in 1756 and thus it was tagged the "Seven Year War."

As did Reverend LeJau, during the Yamassee uprising, the minister remained by the bridge assessing the dangers, conveying news as it arrived and persisting with service every Sunday.[183] When hostilities ebbed, he resumed bringing prayer, service and encouragement every other month to the far-flung families at the two distant chapels, especially seeking camaraderie near the camp at the Twenty-Three Mile House Tavern, then, popularly referred to as "Sociable Hill."

Cooper River, Back River and Goose Creek planters frequented that stopover. There, the Goose Creek Friendly Society (sometimes, "The River Club") met monthly within ¼ mile of the sanctuary avenue to the chapel of ease. The club enjoyed a steady membership of approximately twenty wealthy young planters, such as Zachariah Villeponteaux and James Kinloch from the Cooper and Back River lands, and William Allen from nearby Thorogood.[184] They met for food, drink, cards, and discussion and they accompanied their families to the chapel for worship and sacraments. There, William Allen wed Mary Keating, the daughter of the proprietor of the Sociable Hill Tavern. They recited vows before the wooden altar, with many friends in attendance and afterwards all of them journeyed two miles to the couple's Thorogood home.

Reverend James Harrison, like his predecessors, wished to build a school and thus tapped into the sensitivities of the young planters, as well as the old parish tradition of supporting poor children with local instruction or tuition assistance. However, the Ludlam and solicitation money for a schoolhouse were merely collecting interest, until Peter Taylor, the wealthy owner of Bloomfield Plantation, bequeathed a handsome amount. Then, the impatient minister pushed the project farther. He encouraged the vestry to incorporate as a lawful business to facilitate the expenditure of the £15,272 school account. When Henry Middleton generously conveyed twelve acres of land at the intersection of Red Bank and Church Roads for a school and consummated the transaction with the consideration of "a twig and a turf,"[185] the heart of the enthusiastic minister soared. Soon, donated stacks of clay blocks arrived from plantations near and far and masons erected a little brick schoolhouse beneath a ring of five spreading oak trees.

Seven and sometimes more boys attended the little academy. They begrudgingly walked from neighboring farms and plantations where their fathers supervised slaves or husbanded small plots of land, but no girls

183. Reverend James Harrison reported in 1759 that he officiated at the Wassamassaw Chapel five or six times a year.
184. SCHGM, 27: 188
185. Waring, 9.

sought instruction beyond their mothers' knees and kitchen fires. The gleeful minister visited the school almost every day at first to witness his most progressive work, but soon the pressures of the busy crossroads upon the aging man of God forced his tired hands.

Exhausted and worn, the discordance of the busy bridge and noisy tavern near his home increasingly annoyed him. Youthful cowboys disrespectfully hooted and waved, fast carriages and chaises threw up obnoxious clouds of dust, and anonymous travelers incessantly pestered him for lodging and entertainment.[186] Worse of all, some wagon drivers and equestrians sought his company after stopping too long at the nearby Seventeen-Mile-House Tavern, and never found the aging minister to be as jovial as were they.

Much broader tensions contributing to the sour disposition of the good minister permeated the humid air in the summer of 1765, but unlike the angst that shrouded every inhabitant in the days before Pocotaligo, the tensions filtering to them by packet or newspaper were merely aggravations. That winter, the British Parliament passed the Stamp Act to help pay for the recent French and Indian conflict and early that spring the Quartering Act followed, purporting to house a standing army in the colonies as a deterrent to future foreign aggression. Consequently, accusations of "taxation without representation," percolated to the fore of some conversations, and young soldiers sleeping in private homes affronted others who perceived their hearths offended by an over-stepping parliament.

Those unpopular laws and more that followed stirred protests in the northern cities, and editorial debate in the *South Carolina Gazette* reached most dining halls in Carolina encouraging some in Charleston to organize loud resistance against "oppressive British laws." Planters depended upon the British markets to sell the rice, indigo and products of the forests but artisans in Charleston resented the taxes. The rising protests garnered sympathy among the growing number of craftsmen in Charleston and its expanding hinterland including talented, literate men, such as William Johnson of White House Plantation on the Goose Creek neck. He joined the raucous ranks of resistance near the time that Reverend Harrison departed the parish. The good reverend served the crown loyally and harbored no desire for debate and consternation of the laws of parliament. Thus, he resolutely retreated into retirement in St. Bartholomew's Parish, where he rested more years until his demise.[187]

---

186. Hirsch, 87.
187. SCHGM 51: 165 and Smith Papers, 11/404/2.

Figure 3.11: An unidentified man and woman stand near brick indigo vats at Otranto Plantation circa 1977. Isaac Godin employed Charles Hill to construct at least three vats at his Goose Creek-side plantation later named Otranto. Indigo dye was a lucrative industrial export prior to the American Revolution. Workers disassembled one vat and moved it in 1977 from Otranto to another location for public viewing. Courtesy of Lucille Skaggs.

CHAPTER 4

St. James, Goose Creek Church

Reverend Edward Ellington took-up pastoral duties of the sacred places soon after Reverend Harrison departed. The new priest proved to be an ideal personality for the brooding years leading to the American War of Independence. He arrived at the parsonage near the bridge as tensions hastened day by day, and within months of his appearance, "Sons of Liberty" Samuel Adams and Joseph Warren formed the first Committees of Correspondence in Boston to fuel the rising storm of rebellion against Great Britain. As a result, the *South Carolina Gazette* carried conflicting political editorials prompting some Carolinians to consider overt action against the Royal Government their grandfathers welcomed fifty years earlier in exchange for the Lord Proprietors. Within that emotionally unsettling context, some of the protagonists in Charleston gravitated to a stranger arriving on a packet boat from New England.

WILLIAM DILLWYN

William Dillwyn, a tourist from Boston, disembarked in Charleston during the autumn of 1772. He merely wished to visit the southern city and explore its countryside for rest and amusement, but he immediately found the leading men of Charleston seeking his northern views and political opinions. Peter Smith, a well-read merchant and owner of Broom Hall Plantation on Goose Creek, earnestly sought his audience with the promise of a tour of the countryside. Within three days of his arrival, Dillwyn ventured along the Road to Goose Creek by horseback and later, after falling from his spirited mount, rode atop a carriage toward the Goose Creek Bridge.

News of his journey preceded his arrival and interested parties greeted him at various stops. Thus, after pattering over the old Goose Creek Bridge, Dillwyn met the church minister at the parsonage and walked with him to the country church before departing for the Eighteen-Mile-House Tavern for refreshments. Finally, a guide delivered the traveler from the tavern to Broomhall Plantation where he passed the evening enjoying stimulating conversation, dinner and the "finest wines and brandies." The next morning he ventured by horseback along the unkempt Road to Dorchester in search of mythical Crowfield.

Predictably, William Haggett, owner of the aging estate, appeared near the moon pond, greeted the traveler and "politely shewed [showed]" the house and grounds. Two hours later, Dillwyn departed for Charleston the way he came, pausing again at the parsonage where Reverend Edward Ellington reigned and that evening the visitor from Boston penned notes of the day trip:[188]

> Myself with a Negro boy for a guide went to the next plantation (Crowfield) at which has been as much money expended in improvements as I believe has been the case anywhere in America tho [sic] now much in decay...The Gardens, Fishponds and walks occupy about 20 acres, which has been well planned.[189]

During the tenure of the sincere and earnest Reverend Ellington, the wooden conveyance increasingly delivered strangers to his door. Some, like Dillwyn, arrived as curiosities, but others appeared with disparate personalities, and as months faded into years, disputes roiled the countryside until violence erupted into full-fledged internecine warfare.

A HOUSE DIVIDED

Understandably, the proximity of the St. James, Goose Creek Church to the important gateway bridge, hurled the House of God into the center of conflicts and when loyalties divided, the sanctuary descended into frequent discordance. In response, the talented minister assuaged his congregation

188. SCHGM and Smith papers.
189. SCHGM 36: 109 and Henry Ravenel Dwight, *Some Historic Spots in Berkeley* (Pinopolis, South Carolina: Women's Auxiliary of Trinity Church, 1921, reprinted 1944), 23, 24.

with good humor and patient advisement, and as the hostilities hastened, he correctly conducted services to a divided congregation employing the approved, although understandably pro-British, Church of England liturgy. Sarah Smith Coachman, wife of Benjamin Coachman and their children Benjamin Jr., Nancy and Sarah did not protest the protocol of the funeral service for Benjamin Sr. in the spring of 1779 when they sealed the remains of their patriarch in the family vault on the church grounds, but others disapproved of the Anglican deference to the Crown.

A church vestryman, Benjamin Coachman worked the vast Schenkingh lands south of the glebe, becoming one of the wealthiest men in the colony. He served early in the internecine strife, resisted as a captain in the militia when the British navy burst into the harbor in 1776, and reliably reported as a member of a Goose Creek committee, dutifully executing the directives of the infant patriot government. Perishing two years before the British occupied Charleston, his family honored his patriotism by lending £180,000, one of the largest gifts during the conflict, to the fledgling government. The mourning and unflinching Coachman family buried their loved one by way of the prayerful direction of loyalist Reverend Edward Ellington without objection. Notwithstanding, the superior interpersonal talents of the even-handed minister, sensitivities heightened in the months that followed and tempers flared until one irascible congregant literally and figuratively overplayed his hand.

During Sunday service, soon after the Coachman burial, a disgruntled congregant ordered the minister to omit the prayer for the King of England, and threatened to throw his prayer book at the head of the priest if he persisted to recite it. The threat did not dissuade the loyal churchman from employing the sanctioned recitation the following Sunday, and the patriot kept his promise too. The book of prayer flew as predicted and commotion erupted. In response, the shaken Ellington locked the sanctuary doors and promised to shutter the sanctuary until peace returned to the countryside.

The startling, and immensely inappropriate incident at the church service was a mild harbinger to the severe divisions that soon ripped Goose Creek. Understandably, political disagreement riled tempers, and many heated discussions closed taverns and disrupted dinners as families chose sides during roiling political debates. When neighbors assembled into militias and invading armies threaten hearths and homes, emotions rose to unprecedented peaks of hatred in many corners and lingered in bitterness for generations. Such was the case in Goose Creek when patriots such as

William Johnson rallied in early protests against tax laws and continued to resist on the battlements of Charleston and unto his prisoner of war cell. Wealthy Gabriel Manigault acquiesced, along with many when the British occupied Charleston, but later stiffened and reported to the patriot camp in time for redemption. However, notables such as Henry Middleton supported the rebellion until armies assembled. He then prudently retreated behind his doors at his Oaks Plantation for the duration. Some Goose Creekers remained steadfast to the crown, before, during, and after the struggle, keeping unswervingly loyal until the day they died. Within that divisive context, the St. James, Goose Creek Church persevered as a bastion of loyalists even as it suffered at the hands of both warring sides.

Reverend Ellington kept his promise and secured the doors to Sunday worshippers until the British army marched across the Goose Creek Bridge in April 1780. As the siege for Charleston heightened that year, the British walked inland along the Goose Creek Road, to stem the flow of supplies to patriots trapped below breastworks spanning the narrowest breach of the Charleston Peninsula. Easter arrived on March 26, 1780 but the church remained locked as loyalists and patriots worshipped in their separate ways. In the weeks that followed, British cavalry reconnoitered the Goose Creek neighborhood and established camps on both sides of the overpass in preparation for a significant joint maneuver of two powerful British military forces.

LIEUTENANT COLONEL BANASTRE TARLETON

On April 13, 1780, British Lieutenant Colonel Banastre Tarleton established a post at the Oaks Plantation near the gateway bridge. His appearance at the passage coordinated with a pincher movement east of the Cooper River that was to converge near Moncks Corner. Success against partisan cavalry in the countryside depended upon stealth, and with that tactic foremost in mind, Tarlton thrust north toward the western branch of the Cooper River in coordination with Major Thomas Ferguson advancing up the Cainhoy Peninsula along the east branch of the Cooper. The commanders intended to surprise and defeat the patriots at Moncks Corner, and as a result, cut supply lines to patriot occupied Charleston.

Banastre Tarleton ordered the Legion cavalry, a detachment of the 17th Light Dragoons and American Volunteers to depart the Oaks at 10:00 o'clock at night on an eighteen-mile force march to Biggin Bridge above Moncks Corner. Within two hours, they approached the aging chapel of ease at the camp, now grossly unkempt and tottering in the encroaching forest and soon passed near the Sociable Hill Tavern deserted and forlorn.[190] Within a mile of the chapel, near the intersection to the Road to Strawberry Ferry, one of Tarleton's advance scouts captured a slave carrying a letter from Colonel Isaac Huger to General Benjamin Lincoln. From the written message, Tarleton deduced the disposition of the American cavalry and militia near Biggin Bridge, allowing him to coordinate confidently his riders at the appropriate place and time.

Tarleton pushed his men relentlessly, completing the trek in five hours and arriving during the darkest hour before sunrise on Friday, April 14. Without hesitating, he charged, throwing the startled defenders into confusion, sending some running unarmed into the dark forest and others scattering upon the nearest unsaddled steed. When the confusion settled, dozens of patriots sat under guards as prisoners of war and other lay writhing or dead.

The victory at Biggins Bridge sealed a British patrol perimeter around Charleston that soon sounded the death knell for the patriots defending Charleston. Tarlton returned with captured battle accoutrements but more importantly, the strategic bridge at Goose Creek lay firmly in British control. With the bridge, the British controlled the flow of food on the hoof, as well as wagons on the road and boatloads on the creek, which supplied meat and produce daily to British forces marching into town.

Wisely, the occupying British army kept a base of operations on the Oaks Plantation grounds while they occupied Charleston. They unfurled British banners, pitched tents, and lit cooking fires beneath the spreading oak trees, even in the "pleasure gardens" and to the front door of the main two-story house. From the Middleton lands, they commanded the gateway to Charleston as well as its fertile hinterland and with sentries at the bridge, and along all approach roads, they stood poised to strike north, south, east or west.

The suspicious invaders did not damage the Oaks properties, the church or the parsonage, undoubtedly in consideration to Henry Middleton, one of the most renowned Carolinians, and the father of Arthur, signer of the Declaration of Independence. The British army converted some churches in South Carolina into garrisons, hospitals or barracks, and burned other sanctuaries to the ground, but they spared the Goose Creek church and chapels from all indignities in deference to Middleton. Henry Middleton accepted

---

190. The chapel fell out of use by the time of the war. The Mouzon Map shows a "Chapel" at Wassamassaw but does not show the chapel at the camp. There is a plat indicating the Chapel of Ease at the camp in 1782, but it is likely that neglect and wear ruined the structure by the time of the Revolutionary conflict.

the protection of the Crown, and undoubtedly, his acquiescence protected his property and his beloved church that Reverend Ellington reopened in the summer of 1780 to a congregation of British soldiers and loyalists.

British soldiers lived well during their months at the Oaks and at Alexander Garden's Otranto Plantation, west of the bridge. They feasted on roast pork and chicken and marched patrols in the countryside carrying greasy haversacks stuffed with rice and meat. They kept careful contact with their comrades at Fort Dorchester and were always mindful of dangerous flanking movements that might separate them from the main occupying force in town, but they found comfort and support in the loyalist neighborhoods on both sides of the bridge.

MAD ARCHIE CAMPBELL

British officers and enlisted men frequented the church for spiritual and social exchange during the summer and fall of 1780, finding rare quietude and camaraderie with locals. However, the halcyon scene erupted when British Captain Archie Campbell kidnapped Paulina Phipps from her home at 43 East Battery in Charleston and frantically rushed her to the quiet sanctuary to win a wager and[191] satisfy his youthful passions. With both aboard, Campbell sped a carriage out of Charleston keeping a rapid pace until the wheels pattered on the wooden Goose Creek Bridge, and halted at the parsonage door. The wild-eyed officer called out the wary minister and announced his intentions to marry the lovely woman. When the brave servant of God asserted, "Not without the consent of the lady," "Mad Archie Campbell" immediately confirmed his impetuous reputation, drew his pistol and shouted, "Unless you comply, you shall be instantly shot, and the lady's virtue could only suffer in consequence. I say, sir, make haste!" When he pointed the pistol at his lovely captive, she too hurriedly consented and the sacramental proceedings commenced.[192] Incredibly, even though tempers calmed, passion did not and the couple lived happily together until the firebrand warrior died in a skirmish with partisans at Videau's Bridge the following summer, leaving an inconsolable bride and a healthy infant daughter.[193]

191. Margaret Rhett Martin, Charleston Ghosts (Columbia: University of South Carolina Press, 1963), 89.
192. Joseph Johnson, *Traditions and Reminiscences, Chiefly of the American Revolution in the South* (Charleston: Walker and James, 1851), 62-67.
193. Johnson, 68.

COLONEL WADE HAMPTON

Notwithstanding the passions of many young British warriors and their notable victories, within fourteen months fortunes of war shifted in favor of the patriots, when Generals Thomas Sumter and Francis Marion along with Colonels Henry Lee and Wade Hampton rode into the St. James, Goose Creek Parish. Patriot Colonel Wade Hampton rushed along the Wassamassaw Road into British-held territory to secure the Goose Creek Bridge arriving at the church on Sunday morning, July 15, 1780 while Reverend Ellington led prayers.

At that time, the old carriage driveway led directly to the tall front double church doors, opened wide to catch infrequent airs,[194] and allowing Hampton to gallop to the very walls of the sanctuary. His racing horsemen surprised the sequestered congregation, blocked escape, and captured valuable horses. Immediately, Hampton made prisoners of the male attendees, then quickly paroled them and galloped across the Goose Creek Bridge in search of other red coats and loyalists. He arrested a few resisters at Vance's Tavern one mile west of the bridge, and then penetrated menacingly onto the Charleston Neck before withdrawing. When word reached the British command of Hampton's strategic advance, so near the walls of town, they assayed the perilous loss of the Goose Creek Bridge, the potential collapse of their eastern flank and quickly retreated from Fort Dorchester to within the bulwarks of the fortified Charleston peninsula.

Without the protection of the British army, Henry Middleton did little but wait with his extended family and loyalist friends at his beloved Oaks, and when hostilities waned in 1782, Governor Edward Rutledge unsuccessfully prodded Henry to emerge from isolation. He later sent a letter to his son Arthur, mulling:

> I have not seen your Father ...he keeps constantly at Goosecreek [sic]. I wrote him on my arrival at this place, but whether he never rec'd [received] my Letter or is afraid to answer it (tho it contained no Politics) I cannot say. Drayton and his family are with him, as inactive as ever...[195]

Notwithstanding swirling emotions during the waning days of conflict and onto the months and years that followed, Henry Middleton successfully

---

194. Fraser, 17
195. SCHM, 27: 5.

protected his vulnerable plantation and the royal institutions near the gateway bridge. He supported the patriot causes early in the struggle but evaded the destructive hand of the British by accepting the protection of the crown when the occupation forces arrived. Although disturbing to many, his mixed loyalties were more of the rule than an exception among the Goose Creek planting society. Ambiguity railed amidst the sacred places, causing resentment and distrust to divide the congregation for years after the conflict formally ended.

EASTER 1784

According to the canonical calendar, Christians celebrated Easter on April 11 in 1784, the same year the new United States Congress ratified the Peace of Paris and formally ended the conflict that smoldered three years after the terminal battle at York Town. The treaty returned formalities of peace to a countryside greatly in need of moderating personalities, such as Reverend Edward Ellington. His Goose Creek sanctuary was a bastion for loyalists after the British arrived and the unspoken truth was nonetheless, obvious that the remarkable little country sanctuary avoided the torches of warring armies because of the persuasive influence of the wealthy Middleton family. Nonetheless, a myth spawned, purporting that the Royal Coat of Arms displayed over the altar protected the house of prayer, and incredibly, the Royal Crest remained prominently displayed after the conflict amidst patriotic emotions that swept away most references to Royal rule, including the name "Charles Town." One patriot unabashedly employed unsubstantiated logic when he explained, "...not the sternest R[r]epublican would now wish to see these symbols of regality removed, when it is known that they saved the temple of God from the violence of a mercenary and ruthless soldiery."[196]

Within this confusing postwar environment, where mixed loyalties stoked heated debates long after the muskets cooled, Reverend Ellington rose to the occasion with the energy of a younger man. He employed his versatile personality for reconciling differences, and he frequently engaged travelers along the noisy road near the parsonage and tavern. When the highway commissioners razed the neglected bridge for renovations, he hired a pole man, secured a small barge and operated a free-lance ferry service that saved many travelers from lengthy detours.[197]

196. Johnson, 382.
197. Johnson, 384.

The conflicted public sector neglected the glebe during the revolution and the structures deteriorated greatly.[198] The land, church, and parsonage stood as anachronistic icons to the failed British experiment in North America, but that winter, skilled Middleton slaves re-hung all of the parsonage shutters and doors, aligned dry cypress roof shingles, and chinked the crumbling hearth. Moreover, as was the custom for eighty years, and as certain as the spring rains, Africans arrived days before holy week, to plow, manure and prepare the aging cornfields sprawling near the parsonage.

Near sunrise on Easter morning, Reverend Ellington with his aging servant walked the familiar path to the sanctuary. Somebody's slaves came in the day before to modify the obsolete brick oven near the reserve pond and prepare a coal pit for roasting small pigs and sweet potatoes. They camped near the weir and mill on the glebe, within sight of the sanctuary, standing, and doffing their floppy hats as the minister passed. That day opened with gentle breezes sweeping the forest floor and blending the hickory campfire smoke with low misty air. The pleasant cool weather kept lightness in the minister's steps, but as the morning rushed away and early arrivals appeared on the grounds, he focused more intently upon his duties.

Reverend Ellington unlocked the great double doors and entered the place he hoped would assuage lingering resentments, and although the congregation was steadily losing membership to out-migration, he expected most Goose Creek families to remain loyal to their faith. Moreover, he prayed that generational connections would return the stalwart community leaders to the sacred house.

Soon he was busy welcoming patriots and loyalists alike with genuine alacrity as drivers disembarked families from the carriages near the front door, and women and children waited for fathers to return from the coach barn, a hundred yards south of the sanctuary. As was the custom, families nested together in box pews or walked the angled stairway to the balcony, while their "negroes," listened outside the tall windows.

Custom also demanded the presence of the Middleton patriarch at Easter service, but the 67-year-old Henry dictated his last will and testament merely five days prior and suffered from a "tedious," illness in his Charleston residence at 69 Broad Street. His famous son, Arthur, who remained at the Oaks after the conflict, represented the renowned family in their box pew with his wife and younger brother, Thomas.[199] Henry died nine weeks later

---

198. SCHGM, 29: 269. William Dillwyn visited the church in 1772 and reported that it needed repair.
199. *South Carolina Gazette*, 6-17-1784.

in the early afternoon of Sunday June 13. The following day his widow accompanied the cortege to their vault at the St. James, Goose Creek sanctuary where she interred the remains of the patriarch.[200]

Patriot, Archibald Brown slowly descended from a carriage beneath the bas-relief pelican, protecting a festering wound from which he eventually succumbed. The infant State of South Carolina sent Archibald Brown to France in 1776 to purchase war material. He survived the perilous sojourn during the heat of conflict, returned to Boston on the ship "Queen of France" and immediately rode a horse from Boston to Charleston to assume the rank of lieutenant of one of the light infantry companies defending the city. He first saw combat in February 1779 in Beaufort, South Carolina. During that engagement, a sentry thrust a bayonet into his stomach causing a grievous wound. Nonetheless, he endured the injury, participated in the siege of Savannah, Georgia in 1779 and mounted the walls of Charleston as a captain until the British imprisoned him on May 12, 1780.

During the confusing days and weeks after the fall of Charleston, British officials paroled patriot defenders who swore allegiance to the King, and they briefly released Brown. Brown took advantage of that reprieve from duty to wed Mary, daughter of John Deas. Reverend Edward Ellington conducted the marriage ceremony on August 17, 1780 at the home of Mary's father at Thorogood Plantation. Soon after the wedding, British authorities sent Archibald Brown to the prisoner of war camp at St. Augustine for a twelve-month internment.[201] He survived the horrid conditions in St. Augustine and the war, but the stomach wound never properly sealed. Eight years later, at the age of forty-five, at his home near the twenty-two mile marker on the Moncks Corner Road, he succumbed to complications from the injury.

---

200. "Monday last died at Goosecreek [sic] Arthur Middleton Esq: in the 45th year of his age." Notice in the *South Carolina Gazette*, 1-3-1787. Also see "Died: Saturday last on Sullivan's Island, Thomas Middleton esquire...he was buried at St. James, Goose Creek, outside behind the chancel," *South Carolina Gazette*, 8-21-1797. Grandfather Arthur Middleton generously supported the cost of the church construction seventy-five years before and the vestry designated to him "one enclosed Pew or Seat, containing about 5 feet 6 inches by 7 feet of ground...hereby Ordained, Given and Appropriated Solely and only to the use of the said Arthur Middleton, Esq. and his heirs for Ever," Dalcho, 249-50
201. Testimony of Mary Brown before Justice of the Quorum for the State of South Carolina, District of Charleston, 5-24-1840, www.http/southerncampaign.org, Southern Campaign American Revolution Pension Statements and Rosters, Pension Application of Archibald Brown, W21740, Transcribed by Will Graves.

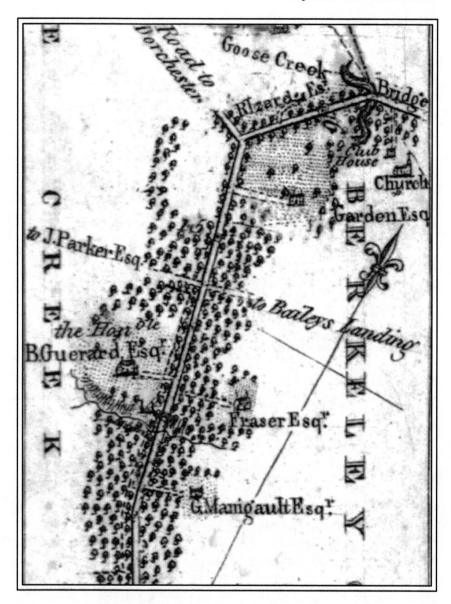

Figure 4.1: The Abernathie and Walker Map published in 1785 shows avenues and main houses of "G. Manigault Esqr.," "Fraser Esq.," "the Hon'ble B.Guerard Esq." "...J. Parker Esq." ""Garden Esq." and "R. Izard, Esqr." intersecting or near the *Road to Goose Creek* south of the Goose Creek Bridge and Church.

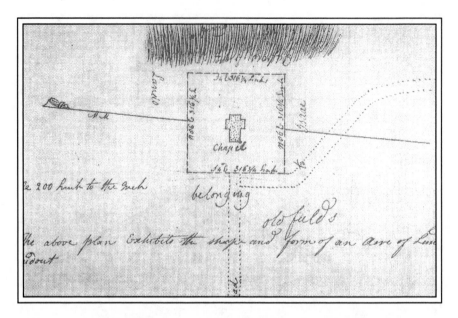

Figure 4.2: The plat shows the one-acre square parcel of land containing the cruciform chapel of ease and cemetery. Isaac Dubose and his wife, Catherine transferred the property on June 20, 1787 to St. James, Goose Creek Church Commissioners. This deed transfer states that George Chicken promised to donate one acre from "the walls of the chapel" in 1725. Isaac Dubose fulfilled that promise, donating the acre as a "burial place." See the Charleston County Deed Book Y-5, 252. The chapel is standing on August 11, 1794 when Benjamin Paul Williams sells the land to Barnard Leitz. See CCDB Q7:257.

Aaron Loocock, Brown's neighbor resided on the Moncks Corner Road between the two Deas avenues. Needed in the defense of Charleston, he deferred and sailed to the safety of England, but regained some of his lost honor and prestige by working in severe conditions for the patriot prisoners-of-war in London. John Deas Sr., vestryman, and wealthy owner of Thorogood Plantation, "mounted the lines," in defense of Charleston, but acquiesced with his immediate neighbors after the fall of the city in order to protect his home, wife and eleven children. He paid a 12% penalty for his wavering loyalty, but regained favored status with the support of his oldest son, who was a minor when the British marched into Goose Creek, but now managed neighboring Mount Holly Plantation. John Deas Sr. survived the bitter post war era with dignity until his wife and children laid him to rest in 1788 at the cruciform chapel of ease near his eastern gate.

One year before his demise, the vestry appointed John Deas senior, and his eldest son as well as, Archibald Brown, and Aaron Loocock as church commissioners to accept ownership of the chapel of ease. The cruciform sanctuary survived the revolution unsullied by the warring sides, but succumbed to age, decades of neglect, and the pressing weight of rotted rafters upon unprotected bricks, prompting the vestry to secure the sacred ground from vandals and brick thieves. The vestry asked Isaac Dubose and his wife, Catherine, the owners of the land, to transfer a one-acre square parcel containing the chapel and cemetery, to the church commissioners who were also the four surrounding neighbors.[202] The families eventually interred all of the commissioners, except John Deas Jr. at the chapel beneath stone markers. Sadly, a thief in the early 1800s plundered the engraved headstone that marked the final resting place of John Deas Sr. and used it for many years as a hearthstone in a nearby cabin. No one recovered the stolen Deas marker and it eventually disappeared. Another stone denoted the grave of his wife, Caroline until it too disappeared after 1927.[203]

Henry Izard arrived at the Easter service by carriage from his renowned Elms Plantation contiguous to the western border of the Oaks. Resting in a box seat, beneath the hatchments displayed on the face of the balcony, Izard was without a doubt the wealthiest landowner and most prestigious head-of-family in attendance. That year the first bale of American cotton arrived in England from the port of Charleston and although the ingenious improvements Eli Whitney made to the cotton gin were eight years away, Ralph Izard envisioned the durability and practical applications of the miracle fiber that sprung forth without much effort from the higher rice lands. He experimented with the curious plant, and later added a cotton gin barn to his well-appropriated settlement, making the Elms one of the best-accommodated working plantations in Carolina, at a time when many landowners abandoned the exhausted soils for better fields farther west.

---

202. Charleston County Deed Book (CCDB) Y-5, 252: South Carolina, 6-20-1787, Isaac Dubose (LS), Wit: Lewis Fogartie, Thos Brodie. Proven in Charleston District by the oath of Thos Brodie 6 Nov 1787 before Phil Prioleau, J.P. Recorded Nov 1787, a plat by Joseph Purcell, Surveyor, included. The record states George Chicken promised to donate one acre from "the walls of the chapel" to the Commissioners of the Chapel of Ease.
203. Alston Deas Papers, SCHS. Also, see William Henry Johnson, the William Henry Johnson Scrapbook. William Henry Johnson, 1871-1934, William Henry Johnson Scrap-book, v. 1, circa 1920-1923, from the photographic collections of the SCHS, 34/0293. William Henry Johnson sketched the cemetery on 5-29-1927 and noted the stone marker of "Mrs. Caroline Deas, 8/1816 age 55."

A celebrated patriot, Alexander Garden Jr. owned nearby Otranto Plantation, but resided in town and divided and sold the ancient estate of his father the following year. His surprise appearance at church as Major Alexander Garden, one-time cornet for "Light Horse" Harry Lee's Legion, and later aide-de-camp for General Nathaniel Greene, was a patriotic spectacle for the congregation who eagerly intoned the emerging myths of heroes.

Figure 4.3: Thomas Middleton (1797-1863), son of Thomas Middleton Sr. (1753-1797) painted the image of the Elms with watercolors. See the Middleton Family Papers (1787-1849) 1168.02.01. The image is courtesy of the South Carolina Historical Society.

Thomas Smith of Broom Hall, like his immediate neighbors at Crowfield and the Oaks, embraced the zeal for revolution at first. His son-in-law, John Mackenzie, of the neighboring Button Hall Plantation, was an ardent resistance leader and member of the "non-importation party," but when the crisis deteriorated into open revolt, Smith retreated to his Goose Creek home to stay above the fray. Nonetheless, he could not avoid the conflict, and like his neighbors, he begrudgingly acquiesced, contributing supplies to the invaders. The previous year, Smith wrote his cousin in Boston that he "…was truly in the way of both parties" causing "distress and trouble" for himself and his family.[204] He and his wife,

204. Michael Trinkley, Ph.D. Debi Hacker and Natalie Adams, "Broom Hall: a good one and in a pleasant neighborhood," (Columbia: The Chicora Foundation Inc. 1995), 58, 59.

Sarah, arrived at church with only two of the youngest of 12 children and departed later that week to enjoy the warmer months at his residence in Charleston. He relied upon fifty slaves to care for Broom Hall while he remained absent in the General Assembly, and four years later reported to the State Convention as a delegate where he helped ratify the Federal Constitution.

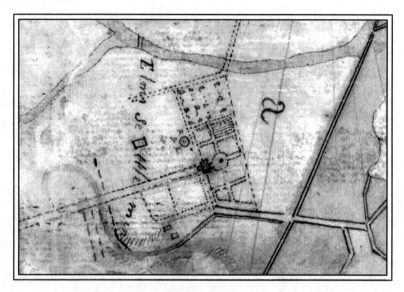

Figure 4.4: The partial plat describes the settlement of The Elms Plantation. The McCrady Plat number 4229 is among the collections of the Register of Mesne Conveyance Office at the Charleston County Office Building, Charleston, South Carolina.

Also absent were John Parker and his bride Susannah Middleton Parker of nearby Hayes Plantation. Remembered by all as a stalwart patriot throughout the painful struggle, he was away as a member of congress. He shot and killed a renegade "red coat," after the assailant fired upon Susannah, and Parker remained an unwavering patriot who somehow escaped the wrath of England. Later, Susannah and his sons laid John Parker to rest under shade trees one hundred yards from the front door of his two-story brick house on the headwaters of Goose Creek north of Windsor Hill.

Smith may have asked for Crown protection. Patriot Ralph Izard, Smith's neighbor, lost slaves and suffered malicious property damage.

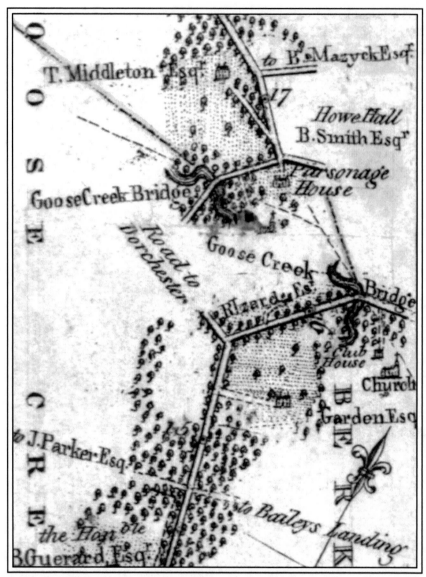

Figure 4.5: The section above the match line on the Abernathie and Walker Map, describes the Goose Creek Church, Bridge, Parsonage House, Road to B. Smith Esq. (Howe Hall), Road to B. Mazyck Esq. (Boochawee), 17-Mile Marker, and the home of T. Middleton Esq. (The Oaks). The segment below the match line shows the avenue to J. Parker Esq. (the Hayes), the 15-Mile Marker, the avenue to Garden Esq. (Otranto), the Road to Dorchester and R. Izard, Esq. (the Elms), the 16-Mile Marker, the Bridge, a Club House and the St. James, Goose Creek Church.

Also conspicuous by their absence were Rawlins Lowndes, his wife Sarah and their daughters. They owned Crowfield within a short ride of the church, but already abandoned the aging manor purchased from William Hagget shortly before the British occupied Charleston. They relocated to fertile fields near Beaufort, South Carolina. Nonetheless, their "capital mansion," once the finest structure in Carolina, now in disrepair, spoke of grander by-gone days. Similarly, no one attended Easter service from Button Hall. The owner, John McKenzie abandoned the one-time showplace rice plantation early in the war and did not reoccupy it, but soon after conveyed the grand old manor with orchards, fishponds, bathhouse and a two-story brick mansion to William Laughton Smith.[205]

A celebrated personality, Benjamin Guerard arrived after a brief ride from Fontainbleu Plantation, which he purchased that winter. He joined the Goose Creek society when he married Sarah Middleton, daughter of Colonel Thomas Middleton of Boochawee and Howe Hall. Merely weeks into his new assignment as Governor of South Carolina, and then a widower, he arrived with his spinster daughter by his side attracting much curiosity from the assembling congregation of old families. He recently purchased an estate on unusually high ground above Steepbrook Plantation, the countryseat of young Gabriel Manigault. Manigault ascended as one of the three most powerful Carolina politicians in the infant republic.

GABRIEL MANIGAULT

The unpredictable circumstances of British conquest of Charleston overwhelmed young Gabriel Manigault, as well as many of his older colleagues. The 23-year-old Lieutenant surrendered amidst the confusing days accepted the protection of the crown and assumed the position of Magistrate for the Charleston District. The British commander awarded that vaulted judicial post to him because of his legal training, but moreover because of his renowned family. The commander hoped that others would follow his example and accept the protection of the king. In mid-August, young Manigault signed a circulated letter congratulating the British victory at Camden. That act encouraged the commander in Charleston and affirmed his trust for the new magistrate, but he was unaware of the turmoil brewing within the young man when he granted permission for him to leave the city late the following winter.

---

205. Wragg Papers 11/467/11 with the Wragg Family Papers, 1722-1859, 1118.0, SCHS

Notwithstanding many rational reasons to acquiesce to the overwhelming British presence, Gabriel Manigault felt the tugs of his Huguenot soul and the pangs of remorse when his fiercely patriotic grandfather died in March of that year.[206] The death of the family patriarch six months after the city fell, turned Gabriel's heart and forced his hands to action.

The family buried Gabriel senior at French Huguenot Cemetery where he long served as vestryman, and in the weeks that followed, they planned and prepared for departure on a short but dangerous journey beyond the walls. In mid-November Gabriel rode horseback along gloomy Meeting Street aside his younger brother and ahead of a carriage with his mother and sister. With a cadre of house servants, the entourage picked its way through the battlements braiding the Charleston neck, and embarked upon the Goose Creek Road for a thirteen-mile trek to their safe house at Steepbrook Plantation.

The derelict byway was busy with wranglers such as Leonard Askew and his two sons. The British employed Askew to deliver cattle from Goose Creek to Wragg's Pasture near the six-mile stone, where butchers portioned the meat for delivery to hungry soldiers encamped on the peninsula. He dutifully repeated the chore every few days, acquiring the animals at Vance's Tavern and driving the herd of one or two dozen beasts ten miles toward the neck.[207] Among the cowhands were streams of unsupervised slaves from many households carrying country produce to the town market and returning with precious pence, increasingly rare within and without the fortified city. Criminals of every stripe roamed the byway, bullying the weak, and preying upon anyone with something of value.[208]

---

206. Gabriel Manigault, Last will and testament, WPA will book 80-B. Also see, *South Carolina Gleanings in England*, the last will and testament of Gabriel Manigault, 1-16-1781, SCHGM, 5: 220, 221. His estate was valued at $845,000. It consisted of 47,532 acres of land, with 490 slaves, storehouses in Charles Town, residences, lots and large sums of money. He was a member of the Assembly, Public Treasurer, Receiver General, and founder of the Charleston Library Society. He assisted poor Protestant immigrants and the Governor appointed him to trade with the Cherokee. Gabriel Manigault and his brother-in-law Benjamin Coachman were ardent patriots with their words and deeds, and both died before witnessing the outcome of the struggle.
207. Peter Wilson Coldham, *American Loyalist Claims* (Washington, DC: National Geological Society, 1980), 17.
208. Robert Wilson Gibbes, *Documentary History of the American Revolution, Volumes II and III, 1776-1782* (Spartanburg, South Carolina: The Reprint Company, 1972), v.II: 215-216. Governor John Mathews wrote to patriot General Francis Marion that a dozen to twenty slaves traveled from Charleston each night to "Goose Creek and up the Cooper River" and returned with supplies. He stated, "The Chs Town markets are now daily supplied with

After riding six miles, the Manigaults paused at Izard's Camp to refresh their horses. Everyone recognized the family as among the class allowed to exchange their beasts if they wished, but the troupe did not tarry long enough to remove the harness, because, unknown perils and more miles remained. Nevertheless, while the postilion brought water buckets to the animals, Gabriel searched every face looking for "Steepbrook people," who slipped bondage or merely visited the Izard slave row, but he identified no one at the camp or along the way. Nevertheless, the landscape was telling. He found the British absent, retreated behind ramparts at Fort Dorchester and Charleston, and the deserted countryside denuded and devolved into a martial vacuum. Furthermore, he found the supply line stretching from Goose Creek to the city brittle due to declining currency from the shrinking military coffers. More telling of the underlying circumstance, the roadway swirled with rumors of gallant exploits of new American heroes who appeared and disappeared along the way, exciting the populace, peaking suspicions and expanding gullible imaginations.

Francis Marion's grandfather, Benjamin Marion immigrated to a nearby farm. His land lay northwest of Steepbrook on the Road to Dorchester that skirted the northern perimeter of the shrinking British-patrolled hinterland. Francis Marion and his small band re-crossed the Santee River the previous month to patrol that familiar neighborhood, assay the progress of the war near Charleston and convey news to superiors. Consequently, with the "Swamp Fox" nearby, Manigault settled his loved ones at Steepbrook and was "obligated" days later to gallop with his manservant across the Goose Creek Bridge to announce his arrival at the tavern near the Eighteen-Mile Stone. It was not long before a whisper directed him to remount and ride to the camp of Francis Marion.

Gabriel Manigault promised loyalty to the patriot cause, and repented for his shortcomings by contributing a huge sum to the impoverished government. He also served in the Governor's camp for the duration of the conflict. In October of that year, General Lord Cornwallis surrendered at Yorktown, Virginia lifting moods throughout the rural campgrounds. With that good news, some patriots journeyed home, but Gabriel remained with the patriot governor and was there when his mother perished at Steepbrook on April 30, 1782.[209] The stubborn British remained behind their ramparts at Charleston until December 14 of that year, when they lit their fortifications, evacuated the moribund municipality and sailed across the bar.[210]

---

the greatest plenty of everything they want."

209. SCHM, 84: 252.

210. During a hearing regarding the will of Gabrial Manigault Sr., Thomas Scottow, Sec-

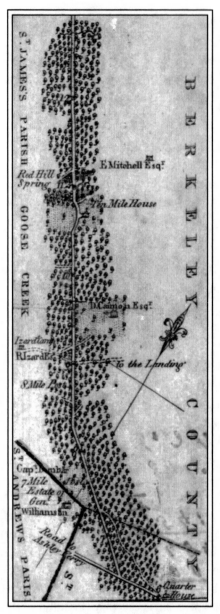

Figure 4.6: The Walker and Abernathy Map shows Izard Camp west of the Goose Creek Road above the eight-mile post. The Izard and Manigault families socialized for many decades before joining by marriage after the Revolutionary War. The Izards owned many plantations including the Elms on the headwaters of Goose Creek.

retary for the Province of South Carolina noted that Gabriel Manigault Jr. was, "without the British lines..." on 3-18-1782.

When or where Manigault reached the camp of Francis Marion is unknown and no record describes the visit or its duration. Nonetheless, within a brief period, a Marion man escorted Manigault on the second leg of the journey to the headquarters of patriot Governor John Rutledge who was preparing to assume his executive duties of a liberated state and needed young legal minds and thick Huguenot blood to stiffen his authority.

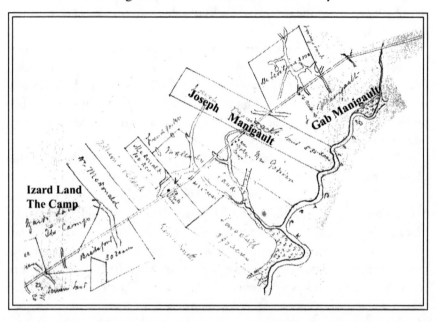

Figure 4.7: This partial plat describes the *Goose Creek Road from the Ten Mile House to Vance's Tavern with the relative situations of the Plantations.* This truncated plat does not show Vance's Tavern, but adds manuscript labels to highlight the Manigault Tracts. Henry Ravenel drew the plat for the South Carolina government to regulate the cutting of timber for the State Road in 1826. Manuscript labels added for this publication indicate the Steepbrook property divided between Gabriel and Joseph Manigault.

Gabriel Manigault made well-reasoned and timed decisions throughout the struggle that kept him on the winning side as the fortunes of war waxed and waned. His final decision to report to General Francis Marion's camp secured his loyalty to the victorious patriots and protected his valuable plantations. He did not attend Easter service in Goose Creek in 1784. He departed early that spring to his Townhouse in Charleston, and the following month he was at Clifton, an estate near Philadelphia, where he eventually retired.

WILLIAM JOHNSON

William Johnson and his large rambunctious family attended Easter service that year. A shaded avenue proceeded one mile north from their Goose Creek-side home connecting to Red Bank Road six miles south of the glebe. Mother, father and now six children conveyed to the church by wagon retracing the last leg of the route that carried them safely home two years before.

What seemed to be a lifetime, Sir Henry Clinton, British Commander at Charleston sent William Johnson to prison in St. Augustine, Florida. There the thirty-nine year old warrior suffered with other Carolinians until released in a captive exchange fourteen months later. Anguishing for his family and learning that the British command banished all of them from war-torn Charleston, he set sail in pursuit of them.

During the British occupation most of the wives and children of the Goose Creek patriots sequestered in their country homes. Mary Loocock of neighboring Red Bank Plantation,[211] Sarah Middleton of the Oaks, Sarah Lowndes of Crowfield and Elizabeth Brown of Back River were among Goose Creek mothers who remained with their children near familiar hearths during the entire occupation. In each case, their husband accepted the protection of the crown and terms of parole. William Johnson refused all terms and as a prisoner of war received little consideration for the safety of his loved ones.

Sarah Johnson sought the security of her rural White House Plantation, hoping for solace in its relative isolation on the northern bank of Goose Creek above the neck, but like most remote places near Charleston, hungry marauders found them, demanded food and drink, stole livestock and bullied the occupants. The British commander ordered commissaries to seize cattle, horses, forages, rice and other articles useful to the army from abandoned "Habitations and Plantations" of "rebels," but many ignored the word "abandoned," causing women and children of patriots to suffer.[212] Nonetheless, the British commander took no action against landowner, Archer Smith when he shot and killed an intruder at Palmetto Plantation across the creek and within sight of White House. In addition, the commander sent a thank-you note to planter, John Parker for shooting

---

211. Aaron and Mary Loocock also owned a home near Thorogood on the headwaters of Back River.
212. Carl Borick, *A Gallant Defense, The Siege of Charleston, 1780* (Columbia: University of South Carolina Press, South Carolina, 2003), 243.

and killing a wayward red coat at the Hayes Estate. Nonetheless, Sarah Johnson dared not resist the intruders at White House. Her oldest son was not yet twelve years old and no slave or overseer dare stand against the raiding dragoons. Consequently, she bravely complied as lonely months passed and more horses, cows and other items of sustenance disappeared.

In the summer of 1781, fourteen months after the fall of Charleston, Sir Henry Clinton ordered Sarah Johnson and her five children deported to British-held Philadelphia where other patriot families sequestered for the duration.[213] However, the gloomy banishment turned to joy after six days at sea. All during that July morning, the three oldest Johnson boys peered over the ramparts as their transport negotiated the dangerous Delaware straits, and all afternoon they watched a square-rigged brigantine shadow them at a thousand yards, tracing each jib and tack until the sun began to slip. Then, when their transport dropped its mainsail at Newcastle Harbor, and the pursuing brigantine slid close alongside, the boys heard their father's voice hail them from the other deck, twenty yards away, and five hundred sea miles from home.[214]

The brigantine carried many captured heads of families recently exchanged for British officers, and more exhilarating reunions erupted that summer and into the early fall to soften the extreme conditions of wartime Philadelphia. Their moods soared again in October 1781, when all the "Dutch watchmen" went about the streets after mid-night crying, "bast twelfe o'glock and Cornwallis es dagen!"[215]

Unbeknown to the weary travelers, circumstances shaping the emergence of the new republic were playing out even as they sailed up the Atlantic Seaboard in July. The armies and navies of Great Britain, France and the rebellious colonies were converging near Yorktown, Virginia for the last major engagement of the war. There, Lord Charles Cornwallis surrendered on October 19, 1781 to General George Washington and French allies, thus numbering the days of British rule in the colonies.

Notwithstanding the shocking defeat at Yorktown, the British remained in Charleston until the following Christmas, delaying the return of the Johnson family to their White House sanctuary. Daniel Latham, a distiller in Philadelphia graciously welcomed the Johnson refugees into his home

213. A tombstone in the Prioleau cemetery near the Johnson tract bears an engraving that states, "Carolina Dawson, Born in Philadelphia July 15, 1782, during the banishment of her mother from Charleston and died in Charleston May 1st 1870."
214. Johnson, 381.
215. Johnson.

until William rented a small cottage for his large family. After eighteen months in exile, impatient William, Sarah, their children and several other families loaded wagons behind horses and embarked on their return to South Carolina. After weeks of deprivation, they reached Charlotte, North Carolina and waited there all of November 1782 as the British retreated behind their fortifications in Charleston and prepared to evacuate.

The Johnson family walked more than two hundred miles from Charlotte before entering their home parish at the end of the first week in December. Trudging along the Road to Moncks Corner, they passed the derelict chapel of ease, its rotten roof near collapse, but marking the familiar center of an aging Back River community of old families and virulent patriots. Near the chapel appeared the mile-long avenue to Thorogood Plantation, home of John and Mary Deas. The Deas' path intersected the byway near the twenty-two mile stone. With waning energy, the travelers followed it west until the main house emerged beneath live oaks framing a wide expanse of gray, dormant rice fields.

Comrades in arms, John Deas and William Johnson "slept on the ground," and "mounted the lines" in Charleston in 1776,[216] but unlike Johnson, Deas acquiesced when the British invaded the second time and dominated the countryside. He feared for his large family, his oldest son was too young to fight,[217] and marauders from both armies stole whatever they coveted from his land. Consequently, when Sir Henry Clinton offered the "king's protection," Deas accepted and retreated to his Goose Creek home, where he waited for hostilities to end, and then greeted his old colleague after a two and a half year hiatus.

John and Mary Deas and their sons and daughter enthusiastically welcomed Sarah, William, their four boys and daughter upon their arrival to the Deas home in December 1782. The Deas family entertained the growing Johnson clan while William senior "went down on Goose Creek Neck" to inquire about his White House Plantation.[218] Upon arriving at White House, Johnson discovered marauders stole all of his livestock, but the resourceful servants produced "a good crop of provisions."[219] Incredibly, not a single slave departed during the chaos of war, remaining loyal to

---

216. SCHM, 24: 21.

217. John Deas jr. was fifteen-years old in 1780.

218. Joseph Johnson recalled the visit but referred to the place as "Thorough Good." An avenue to Thorogood Plantation, the home of John Deas and his large family, intersected the Road to Moncks Corner near the twenty-two mile marker.

219. Irving/Stoney, 74.

their ancestral village,[220] and Johnson sent two of them with a wagon the following day to retrieve his exhausted family. That evening, long after sunset, from the lowest point of his property near Red Bank Landing, he watched the southern sky glow. The British were evacuating the city and torching their abandoned fortifications as they departed. All during the night of December 14, flames lit the chilled sky beneath a brilliantly waxing moon.

During the early days of winter, the Johnson family settled into familiar routines on Goose Creek, and in late December, they sailed to Charleston to assess the devastation. Much work and responsibility confronted each of them, but it was Christmas Eve, a time for reflection and celebration. As William stowed the oars of his skiff at the city wharf, he caught the glint of a lost shilling in the pluff mud. With it, he purchased a bundle of raisins that Sarah baked into a pudding. Many years later, Joseph Johnson recalled the Christmas of 1782 when the family gathered around the raisin pudding; "Never had we enjoyed a happier Christmas...!" William Johnson, blacksmith and planter, chanced his family and fortune for patriotic principals and emerged a wealthy man in multiple ways.

MAJOR GENERAL WILLIAM MOULTRIE

None of the famous Moultrie boys attended Easter service at Goose Creek in 1784. Dr. John Moultrie, patriarch of the famous family and his bride, Lucretia Cooper joined the congregation more than fifty years before, conveniently residing on the waterway five miles south of the bridge. Their robust family eventually counted four sons, all of whom attained prominence in public service. Eldest son, John Moultrie became Lieutenant Governor of East Florida under the Royal Government, and supported the British Crown during the Revolutionary War. Third son, James became Chief Justice of East Florida, and Thomas rose to the rank of captain, but perished in 1780 during the brutal siege of Charleston. A fifth son, Alexander Moultrie descended from Dr. John Moultrie and his second wife Hannah Lynch. Alexander planted fields contiguous to the Chapel of Ease at the camp. Alexander called his inland rice estate "Richmond Plantation," and like his famous father, served the state of South Carolina

---

220. United States Census, Enumeration Schedule, Charleston District, St. James, Goose Creek Parish, records that William Johnson only owned 16 slaves in 1790. Will of William Johnson, Will Book Volume 33: 1409, (1807-1808), 10- 25-1808, William Johnson kept "negro blacksmiths" and "such other town negros [sic]."

in public office. The governor appointed him Attorney General and that Easter morning, many attendees searched for him, the other Moultrie brothers, and especially William, the hero of Sullivan's Island.

William Moultrie, the boy asleep on his mother's lap at Easter service fifty-two years before, ascended as an iconic South Carolina hero. Rising to the rank of Major General in the Continental Army during the Revolutionary War, William Moultrie subsequently led as a lawmaker and governor of the infant State of South Carolina. Although he grew up on Goose Creek, life callings carried him away from his childhood home and he typically attended services at St. Philips Church, near his town house overlooking Charleston Harbor. Merely three years before, naval vessels roiled that waterway with all the canons ablaze, but now the peaceful harbor laid still and silent in want of commerce for the fledgling nation.

Reverend Edward Ellington arrived in Goose Creek before the canons of war sounded in Charleston harbor, but amidst mounting calls for revolution. As months turned to years and the shrill call to arms hastened, the good pastor led an increasingly disparate congregation that polarized into warring camps. The bitter flock presented daunting challenges to Reverend Ellington but throughout those trying times, he led unwaveringly, finally bringing his followers together again on Easter morning in 1784. That day he worked to salve the wounded souls of his tattered parishioners through skillful reflection and he hoped to reunite them spiritually through prayerful introspection. One attendant of the church recalled that, "[Reverend Ellington was] pious, talented, eloquent, and zealous in his parochial duties…."[221] The "talented" minister endeavored to unite his followers before, during, and after the conflict and until he retired in 1793. Notwithstanding his vaulted interpersonal skills, he did not avert an ecclesiastical decline. As the 18th century waned, neither he nor his successors thwarted the dynamic political force weighing mightily upon the hundred-year-old parish, besmirching all things British, and eroding the little sacred places.

---

221. Johnson, 383. Joseph Johnson described Reverend Ellington in his *Traditions and Reminiscences, Chiefly of the American Revolution in the South*, published in 1851. He likely gleaned some of his observations during the 1784 Easter Service when he attended the service with his father, William Johnson, and his family.

CHAPTER 5
Little Places

Walking to church clutching his handwritten sermon and resting a fishing pole on his shoulder, Reverend Milward Pogson stopped on the Goose Creek Bridge to test his luck. Spring arrived late in 1798, and the warming creek waters enticed the famished bream and trout to the surface, stalking and snatching insects and flies. The sporty minister did not pass up an opportunity to catch supper, and soon with patience and skill, he hooked an enormous trout. As the fish fought for its freedom, the good minister fully engaged in the excitement of the sporting moment and forgot his sermon tucked under his arm. The papers slipped into the water several feet below the overpass and floated beyond his reach. Consequently, the priest arrived at the sanctuary door that Sunday with his dinner but no message for the congregation.[222]

Reverend Milward Pogson assumed the responsibilities of the St. James, Goose Creek Church congregation near the turn of the 19th century. He found the parsonage uninhabitable with one wall partly fallen and the roof sagging ominously. However, the resourceful churchman was the husband of Henrietta Wragg, daughter of an old Carolina family with town and country property and multiple connections to landed gentry. She nurtured her gentility with the ancient clans of Carolina and as a result, a favored uncle invited the popular priest and his bride to reside in the well-accommodated Otranto Club House near the western approach to the bridge. There, Pogson

---

222. Waring, 1897, 17. The vestry elected Milward Pogson rector of St. James, Goose Creek Parish, 3-28-1796. He served until Reverend John Thompson replaced him. Milward Pogson resigned 2-26-1806 but served the same parish briefly a decade later. www.jstor.org/stable/27569761.

assumed the appearance of a well-healed country gentleman while drawing a modest salary from the shrinking rural Anglican congregation.

Reverend Pogson walked across the Goose Creek Bridge every Sunday generally oblivious to the persistent but subtle changes in the habits of people he passed every day. During the early decades of the 19th century, the neighborhood served by the Episcopal (Anglican) Church[223] devolved from a collection of large prosperous estates to a community of marginally successful planters and farmers. Investors steadily shifted available capital away from the exhausted inland rice fields to lands along tidal influenced rivers. Some successful planters abandoned the exhausted estates of their fathers and grandfathers and sought cotton fields in the west. Others despaired and turned to crime, prompting one Goose Creeker to recall, "persons rarely ventured to travel the Goose Creek road without arms," because highway robbery and horse stealing were so common.[224] Moreover, the persistent and mysterious malaria that plagued the parish for more than a century forced some to seek healthier environments.

The predictable summer fevers prompted wealthier planters to seek the harbor breezes of Charleston during the warmer times of the year while the less affluent residents traveled to nearby but well-drained pine forest communities such as Summerville, Pineville, Barrows and Pinopolis. Other Goose Creek planters such as James Withers and James Graham enjoyed entire seasons on Sullivan Island near the cool sea air until the first frost prompted their return to the countryside.[225]

The seasonal exodus, the shift to tidal rice culture, and the exhausted fields diminished the wealthy population that long characterized the eastern third of the parish. By 1810, overseers employed by absentee landowners, marginal planter/farmers, tenants and African-American slaves dominated the demography of the parish and that trend toward a less affluent population persisted for decades as more families employed overseers to manage the workers and care for the land during most of the year. Consequently, among 154 heads of households in the parish in 1810, there were 36 (23%) families not present 20 years earlier and those additional heads of households were not landowners, but overseers and their dependents.

---

223. Part of the Anglican Communion, the Episcopal Church in the United States descended from the Church of England in 1789. After the Revolutionary War, Anglicanism in South Carolina almost collapsed.

224. ·Samuel David Dubose and Frederick A. Porcher, *A Contribution to the History of the Huguenots of South Carolina* (New York, New York: The Knickerbocker Press, 1887, Columbia, South Carolina: Reprinted from the Original, The R.L. Bryan Company, 1972), p. 8.

225. SCDAH, S165015, General Assembly Petition, Number 1501.

Overseers became increasingly important, and in some cases worked their own slaves side by side with those of the absentee owner. In 1810, Goose Creek overseers William Browning, William Campbell, Joseph Cantey and Andrew Dehay owned 129, 137, 69 and 6 slaves respectively.[226] Obviously, some overseers supported relatively wealthy households, but most owned few or no bound laborers and were far less wealthy than were their property owners.

Additionally, during the first decades of the new century, more "free colored" labored upon the worn properties. In 1830, sixty-one emancipated African-Americans worked Goose Creek farms with varying levels of responsibilities.[227] Some managed the entire plantation in the absence of the owner while others worked mundane tasks. Only 40% of the landowners in the eastern section used white overseers, relegating the other plantations (60%) to the talents of non-white drivers.

Some planters, such as Benjamin Paul Williams, who purchased George Chicken's plantation,[228] and John Bowen, who purchased the Coachman (Schenckingh) lands on Goose Creek, were well-to-do owners of successful estates. These men kept homes in Charleston where they endured the unhealthy months and depended upon the loyalty of multi-generations of African workers. They relied upon employed "free colored," as well as their own bound help to manage successfully the properties in their absence, but many only marginally kept the family and workers fed and others failed at that.

Contemporaries noted that some, "call themselves Gentlemen" but many members of the old families were bankrupt or nearly insolvent, and some of the best-known families struggled mightily to keep the appearance of propriety with little more than exhausted fields and worn implements. During those anachronistic years, Reverend Pogson was the first minister ordained in the Episcopal Diocese of South Carolina. The state no longer sanctioned the Church of England; services long ago vanished at the rural chapels of ease due to the lack of worshippers and the congregation persistently dwindled throughout his decade-long tenure. Therefore, at the turn of the new century, the Goose Creek Bridge conveyed fewer wealthy patrons to their rural homes and sanctuaries, but carried more hungry families to small farms scattered wantonly throughout the central and

226. 1810, United States Census and Slave Schedules, St. James, Goose Creek Parish.
227. 1830, Census.
228. Isaac Dubose sold Cedar Grove Plantation to Benjamin Paul Williams on 6-8-1787. Exclusion for the chapel of ease is included in the deed, CCDB Z5:293. The chapel is in ruinous condition, Dalcho, 493-98.

western sections of the parish where few, if any confessed ties to the obsolete institutions of England. Nevertheless, a few families of powerbrokers on both sides of the bridge, persisting from the colonial era, emerged as members of the new United States Federalists Party led by Alexander Hamilton.

THE FEDERALISTS

Wealthy Gabriel Manigault of Steepbrook Plantation married Margaret Izard in 1786. She was the sixteen-year-old daughter of Ralph Izard and Alice De Lancey Izard of the renowned Elms Plantation. Ralph Izard was a member of the Continental Congress, a United States Senator from South Carolina, and the father of six, including Charlotte, who married William Loughton Smith, a wealthy and dynamic politician residing at nearby Button Hall Plantation. These marriages united the Manigaults, Izards and Smiths into a political faction that dominated South Carolina for almost sixteen years and influenced the national Federalist policy during the presidencies of George Washington, John Adams and Thomas Jefferson.[229]

Dining rooms, parlors, libraries and verandas at the Elms, Button Hall and Steepbrook manors lay within a four-mile triangle straddling the dynamic little Goose Creek Bridge, and each abode provided a venue for dinners and other parlays where the three influential men debated relevant issues of the new state and republic.[230] The Izards kept an elegant countryseat and a five-acre "pleasure garden" at their Elms Plantation. Their home featured an octagonal drawing room as well a large hall where the newest leaders of the republic communed. The Steepbrook mansion, a large, square, two-story wooden structure, sat atop a high basement overlooking Goose Creek. The hipped roof splayed above one-story porches spanning the front and back of the house. Important conversations ensued on the verandas as well as in the elegant wainscoted dining hall. William Loughton Smith sometimes greeted his visitors in the parlor of his two-story brick abode, but he preferred to meet in his library with books valued at more than £2,100.[231]

---

229. Friday, 5-23-1788 Gabriel Manigault assented to ratify the Constitution of the United States along with Goose Creek representatives, Ralph Izard, Peter Smith, Benjamin Smith, William Smith, John Parker, Jun., and John Deas, Jun.
230. Walter B. Edgar and N. Louise Bailey, *Biographical Directory of the South Carolina House of Representatives* (Columbia: University of South Carolina Press, 1974), 3: 471, 472.
231. Shelley E. Smith, *The Plantations of South Carolina: Transmission and Transformation in Provincial Culture*, UMI Dissertation Services, A Bell and Howell Company, Ann Arbor Michigan, 1999, 154, 177. Artist George Roupell, painted a description of the Steepbrook

Figure 5.1: Charles Fraser painted *Mr. Gabriel Manigault's Seat at Goose Creek,1802*. The painting is from *A Charleston Sketchbook*, 1796-1860. The painting of Steepbrook Plantation is courtesy of Mrs. Carolina Cohen.

Each patriarch accomplished much and held lofty offices: Ralph Izard ascended in the United States Senate to its President pro tempore, William Laughton Smith emerged as Emissary to Portugal, and Gabriel Manigault, among many accomplishments, represented the St. James, Goose Creek Parish at the State Convention, where he assented to the Federal Constitution. Furthermore, each parlor hummed with relatives and rising business leaders, reaping new money from fascinating opportunities, some of which employed innovative engines (gins) that extracted stubborn seeds from cotton. Some garnered profits from public works projects, such as the Santee Canal connecting the Santee River to the Cooper River and the highly touted State Road that originated at the Goose Creek Bridge. Notwithstanding these exciting innovations for commerce and convenience, few congregants greeted Reverend John Thompson when he replaced Milward Pogson at the St. James, Goose Creek Church in 1801. Thompson was the last priest to lead regular Sunday service at the country church where more parishioners once attended Easter service than the largest congregation in Charleston. Three years later, the one-time busy crossroads for planters, traders, herders and craftsmen lay silent when a hero of the American Revolution, General William Moultrie, passed over the bridge via carriage in pursuit of his final place in history.

---

dining hall entitled *Mr. Peter Manigault and His Friends*, Goose Creek, South Carolina. See, "Notable Libraries of Colonial South Carolina," South Carolina Historical Magazine, v. 72, p. 109, South Carolina Historical Society, Charleston, South Carolina 1971.

Michael J. Heitzler, Ed.D.

WINDSOR HILL

Major General William Moultrie, warrior for independence and hero of the
American Revolution, died on Thursday, September 27, 1805, in a small, run-
down, two-story clapboard house on the corner of Magazine and Logan Streets
in the "jail bound" section of Charleston.[232] As was the practice of that day,
city officials rented small houses near the Charleston jail to sequester people
imprisoned for unpaid debts. The aging seventy-four year old warrior lived
"jail bound" and nearly alone with William, his manservant while officials
investigated his financial insolvency. As was a common expectation thirty
years before, he selflessly signed vouchers to supply his hungry infantry and
artillerymen during the Revolutionary War. Confidently, he expected the
victorious American government to pay the vouchers, settle all debts and clear
his obligations after the conflict. Unfortunately, he pledged his own assets
against public accounts and inexplicably included private expenses. As a result,
his financial status devolved into an embarrassment, even as he ascended to the
state senate in 1790 and the governor's office in 1792 and 1796.

Within that disturbing context, the general lay in his side-yard portico
all night and into Thursday morning, weakening and fading. Days before,
William the manservant threw wide the wooden shutters to admit as much
of the harbor breeze as possible, but because of the unrelenting humidity,
he dragged the soldier, bed and all onto the little porch aside the garden
where the general rested more comfortably.

Optimism reigned within the old warrior for many reasons even as he
suspected his approaching demise. General Moultrie ended his public service
as the sixth governor of South Carolina eleven years prior, and for decades,
he witnessed the fledgling nation resist jealous European navies, as did he
with canon fire nearly three decades before. He also listened as critics sullied
his war as a great folly that birthed a fledgling republic and set it to flounder
without the markets of the empire. Nonetheless, he found comfort in his
accomplishments and sought reprieve by penning his memoirs for nearly a year
in the modest townhouse, as the investigation into his solvency swirled.[233]

---

232. "Magazine Street, Old City Thoroughfare, Losing Identity," *News and Courier Newspaper*, 9-6-76, Charleston, South Carolina. The article uses a 1900 photograph of the
residence of General William Moultrie, when he was "jail bound for debt."
233. SCDAH Series S165029, Year ND, Item 85. Also, see: John Bennett. Wooden, "House
Where General Moultrie, Jailbound for Debt, Wrote his Memoirs, Is Being Stripped for
Firewood." *News and Courier*, 3-28-1938. Also see, William Moultrie, *Memoirs of the American Revolution* (New York: Daniel Longsworth, 1802). The publication date is three years
prior to the death of the general.

Figure 5.2: This section of the Walker and Abernathy travel map describes Charleston near the time the funeral cortege carried the remains of General William Moultrie, from the "jail bound" section of town along Meeting Street, across the neck of the peninsula to the Road to Goose Creek. The Road to Goose Creek commenced at the six-mile stone, near the intersection of a road west sometimes called, the Road to Ashley Ferry.

That Thursday, as the old general lay on his portico, President Thomas Jefferson waited enthusiastically for news from Meriwether Lewis and William Clark exploring an expanse called the Louisiana Territory. The United States of America was the youngest nation on earth, but already one of the largest. Moreover, the new country held immense potential that sparked the imagination of many. Some whispered about potential fortunes from fur trade in the British Northwest and others envisioned greater riches from the untapped Pacific Rim.

All that Thursday afternoon, family and acquaintances stood near the narrow foyer outside the front door on Magazine Street, while others moved stolidly about the humid parlor as the general faded into paralysis. When he lapsed into a deepening unconsciousness, a runner hurried through the musty city to spread the heartrending news.

That evening, loved ones carried his casket and body three blocks to its place before the altar in St. Philips Church. A few kept vigils all night and in the darkest hour of Friday morning, the clang of the front door latch awoke William, the manservant from his fitful nap. Both church doors swung wide and remained agape as the first light broke above the seaport, and townspeople appeared to watch the funeral wagon with cortege roll toward the city limits.

The procession commenced the seventeen-mile trek by pattering north on Meeting Street through the remnants of ancient fortifications. There, upon an earthen redoubt, twenty-five years before, Thomas Moultrie, younger brother of the general met Hessian infantrymen and perished from battle wounds. Still, that narrow cross section of the peninsular neck lay replete with old ditches awash with briny water and eroded banks that once defined a formidable rampart reaching from the Ashley to the Cooper River. Now the fallen infrastructure spanned uselessly beneath an orange sky rapidly diffusing above the Atlantic. Beyond those nauseous ditches and drains, the funeral party embarked the dusty Road to Goose Creek at the four-mile stone and continued two more miles to the Road to Ashley Ferry branching toward the west.

The old Road to Ashley Ferry passed near Windsor Hill at the head of Goose Creek, and at an earlier time, it was the preferred ingress, but a shorter route evolved through the St. James, Goose Creek Parish after the State Assembly in 1786 designated the little town of Columbia as the Capital of South Carolina. By the turn of the century, more carriages and equestrians preferred a short cut proceeding east from the wealthy Ashley River neighborhood to the State Road. Thus and coincidently, the most convenient route to the cemetery in 1805 carried the entourage past the boyhood home of the general and traced the original path west (later Ashley Phosphate Road) to the small hilltop family cemetery at Windsor Hill.

A respectful silence pervaded the procession, even as spectators gathered in small groups along the way and more waited near private avenues every quarter of a mile or less. Allen Fawsworth witnessed the passage of the hero. He resided with his large family near the 8-mile stone, where he supervised bound souls for the property owner, Thomas Baldric.[234] Similar land management arrangements characterized most properties along the way, including the next plantation owned by John Brailsford who employed Thomas Screven as overseer. Perry Philips supervised the properties that followed.[235] All gentlemen, overseers and male slaves doffed their hats while the ladies stood in silent deference with their children in hand to witness the passage of an era.

John Philbing respectfully watched the entourage approach for three hundred yards. He purchased the Ten-Mile-Tavern merely two years before from Thomas Tims and now viewed the long straight ascent of the Road to Goose Creek approaching from Charleston. The old spring at the ten-mile stone refreshed men and beasts for hundreds of years and the tavern remained the most popular way station to Columbia. Proprietor Philbing brought cider and bread to the sojourners when they paused to water the horses, and Alexander Burn and William Tate stopped their carpentry chores to pay respects.

Soon after the funeral party departed the Ten-Mile-House-Tavern, the old Moultrie family home came into view. The direct avenue permitted travelers on the road to see the main house at the end of a two-hundred yard long shaded avenue. The Moultrie family plantation conveyed to William and his brothers when their father, Dr. John Moultrie died in 1771, and the sons sold their family plantation in two parcels. John Fisher, "cabinet maker," purchased the southern section and relied upon its mature forests to supply lumber for his carpentry and furniture business. Dr. Charles Drayton purchased the northern portion with the old Moultrie settlement that included the two-story brick main house, nine slave-houses, many outbuildings with expansive lawns and gardens. Wealthy Drayton

---

234. Richard Hrabowski, *Directory for the District of Charleston Comprising the places of residence and occupation of the White Inhabitants of the Following Parishes to wit...St. James (Goose Creek)* (Charleston: John Hobb, no.6 Broad Street, 1809). The directory is among the collections of the South Carolina Historical Society, Charleston, South Carolina.
235. Hrabowski.

offered no assistance to the patriot cause during the darker days, preferring to sequester with the Middletons in the loyalist neighborhood near the St. James, Goose Creek Church, and he seldom visited the old Moultrie homestead after the war, preferring his plush Ashley River home. That day the entourage passed the general's boyhood home unnoticed.

When the cortege approached the twelve-mile stone, the tollgate pole rose sharply and remained steadily erect as if mocking Archibald McKelphin. McKelphin, an aging militiaman, stood alongside the gate, as rigid as the turnpike, presenting parade dress in honor of the general, while his curious grandchildren scampered along and atop the fence, and his workers paused in the bursting cotton fields until the funeral procession faded.[236]

The improved passage west diverged from the Road to Goose Creek near the 14-mile marker and skirted above the reaches of the Goose Creek waterway through three miles of forest and farmlands. The unusually straight byway undulated slightly, but often flattened and straightened sufficiently to allow travelers to gaze hundreds of yards ahead before bending into the woods. Occasionally when the path curved northwest, it lined up like a compass rose upon the rising mount. Then, Windsor Hill showed high and prominent above the horses' heads with the lowland forests sprawling against the horizon. One traveler noted "the elevation on which Windsor Hill stood [was] in full view of the much used highway...a fitting place of repose for a man of his national stature."[237] Late that afternoon, the servants and loved ones interred the general next to his son, in compliance with his "earnest request,"[238] and the exhausted procession retired in silence and without marking the grave. Sans a gravestone, the family hoped that creditors would be unable to find the site, nor seize the body and hold it for family ransom, as was a sordid myth of that day. The next morning, the *Charleston Courier* newspaper provided a glowing testimonial of the general and reported the "...most honorable and respectable burial," but gave no hint of the location of the grave.[239]

---

236. William Allen Deas owned the land at the 12-mile-stone in 1805, where the tollgate operated. He employed Archibald McKelphin, a militiaman as his overseer.

237. Mrs. Ainslie Brailsford Lawrence copied the following on 3-1-1875 from page four of the Moultrie family *Bible*, "General William Moultrie was buried at Windsor Hill, next to his son at his earnest request..."

238. The family *Bible* kept by Alexander Moultrie recorded the desire of the general to be buried aside his son, William.

239. Swamp vegetation surrounds the site except along the southwest section, where the hill connects with additional upland known as "Windsor Hills."

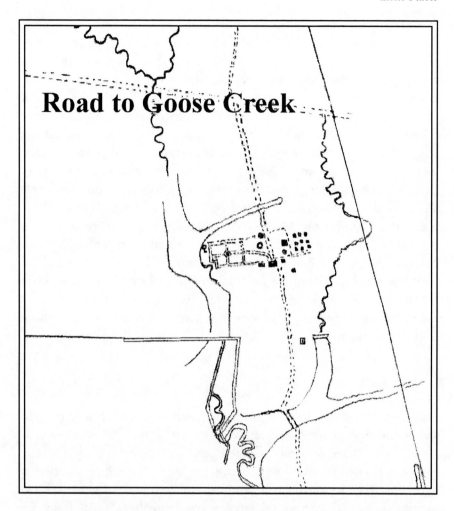

Figure 5.3: The partial plat describes the boyhood home of Major General William Moultrie. A survey produced this partial plat of property owned by Cyprian Bigelow in 1805, the year Major General William Moultrie died. The survey indicates the orientation of the Road to Goose Creek, as well as the settlement where the general was born and resided throughout his childhood. The main house with several large barns, carriage houses and other structures appear accessible by way of the main avenue that intersected the Road to Goose Creek. The plat describes an ornamental lawn with a center circular feature and walkways to the west of the main house. In addition, the plat indicates nine slave quarters north of the main avenue.

All of Carolina honors the memory of General Moultrie every day when the indigo blue South Carolina State flag ascends alongside the stars and stripes of the nation and all appreciate his role as a famous patriot whose gorget insignia and iconic palmetto tree graces the state banner. Nonetheless, when loved ones carried the remains of the general to a resting place high on the hill, no one accounted for the full measure of that man or the significance of his passing from the national stage. As his procession carried him beyond the ramparts of the city, into his home parish, past his childhood abode, and alongside diversifying Carolina businesses and farms, the journey recalled the long colonial legacy of which he and his family played essential roles. That long day recounted his lifetime as well as framed a moment in time, when his tenacity behind the guns on Sullivan's Island sufficiently stiffened the resolve of the founding fathers in Philadelphia. Those men signed the famous Declaration of Independence a few days after the cannonade, and consequently transformed a tentative union of colonies into a confident competitor among the leading nations of the world. Moreover, during the fateful years that followed, the novel ideas forged from fire, steel and revolution led to further originality when the founders listed specific rights for every white male, including freedom of religious worship.

HOUSES OF PRAYER

During the first two decades of the 19th century, John Hinds enjoyed steady business at his Seventeen-Mile House Tavern one-quarter mile above the shuttered St. James, Goose Creek Church and fallen parsonage. His business persisted as a popular stop for wayfarers seeking Charleston and conversely, in pursuit of Columbia and beyond.[240] The State Road expedited long land trips and saved many struggling family farms by connecting the agricultural products to the city markets, but no Goose Creek plantation fully recovered from the destruction of war. Moreover, the estranged Church of England in Carolina left a religious vacuum in the moribund society hungering for spiritual sustenance.

In 1784, John Wesley chartered the Methodist Church and late that year the Methodist Episcopal Church in the United States officially assembled in the "Christmas Conference" to organize its missions across the nation. Soon after, Francis Asbury, one of the assembly leaders, rode into the St. James, Goose Creek Parish as the first Methodist "circuit preacher" in Carolina. He brought together numerous prayer groups

---

240. Hrabowski.

under brush arbors in the center and western sections of the defunct parish, establishing long-standing congregations. Francis Asbury laid the foundation for Methodism in the old parish, but the tenacious Baptists assumed many of the spiritual responsibilities of the St. James, Goose Creek vestry, including the stewardship of the two fallen Anglican chapels in the "wilderness," and the little "Ludlam" schools.

In concert with the rising protestant congregations, the resilient St. James, Goose Creek vestry sought ways to protect their sacred places and appropriately use the Ludlam dollars to educate the poor. Although the funds depreciated considerably during the war, sufficient money remained to build a second brick schoolhouse.[241] The school arose in 1800, close to the site of the previous academy, and in 1814, Mrs. Rebecca Smith bequeathed a legacy to Benjamin Tyler, the "schoolmaster of the Ludlam School." Her gift minimally sustained instruction at the academy but financial challenges mounted and eventually overwhelmed the vestry.[242] The vestry aspired to advance the noble Ludlam mission originating almost a century before, but that well-intentioned experiment faltered when donations declined and fewer children attended until the church leaders abandoned the little institution of learning.[243] Nevertheless, the dogged church leaders persevered to train the parish poor by beseeching the rising Baptists congregations for help. They asked the Baptists to operate the schools in their stead on or near the sacred chapel sites.[244]

---

241. Smith Papers, 11/404/2, SCHS. The date of the construction is unknown, but Henry Smith visited the schoolhouse site observing its ruins near the end of the 19th century and reported that the vestry built the brick schoolhouse sometime between 1765 and 1770. He noted that the site was, "...about a mile to the north-east along the road that passes in front of the church."

242. Langdon Cheves, the Langdon Cheves Papers are among the collections of the South Carolina Historical Society, Charleston, South Carolina, 34/0320.

243. Smith Papers, 11/404/2 and Smith Papers plat on microfilm 1102 at SCHS. Charles Graves used the school building as a dwelling as late as 1852, when it fell into ruin. One could still trace the foundation during the first decade of the 20th century. According to an 1888 plat, the school stood at the intersection of Snake and Red Bank Roads. This may be the site of the school built circa 1765-1770 and the vestry probably erected it on the 12-acre school tract given by Henry Middleton for "a twig and a turf." Today, that school site is opposite the Goose Creek Rural Fire Department on Red Bank Road.

244. Smith Papers, 1102.00. Henry Smith recorded in his notes that the vestry purchased land and erected a "red brick" schoolhouse near 1800. It was located approximately two miles from the church and was operational in the early 1800's.

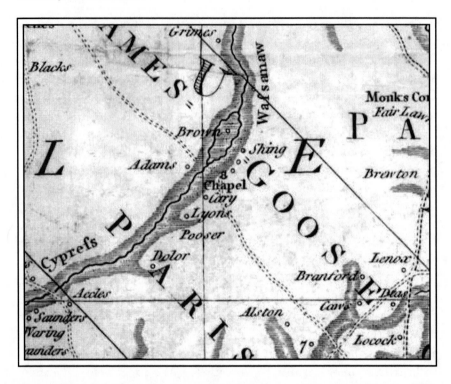

Figure 5.4: The Henry Mouzon Map shows the St. James, Goose Creek Chapel of Ease at Wassamasaw in 1775.

The Wassamassaw Baptist Church rose upon the St. James, Goose Creek Parish Chapel land in Wassamassaw, near the spring and ancient corrals, where Thomas Smith donated property for a school building a hundred years before.[245] Reverend Ralph Bowman was the first pastor at that Baptist assembly.[246] Richard Furman later engaged in missionary work there, setting the stage for future church leaders such as Reverend Matthew McCullers, who came to Wassamassaw during a revival in 1804, and afterwards traveled to the camp. There, at Colonel George Chicken's ancient campsite, he occupied the vestry chapel property and prepared a place for a congregation of worshippers.[247]

---

245. SCHGM 16: 43.

246. Ballentine, George H. *Church Record Book of Wassamassaw Baptist Church, Wassamassaw Section, Berkeley County, South Carolina, 1875-1919.* Private Publication by George H. Ballentine, 2714, Phyllis Drive, Copperas Cove, Texas, 2001 and see W.J. Townsend, H.B. Workman and George Eayrs, eds. *A New History of Methodism,* 2 vols. (London: Hodder and Stoughton. First ed. 1909), v1: 53.

247. *Bethlehem Baptist Church, Ledger of the Solemn Covenant of the Bethlehem Baptist Church in*

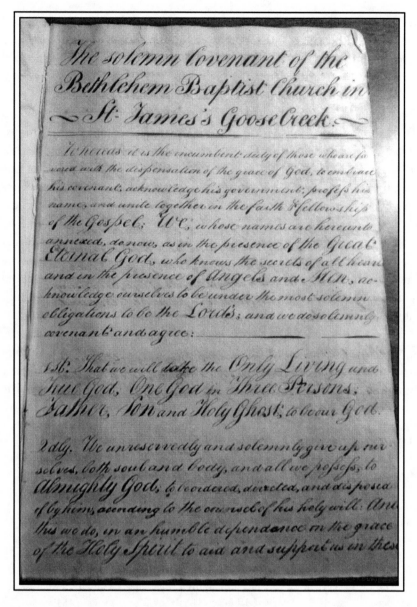

Figure 5.5: The title page of the "Bethlehem Baptist Church Covenant Book" gives the principal beliefs of the congregation. Twenty-two members, including eleven males and eleven females signed the covenant. Reverend John R. Hyatt served as pastor at the time.

St. James, Goose Creek, 1811-1871 (Book of the Covenant). The ledger book is among the collections of the Charleston Museum, Charleston South Carolina, 2007, 035, 002. Also see Ballentine.

Where a heap of bricks marked the place of the cruciform chapel, Reverend M. W. McCullers met with eight "brethren," on June 13, 1812 to organize a new Baptist assembly. With the fervent aid of Hephzibah Townsend[248] and help from J. H. Grumes (Grooms), church secretary, Reverend McCullers and two deacons significantly expanded the group.[249] Soon, the congregation hammered together a twenty-by-thirty-foot clapboard structure contiguous to the crumbled sanctuary using some of the tumbled bricks for the new foundation and front steps.[250] After McCuller died in 1817, successors kept the little sanctuary vibrant and provided for the spiritual requirements of the black and white Christians in the vicinity until after the Civil War, bringing soul lifting hymns to the countryside, and baptizing, marrying, and expanding the cemetery.[251]

Baptist congregations consistently ascended and missionaries busily erected new meetinghouses for vibrant growing memberships as the Episcopal institutions retreated. In 1825, Reverend C. P. Elliott attempted once again to revitalize the congregation at the St. James, Goose Creek Church, but found only four consistent communicants. Resolutely, he locked the doors one more time and passed the keys to Major Edward H. Edwards, the church deputy. Edwards acted as a land steward, renting glebe fields to families and with the nod from the vestry in 1828, sold the aging brick school building to Charles Graves for a family residence. The vestry did not abandon the church but combined $800.00 from tenant

---

248. Ballentine, 107.

249. Book of the Covenant and ledger book is among the collections of the Charleston Museum, Charleston South Carolina, 2007, 035, 002.

250. Remnants of two brick footings of the wooden church remain indicating the foot-print of the sanctuary. The *Map of North and South Carolina*, 1827, prepared by Henry S. Tanner shows a church at that location. The map is among the collections of the North Carolina State Archives. Frederick Dalcho reported in 1820 the chapel "crumpled" and, "...there are several tombstones around it; the oldest inscription upon them, that is leg-ible, is 1757." Mrs. Elizabeth Poyas visited in the mid-1800s and reported the "Baptists have a neat wooden church adjoining the ruin, from which they have used a few bricks for their steps..." Poyas, 192. A Ministerial License issued to George Lynes in 1849 states, "George Lynes...a man of good moral character, real piety and sound knowledge... is hereby authorized to... preach the gospel...this 10th day of February, 1849...." The minis-terial license is among the Lynes Family Papers.

251. The Book of the Covenant lists "colored" congregants accepted to the congregation after baptism. The book notes 8-11- 1810 "...Nanny and Betsy Sue...and the follow-ing servants of Mr. James Carson...of Dean Hall." Other entries list "...servants of Mr. Keckly," of Spring Grove Plantation, as well as servants belonging to George Lynes, James Fergusan and others.

rents with a $500 gift from St. Michael's Church in Charleston to bind the leaning sanctuary walls with iron rods, strengthen the roof, re-plaster the interior and recast the rough exterior stucco.

Before and after the Civil War, in exchange for the use of chapel lands, the Baptist congregations supervised the Ludlam supported schools, delivering instruction within a "faith based" arrangement with the State of South Carolina. The churches provided instruction in the lower parish and the state opened two schools north of Wassamassaw. The vestry employed teachers and paid their salaries with Ludlam dollars, but the Baptists selected the students and supervised the locations. Consequently, when the state legislature appointed school commissioners in 1827 to audit the Ludlam account[252] they found a school in Groomsville supervised by the nearby Bethlehem Baptist Church, and another school at the Wassamassaw Chapel of Ease overseen by that Baptist congregation.[253] Each Ludlam schoolmaster earned $300 annually, the same amount as public school teachers. A dozen or more students from poor families attended free of charge, prompting one visitor at the camp near mid-century to note that a young male teacher led "a few scholars from the lower class."[254]

The faith based arrangement between the parish and the State of South Carolina, in concert with the church-school partnership between the Baptists and Episcopalians, endured even as families steadily out-migrated in pursuit of fertile cotton fields. Those staying behind contended with worn soil and an anachronistic labor system based upon involuntary servitude that was no longer profitable in Goose Creek. Consequently, when promising new railroads spiked across the parish near mid-century, the rural residents remained entangled with a slave-based labor system that bound them to a failing way of life. Nonetheless, the great-railed behemoths of iron and steam gave hope to those who chanced that emotion, and when loading stations punctuated the countryside, some European-American families clustered. They erected sawmills, gristmills, blacksmith shops,

252. SCDAH, S165018, Year 1828, Item 32. In the minutes of the Wassamassaw and Mt. Olivet Churches frequent references cite the "Goose Creek Church" (Bethlehem Baptist) and "victors from Goose Creek," indicating a close fellowship between the three churches. It is likely that these sanctuaries shared pastors. In 1871, the Goose Creek Church contributed $2.00 towards the construction of the new house of prayer at Wassamassaw.
253. SCDAH, S165029, Item 2.
254. Poyas, 193. The little community near the camp acquired the name, "Strawberry," when the Northwestern Railroad Company erected a depot with that title near the intersection of the Road to Moncks Corner and the Road to Strawberry Ferry (today Cypress Garden Road).

little stores, and endeavored to use the newest conduits of commerce to exert their dwindling control over the surrounding black majority. There, they asserted sole mastery over a tiny universe, filtering whatever entered or departed their countryside by way of the trains, and confronted the wider community from the depot platform that was, for the next one hundred years, their sole "window to the world."

TRAIN DEPOTS – WINDOWS TO THE WORLD

The Northeastern Railroad (later the Atlantic Seaboard Railroad Company and today CSX Transportation Inc.) was one of three rail lines that radiated from Charleston through the St. James, Goose Creek Parish. The State of South Carolina granted a charter to the Northeastern Railroad in 1851 to connect Charleston to Florence in the northeastern section of the state. From Florence, the Wilmington & Manchester rail service connected to points north and west.[255] Private companies with state incentives laid the rail lines after successful years of public bridge and road construction.

A toll system replaced the unfair and impractical methodology of assessing contiguous landowners for road upkeep, and tolls combined with other state revenue affected considerable improvements along the State Road. Mary Blackman, one of many landowners, who hired out their slaves for road and bridgework, assigned five of her bound workers as "... hands liable to work the High Roads..." Notwithstanding considerable success, not all travelers were impressed with the improvements and one northern tourist humorously criticized the Goose Creek Bridge:

> ...other materials failing, they have split small logs in half & have lain [sic] them bridge fashion, the flat side upward & covered them with a few inches of clayey sand. As the chairs or gigs of this country have no springs, this kind of road keeps your bodies in a perpetual quiver, & you are left to apprehend that your brains may be shaken out of place or addled ...[256]

---

255. The state chartered the Northeastern Railroad Company in 1851. The company began construction in 1854 and completed the project in 1857. It tied Charleston with the northeastern section of South Carolina. The Atlantic Coast Line Railroad formed in 1898 as a consolidation of several roads including the Northeastern service
256. SCHM, 68: 244. Also, see the work contract between Mary Blackman and Thomas Mallard, Road Commissioner, March 31, 1840, among the Lynes Family Papers. Masters "hired out" slaves for approximately $7.00 a month. "Old Mrs [Elizabeth] Donnelly" and her children stayed at Foxbank temporarily and hired out their slave Jack until he became

Shortly after the traveler's bumpy ride, the state replaced the Goose Creek Bridge with a substantial covered structure, 200 feet-long, featuring wooden floor planking, brick abutments at both ends, a heavy wooden support in the middle, and a roof covered with cypress shingles that retarded weathering.[257] It was a significant public works success, one of several local transportation improvements completed during the first half of the 19th century, and a source of hope for the struggling St. James, Goose Creek Vestry.

The relentless vestry crossed the old bridge in 1844 to inspect contracted repair of the coat of arms in the St. James, Goose Creek sanctuary that vandals defaced. Additionally, an artist duplicated the bas-relief pelican and hatchlings above the church front doors and craftsmen repaired the pulpit stair railing, re-laid the flooring, and cut down the boxed pews to remove the rotting lower edges. Finally, woodsmen chopped away the encroaching forest from the church walls to protect the exterior and expose the ancient cemetery. Soon after, for the first time, because there was no bishop during the colonial era, the Bishop of South Carolina consecrated the freshly renovated St. James, Goose Creek house of prayer.[258] The enthusiastic vestry expected the expensive renovations to rejuvenate interest in the ancient sanctuary, but neither donations nor membership increased. Hope returned after workers completed the new bridge in 1851 and the Otranto rail stop in 1854, but although the refurbished sanctuary nestled a short walk from the new station through the covered bridge, church membership continued to shrink.

Rail lines were essential during the 19th century because they carried products from the fields and returned fertilizer for the depleted soils; keeping farms sufficiently productive to sustain small groups of families and businesses near the depots. Each depot in the St. James, Goose Creek Parish were "flag stops" that required the station manager to wave a banner

---

too ill to work. Elizabeth Donnelly sold him at the 22-Mile House for $256.00 and traded Jack's work time and an "old saddle." to settle debts, 2-2-1850. The receipt is among the Lynes Family Papers. A letter dated 4-11-1856 from J.S. Drayton to John F. Poppenheim states he cannot afford to purchase [slave] Julia and her two children but promises to lease them for $7.00 a month. The arrangement persists into the Civil War years. The relevant letters are with the Simons and Simons, Poppenheim Family Legal Papers, 1854-1876, 0431.02 (P) 10-02, SCHS.

257. SCDAH, S165029, Year 1851, Item 6.

258. SCHS, St. James, Goose Creek Parish Vestry Minutes. The minutes were on temporary loan to SCHS.

at the approaching engine to signal the presence of waiting passengers or cargo. Without the signal flag, the chugging, steaming locomotives from Charleston sped fifteen miles past Otranto Station, hurried three miles farther to Mount Holly, four more miles to Strawberry Station and pulled on to Moncks Corner, ten miles distant. The little depots were essential connectors to markets, allowing farmers to buy and sell. They were also important social centers connecting isolated families to urban centers. Mount Holly Station emerged at the center of the most notable parish community in the 19th century.

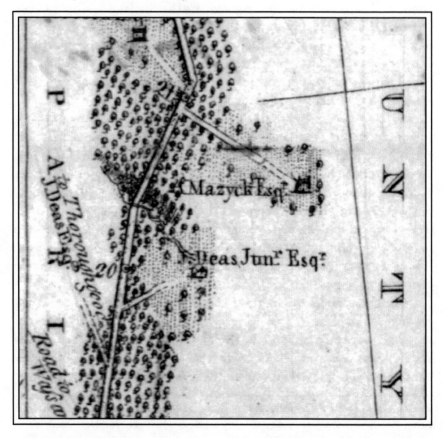

Figure 5.6: This section of the Abernathie and Walker Map published in 1787, shows the main avenue to "Deas Junr. Esqr." (Mount Holly Plantation main house) intersecting the *Road to Moncks Corner* near the convergence of the avenue to Thorogood Plantation, owned by John Deas Esqr. The Mount Holly Rail Depot was constructed seventy years later south of the 20-Mile Marker shown above the avenue to Mount Holly.

The Mount Holly Station takes its name from a nearby plantation, once owned by John Deas. The Deas manor house sat atop a slight rise near inland swamps where sports enthusiasts constructed Dennis Park and a baseball field two hundred years later. The main house, a simple wooden structure, rose at the center of a settlement of outbuildings approached by a private tree-lined avenue leading east from the Road to Moncks Corner. When Elizabeth Allen, daughter of the owner of Thorogood, married John Deas, he assumed stewardship of the Thorogood Estate, and by the end of the Revolutionary War, his son, John Deas Jr. resided on the Mount Holly section of the family land.

The younger Deas inherited his father's estates at the age of 27, including Thorogood, Cypress and Mount Holly Plantations.[259] Thus, he was a wealthy planter when he married Maria Smith, the daughter of William Laughton Smith and Elizabeth Inglis, well-heeled owners of Button Hall Plantation, a short walk south along a cart path from the Mount Holly House.[260]

John Deas Jr. died in 1790, the same year he inherited his father's estate and the properties passed to his brother, William Allen Deas and by 1806 to another brother, David Deas. David sold the land outside of the family and it subsequently changed hands three times until it conveyed with only 500 acres to Benjamin Donnelly in 1853.[261] That year, the Northeastern Railroad Company began to lay ties and rails through the parish to farms that depended upon unreliable rural roads to access Charleston markets.

WASSAMASSAW

The Wassamassaw Baptist Church thrived among the well-irrigated farms near the State Road that connected rural families to the Charleston markets. The rich estates that characterized the eastern sector of the parish during the colonial era dwindled and never resurrected. Edmund Ruffin, the southern agricultural reformer, described Goose Creek near mid-century, "…as much a scene of desolation as any…."[262] A few diversified estates, such

259. S.C. Archives Plat Series L10005 Reel 3, Plat, 547 and Reel 8, Plat 4261.
260. Bailey and Cooper, 1988, 180 and Census, 1790.
261. Smith Papers, 1102, 381 and MCO Book X 312:79.
262. William M. Mathew, ed., *The Private Diary of Edmund Ruffin, 1843, Agruiculture, Geology & Society in Antebellum South Carolina* (Athens and London: The University of Georgia Press, 1992), 61. Also see, Michael Trinkey, Debi Hacker and Natalie Adams. *Broom Hall*

as Medway Plantation, persevered in the eastern section producing rice, bricks and lumber. However, less affluent farms in the central and western parts increasingly dominated the parish near the middle of the 19th century accompanying a notable shift of political influence to those quarters.

As the central and western sections emerged as viable economies for smaller landowners and yeoman farmers, leadership adjusted westward to farmers such as John Willson of Wassamassaw. He became relatively wealthy and rose to political prominence on the local and state level, but with few exceptions, most of the white Goose Creekers remained marginally successful until the trials of the Civil War eradicated slavery and collapsed the fragile economy.

Political disputes and labor strife sometimes converged during the 1850s. That year, the State Legislature authorized an election to select delegates to a convention in Columbia for consideration of abolition issues. Delegates to the convention from St. James, Goose Creek included West Williams and Isaac Bradwell, Jr.[263] Protest meetings hinting at secession became common because most white farmers depended on slave labor for their meager subsistence. Thus, the concept of emancipation was unthinkable. As a result, some farmers met during the summer of 1851 and produced another resolution; this time to defend slavery at all costs, indicating the rising temperament of an increasingly desperate population.[264] During this period, slavery, states rights and secession was on the minds of most, and they drew bitter lines leading to conflicts, but an unexpected crisis that was nonetheless symptomatic of the obsolete labor system erupted near Mount Holly Station in 1855, temporarily shifting attention away from the slavery debate.

STRIKE AT BUTTON HALL!

Paid labor steadily replaced the anemic slave system in Goose Creek that long migrated away from the failed inland rice fields to western cotton plantations. Construction bosses paid daily wages to work crews consisting largely of young Irish immigrants, to lay wooden ties and rails for the new line. The crews labored in ten-hour shifts, six days a week,

---

Plantation: "A Pleasant One and in a Good Neighborhood," (Columbia: Chicora Foundation Inc. 1995). 51.

263. Maxwell Clayton Orvin, *Historic Berkeley County, 1671-1900* (Charleston: Comprint, 1973), 171.

264. *Charleston Courier,* 9-10-1851

and boarded in company quarters. The wet, soft ground of the long idle Button Hall Plantation rice fields lay overgrown with water oaks, tupelo, elms and willows. They sprawled menacingly before the intended route near the Eighteen-Mile rail marker. The route depended upon 400 yards of trestlework to traverse those wetlands, and in 1855, within one mile of the unfinished Mount Holly Depot, the laborers stopped work in the first railroad strike in South Carolina.

The workers protested low wages and poor living conditions, but the company countered by rushing replacements to the scene. A melee erupted when the replaced workers refused to give way, prompting the company officials to appeal to civil authorities for help. In response, the South Carolina Attorney General issued a special endorsement that authorized the local sheriff to execute warrants for the arrests of thirty-three identified workers. When the sheriff, accompanied by Northeastern railroad officials, attempted to incarcerate the Irishmen, workers opposed them with bludgeons and one pistol. One laborer announced he would not be "taken alive," but mercifully, cooler heads prevailed that day and the sheriff retreated from the scene.[265]

Angry workers followed the retreating sheriff on foot. They walked eleven miles toward Charleston brandishing their weapons and alarming the general population until the sheriff met them the following day at the seven-mile-pump house station. There, the lawman confronted the strikers with overwhelming re-enforcements, including the Washington Artillery, Washington Light Infantry, Charleston Riflemen, and the Charleston Light Dragoons.[266] The sheriff arrested thirty-three workers and housed them in the Charleston jail to await trial, and with little public support for the outnumbered strikers, work soon commenced through the wetlands.

The rail line traversed the Button Hall rice fields, crossed the Mount Holly Plantation Avenue and continued slightly more than one tenth of a mile to the new depot. Predictably, the company named the rail stop, "Mount Holly" after the nearby plantation and as families settled near the convenient station, the Mount Holly name attached to the broader

---

265. *Charleston Courier*, 3-9-1855, 3-10-1855, and 3-12-1855. The newspaper expressed no sympathy for the workers, touting the long experience of the railroad managers and listing the "liberal supply," of beef, pork, fish, flour, coffee, tea and molasses available at the barracks for the laborers.
266. The legislature of South Carolina, allowed the incorporation of the Northeastern Railroad Company in 1851 and four years later granted tax exemption status to it.

neighborhood. The Northeastern Railroad Company completed its full length without further labor strife and commenced its maiden run in 1857 evoking optimism among many, including the St. James, Goose Creek Vestry, who persisted with the Baptists and the State of South Carolina to educate the poor until the outbreak of Civil War.

CHURCH SCHOOLS

Until the outbreak of war, the South Carolina School Commissioners, the local Baptist congregations and the St. James, Goose Creek Church vestrymen collaborated to instruct as many poor children as possible. Together they educated more than 20% of the parish youth, but as the Civil War threatened; their combined efforts barely paid the salaries and funded only $40 annually for school supplies.[267] Nonetheless, George C. Smith taught 20 to 30 students each term at the Wassamassaw School, while Henry Nichols taught at least that many scholars at the school in Groomsville.[268] Remarkably, one year prior to the cannonade upon Fort Sumter, the vestry educated 57 scholars. Those numbers included 19 children at the Thorogood School one mile west of Chicken's old camp, 10 at Groomsville School west of Strawberry Station, 16 at the Wassamassaw chapel site, and 12 students at the St. James Academy on Red Bank Road.[269] As the war years beckoned, John J. Singletary, "church clerk" for Bethlehem Baptist Church, received a Charter of Incorporation from the State of South Carolina authorizing the church to hold real and personal wealth up to $50,000. Also prior to war, the vestry changed the name of the "Bethlehem Baptist Church," to "St. James Baptist Church,"[270] and sent representatives to the Baptist conventions in Charleston. Sadly, war scattered the congregations when the men reported to the war fronts and the church leaders diverted their shrinking resources to daily survival.

The Civil War halted the Ludlam education funding when the St. James, Goose Creek Vestry pledged that money and more to the Confederate

---

267. SCDAH, S165029, Year 1854, Item 20.

268. SCDAH.

269. SCDAH. S165029, Year 1860, Item 6.

270. St. James Baptist Church Petition with Supporting Papers, to be Incorporated, John J. Singletary, Signatory, S.C. Archives General Assembly Petition S165015, Year 1855, Item 5. The vestry may have sought a new title in deference to the old St. James, Goose Creek Parish.

Government. Nevertheless, and even as the male membership departed for distant fronts, stalwart Christians led the dwindling parish congregations, including the vibrant assembly at the Wassamassaw Baptist Church, the tiny St. James Baptist Church (Bethlehem Baptist Church) at the camp, and the ancient St. James, Goose Creek house of worship near the Goose Creek Bridge. As war raged, the church leaders baptized new members and brought spiritual sustenance to the white and "Collered [sic]," congregants until years of bloodshed and disorder tore the little places all asunder.[271]

271. *Book of the Covenant,* 1812, 1815, 1817. After emancipation, the African -American congregants connected to the Morris Street Baptist Church in Charleston.

CHAPTER 6
"The Bridge is Torn Asunder!"

Road traffic over the Goose Creek Bridge increased significantly during the Civil War (1861-1865) as the declining Confederacy consumed more of the resources of the countryside. As warring fronts on land and sea shifted nearer to Charleston, authorities diverted locomotives and train cars to support the resistance, requiring more military suppliers and private entrepreneurs to use transport wagons and the roadways, instead of rail lines, to deliver resources to the city. In addition to the wagon traffic, increased activity at the St. James, Goose Creek Church brought pedestrians to the bridge in 1863. Reverend L. Philips, Minister of St. Stephen's Church on Anson Street in Charleston sought the inland safety of St. James, Goose Creek Church when the blockading Union Navy shelled and badly damaged his downtown house of worship. He led seven church services in Goose Creek in 1864 and most of his attendees disembarked at Porcher (Otranto) Station on the western side of the bridge. After Sunday services, Reverend Philips traveled one mile along the Road to Howe Hall to pray with eager African-American workers at James Vidal's plantation. Vidal, a first generation South Carolinian from Germany encouraged Christian worship among his workers and a vibrant congregation emerged. Reverend Philips baptized new believers at Howe Hall as well as other nearby slave communities and believed the parish church, conveniently accessible by rail and bridge, availed excellent opportunities for missionary work. However, his optimism waned when Union forces pressed upon the parish and the rural neighborhoods descended into chaos.

During the years leading to conflict, Mount Holly and most other Goose Creek plantations subdivided into farms that were less self-sufficient and more dependent on the wider community for essential goods such as seed and fertilizer and services available at sawmills and blacksmiths. Consequently, rural families increasingly depended upon the nearest railroad station and its nearby commercial outlets to purchase necessary goods and services, send what they produced to markets and listen as ideas of secession percolated. When war erupted, the trains brought the war to the farmhouse doors by transporting human and material resources to the battlefields and returning with news from the fronts.

Station	Distance from Florence	Station	Distance from Florence
Florence	NA	St. Stephen's	57
Effingham	9	Bonneau's	65
Coward's	16	Monck's Corner	73
Graham's	23	Strawberry	79
Cade's	30	Mount Holly	83
Kingstree	38	Porcher's	88
Salter's	44	8 Mile Turn Out	94
Lane's	49	Charleston	102
Gourdin's	52		

The chart information derives from a section of the *Hill & Swayze's Confederate States Railroad & Steam-boat [sic] Guide*, giving the stops for the Northeastern Railroad in 1862.

Confederate General, Roswell Sabine Ripley ordered the erection of Charleston Harbor defenses late in 1861, and directed William Bell to secure sufficient labor for the huge task. Bell and his unit, the Charleston Light Dragoons undertook the assignment by requisitioning one-fourth of the enslaved labor force of his Pine Grove Plantation, and from his father's contiguous Back River lands. Both of the plantations lay within walking distance to Strawberry and Mount Holly Railroad Stations and soon dozens of workers boarded cars bound for Charleston.[272] William Bell and his father's generous contributions encouraged the cooperation of the neighbors, who soon marched their work gangs to the nearest depots too. William Bell's success replicated throughout the Charleston hinterland until thousands of slaves reported in thirty-day cycles to erect harbor defenses. Two years later, the rail cars delivered workers to the Charleston neck to erect breastworks in anticipation of a Union land assault.[273]

As Charleston braced for invasion, and the Union blockade tightened, all commodities became increasingly scarce. Production efficiency steadily worsened with family heads and strong sons absent at war, and many necessities became difficult to find and some unattainable due to the lack of production and transport. As the military commanders reassigned more rail cars to deliver supplies to the warring fronts, shipments of food and firewood from depots close to Charleston steadily increased. Thus, workers at Porcher, Mount Holly and Strawberry Depots remained busy loading food and firewood on boxcars shuttling to town every day, but the spike in sales from the St. James, Goose Creek Parish plantations provided little solace to loved ones whose hearty husbands and sons languished on distant fronts. Furthermore, the business boom ended when available food and fuel dwindled, and costs spiraled beyond the reach of most. Eventually, Charleston City Councilmen called for donations of food and firewood from the countryside, and by late 1863, train cars rumbled to town from Mount Holly with donated cords of firewood to warm chilled families hunkering in the City damaged by persistent naval bombardment. In addition to procuring slaves, food and firewood for the city, Goose Creek men such as Charles Graves and John Earnest served on the *Board of Soldiers Relief* disbursing increasingly meager support to ninety destitute families (26% of the families) in the St. James, Goose Creek Parish. In March of 1863, T.C. Warnock, Chairman of the *Board of Soldiers Relief* reported that the support for the "pressing needs" of the families was "too small." His written report exposed a steady increase in the number of hungry people in Goose Creek, a decreasing amount of available money

---

272. Paul Gervais Bell, Jr. ed., *William Bell, Company K, 4ᵗʰ South Carolina Calvary, Charleston Light Dragoons* (Houston, Texas: 2007), 11. The plantations owned by William Bell and his father lay between the Road to Moncks Corner and Back River in the vicinity of Chicken's camp. For a plat of the plantations, see McCrady Plat number 1546, William Bell, 4572 acres, number C3182, SCDAH.

273. *Charleston Mercury*, 5-6-1863 and *Charleston Courier*, 7-14-1863.

and a correlating reduction of help per household.[274] Families suffered from the absence of able-bodied men most grievously.

Phillip Porcher Jr., the oldest brother at Otranto Plantation reported to duty at the first call and protected Charleston Harbor as a seaman. He wrote to his sister at Otranto from the *Steamer Juno,* in late December 1863, regretting that he had been unable to have Christmas dinner with her. Three months later, the stunned family learned that the twenty-eight year old sailor drowned at sea.[275] That same year and within days of his seventeenth birthday, second son, Harry Porcher galloped up Otranto Avenue announcing that he joined General Wade Hampton's Cavalry. "How soon can you get me ready girls?" he shouted! Reluctantly but obediently, the despondent family bid farewell to Harry as well as "Kent" a young, tall manservant and the "flower of his flock."[276] Encouragingly, Martha, the family cook and Kent's "mama" promised "I jus[t] tell him [Kent] he need not come home if he let anything happen to 'Mas Harry.'"

William Bell rode out with the Charleston Light Dragoons in 1863 but received serious wounds a year later. His commander declared him unfit for service and released him on a sixty-day parole from his duties in Savannah, Georgia, where the southern defense shifted in expectation of United States General William T. Sherman's push to the sea. In mid October, 1864, Bell found his way to Charleston, and walked across the city to board a Northeastern Railroad mail car. It carried him to Mount Holly Station, where he surprised his wife waiting for a package delivery.[277]

After fifty-nine "glorious" days with his family and "well fed," he rode the train to Florence, transferred to Columbia and reported to Confederate Major General Matthew Calbraith Butler. Surprisingly, the general advised

---

274. Records of the *Board of Soldiers Relief,* 1863, SCHS, and SCDAH, Miscellaneous Communications, Number 3. Also see *Charleston Mercury,* 10-21-1864, "...we would remind the planters on the immediate lines of our railroads that donations of wood will be very acceptable..." Also, see *Charleston Mercury,* 5-6-1863 and *Charleston Courier,* 7-14, 1863.

275. The Ford Family papers, 5-21- 1810-7-28-1907, A letter dated 2 September 1885, certified that "Lieut. Philip Porcher ...was drowned at sea off the coast of South Carolina, on the 10th of March, 1864." The papers are among the collections of the South Caroliniana Library, Columbia, South Carolina.

276. Arthur Peronneau and Marianne (ne Porcher) Johnstone Ford (hereinafter Ford), *Life in the Confederate Army: Being Personal Experiences of a Private Soldier in the Confederate Army; Some Experiences and Sketches of a Southern Life,* (New York and Washington: Neale Publishing Company, 1905), 73.

277. Bell, 11.

Bell to return home and relocate his family immediately in advance of the planned evacuation of Charleston. It was near Christmas and Union forces were scouting the banks of the Savannah River overlooking South Carolina when Bell arrived at his Pine Grove Plantation home. He packed his wife, children and "white nurse," and rushed them to the Mount Holly Station where they boarded one of the last northbound railcars to seek sanctuary at her family home in Camden.

Daily train service stopped temporarily in early December as the shifting fronts in Georgia required more railcars,[278] and regular service ceased entirely near Christmas 1864, when the Confederate forces turned away from Savannah. The southern cause faded precipitously during the early days of 1865 forcing Confederate General William Joseph Hardee to order the evacuation of the southern regions of South Carolina. Governor Andrew Gordon Magrath in Columbia, South Carolina pleaded with Hardee, "…the retreat from Charleston will be the death march of the Confederacy. Your army will be a funeral procession."[279] Begrudgingly, Confederate Brigadier General Pierre Gustav Toutant Beauregard directed the evacuation of Charleston and within hours of these commands, the roads north jammed with activity.

Confederate units decamped on James and Johns Island and began marching through St. Andrew's Parish toward Bees Ferry. They crossed over the Ashley River and joined streams of soldiers fleeing the port city along the State Road. They pursued the State Road past Otranto Plantation, over the Goose Creek Bridge and through the long St. James, Goose Creek Parish while Columbia smoldered in the wake of Sherman's army, marching toward Charlotte, North Carolina, hundreds of miles north of the increasingly dispirited line of humanity in Goose Creek.

---

278. *Charleston Courier Newspaper*, 11-13-1863 and 12-12-1863. The North Eastern Railroad delivered 400 cords of firewood on November 12. The *Charleston Courier* reported on December 12, 1864 that the Northeastern Railroad daily run was suspended until further notice. Telegraph message from Charleston to Major F.W. Sims, December 15, 1864 explains that the rail cars are to be diverted to Georgia. A. Myers, Quarter Master General, Confederate States of America, Quarter Master General Office, Richmond Virginia, letter to A.F. Ravenel, President of the North Eastern Railroad, Charleston, South Carolina, January 12, 1864, stating that troops were to be transported at two cents per mile, per man.

279. Foster, Lisa, *Janie Mitchell, Reliable Cook, An ex-slave's recipe for living, 1862-1931,* (Charleston, South Carolina: Evening Post Publishing Company, 2011), 39.

Figure 6.1: The photograph shows Philip Porcher, owner of Otranto Plantation, father of Marianne Porcher and Captain of the Goose Creek Militia. The image is with the Frederic A. Porcher Papers, 1826-1922, number 1082.02.01, among the collections of the South Carolina Historical Society, Charleston, South Carolina.

Marianne (later Marion) Porcher was the sixteen-year old daughter of Philip Johnstone Porcher, Captain of the Goose Creek Militia, commonly known as the "home guard." Her father owned Otranto Plantation and served the war years near Otranto commanding forty men who were too old, too young, too feeble or otherwise excused from the front lines. Under orders, he and his militia relocated two weeks before the evacuation began. They marched ten miles northwest of the Goose Creek Bridge to the town of Summerville to shore up the coastal defense. Soon after, new orders joined them with the exodus, leaving the parish devoid of healthy adult white males.

Marianne Porcher, her younger sister, mother and two aunts first witnessed the passage of the retreating confederates from the upstairs windows over the portico at Otranto House. They scanned the main plantation avenue for movement at the farthest extent of the vista at the State Road. At first, there were only a few gray cavalrymen passing but soon the lines thickened until men persistently moved by from morning until night for ten consecutive days. The drab lines of retreating soldiers greatly concerned the women at Otranto but Marianne, a resilient teen reconciled, "…we are left in the enemy's lines by [with] the hope that our army, strengthened by the coast troops, may defeat Sherman."[280]

Figure 6.2: The photograph shows the main avenue at Otranto Plantation from the perspective of the main house toward the road. William Henry Johnson (1871-1934) produced the photograph. The image is in the William Henry Johnson Scrapbook, circa 1920-1923, among the visual collections of the South Carolina Historical Society (34/293), Charleston, South Carolina.

Men in unkempt woolen buff gray or butternut uniforms with night rolls of all descriptions streamed past Otranto daily, and dozens camped nightly under the moss-draped oaks along the main avenues at Otranto, on the western side of the Goose Creek Bridge, and along the avenue of the Oaks Plantation on the eastern side. Some soldiers appeared sheepishly at the back door of the Otranto house seeking something to supplement their meager rations. Marianne Porcher and the other women of the house distributed cornbread from the back stoop, "sometimes [with] a little

280. Ford,106. Marion (affectionately called "Min") J. Porcher (later Marion Johnstone Ford) wrote letters to her cousin, Clelia Missroon concerning her observations at Otranto in February and March, 1865. She also wrote letters from Charleston later that year.

milk."[281] The women dutifully kept the oven hot all day, baking salt and corn flour for the "gallant fellows" who kept the trappings of southern pride even as the well supplied, better equipped and greater manned Union army pursued them.

Figure 6.3: The photograph shows the Otranto main house. William Henry Johnson (1871-1934) produced the photograph. The image is in the William Henry Johnson Scrapbook, circa 1920-1923, among the photographic collections of the South Carolina Historical Society (34/293), Charleston, South Carolina.

During the third week of February, John George Vose traveled on one of the last evacuating Northeastern Railroad cars through Goose Creek with orders to depart Charleston and reassemble in Florence, South Carolina. With Vose and as many riders as possible, the train paused at Porcher Station, crossed the long trestle over Goose Creek, and immediately passed within sight of the Eighteen-Mile-House Store, his boyhood home. The temptation was too great. John George Vose disembarked at Mount Holly

---

281. Marianne Porcher letter to Clelia Misroon, typeset pages, Charleston, 5- 25, 1865, item 11/315/04 with the Frederic A. Porcher Papers, 1826-1922, 1082.02.01, SCHS. Also see Ford, 108.

Station and walked back two miles to surprise his father, Carsten Vose and stepmother. He relished a home-cooked meal, a warm bed and recalled, "[I] spent the night with ma and pa, washed up and continued the journey the next day."[282] He did not eat that well again for many months.

The Confederate army struggled with too few wagons, failing railroad locomotives and scant supplies. Rations were so limited that commissary officers allocated only seven ounces of bacon and one pint of cornmeal per man each day during the evacuation. Sometimes when wagons bogged down far from hungry ranks of soldiers, men fell to sleep with nothing to eat, and sometimes they went hungry the following day as well. One evacuee recalled, "We were glad of an opportunity to beg at any farm-house for an ear of corn with which to alleviate our hunger." The poorly equipped evacuating army commenced the march with "as much baggage as they could carry..." but as their vigor ebbed; they dropped all impedimenta and kept only one blanket and the clothes on their backs. The hungry men took turns using two or three frying pans supplied for each company to cook dinner and some waited until eleven o'clock at night to eat. Others wrapped scraps of bacon and cornbread dough around the ends of their ramrods and toasted the food directly over hot coals. Marianne Porcher marveled at the soldiers' impoverished gallantry and declared that while they survived on "miserable rations," and slept by the glow of numerous campfires at Otranto each of ten cold and wet nights, "not one thing, did we miss after them..."[283]

The state road, as well as the two rail lines radiating through the St. James, Goose Creek Parish provided vital connections from Charleston to the interior of the state, but those routes were not strategically important to General William T. Sherman's Union Army. When Sherman's soldiers marched from Savannah, Georgia to Columbia, South Carolina, the blue Union juggernaut skirted northwest of the St. James, Goose Creek Parish bearing directly upon the capital city in the center of the state and leaving Goose Creek and the rest of the eastern flank to Union General John Porter Hatch. That seasoned commander led the coast division that assumed military charge of Charleston in February 1865. Immediately, he sent

---

282. Roland Dordal Family Papers, among the private collection of the Dordal family, 204 Easy Street, Goose Creek, South Carolina, 7. Carsten's mother, Jane H. R. Vose was born in Goose Creek in 1813 and died at the Eighteen-Mile-House at the age of thirty-eight. Hereinafter cited as Dordal.

283. Marianne Porcher letter to Clelia Misroon, Charleston, May 25, 1865, Porcher Family Correspondence, 1865-1866, among the F.A. Porcher Papers, 1082.02.01. Also see Ford, 108.

forty-two year old Brigadier General Edward E. Potter inland by way of the Goose Creek Bridge with cavalry to suppress resistance, pursue confederate stragglers and command important byways.

When units of the Union Army closed, the Confederate rear guard lit the covered Goose Creek Road Bridge ablaze, ripped up the nearby rail and trestlework over Goose Creek and boarded the last engine from Mount Holly Station; riding twenty-six miles to the assembly point at St. Stephen's Depot. The rising smoke from the burning bridge alerted everyone on both sides of the waterway and when the Otranto house servants ran to investigate, one screeched, "...the bridge is torn asunder!"

The rising pallor of smoke shrouded the women at Otranto with a dreadful pall. They were the only white residents remaining on the western side of the waterway and they felt isolated, and at the "tender mercies of the wicked..."[284] The circumstances steadily worsened. The following day, Fannie, a house servant said, "Miss Min there are [sic] some of our pickets coming up the avenue." Marion's sister, Anne looked out and blurted, "They are Yankees, I know them by their blue legs!" Those words set the entire household into confusion. "Momma looked out from upstairs..." winced at the faces staring back at her from the road and reflectively retreated behind the shutters. However, no amount of wailing slowed the blue uniforms relentlessly galloping up the avenue toward the undefended home.[285]

The first interlopers arrived at Otranto astride fast horses securing the front line, seeking Confederate snipers, identifying potential bivouacs and preparing the rail stations to receive re-enforcements. Soon, foraging parties followed in search of fodder and pastures and reconnoitering places for supply depots. The advanced troops arrived merely hours behind the retreating Confederates, and less than that ahead of hundreds of Union infantrymen.

All the following day, as the mood at Otranto plummeted, a steady stream of Union soldiers arrived by road or disembarked at Porcher Station one-fourth mile from the smoldering gateway bridge. The Fifty-fifth Massachusetts Volunteers, under the command of Colonel Alfred Hartwell, supported Union General Edward E. Potter's movements.

284. Marianne Porcher letter to Clelia, November 20, 1864 reports that a shell hit their house in Charleston forcing their retreat to Otranto. A letter dated January 15, 1865 reports that she sequestered at Otranto with her sister, mother and two elderly aunts, Annie and May. Another letter dated 5-25- 1865 described the arrival of the first Union troops at Otranto.
285. Porcher letters, Otranto 2-20-1865 and Ford, 108. The lead rider quickly circled the house to prevent escape.

The Fifty-fifth Massachusetts Infantry, consisting of black enlisted men and white officers, came ashore at Bull's Bay near McClellanville and camped in Mount Pleasant. The entire regiment ferried across the Cooper River and entered Charleston on February 21, 1865. Other units joined Potter's Division as he penetrated the interior. Steadily, the young African-American infantrymen, with equally youthful white officers, supplanted the reconnoitering Union cavalry and persisted along the road to the barns and sheds and to the portico and front door of the Otranto House like "savages… [with] rifles as tall as they."[286] Marianne Porcher recalled the glint of bayonets and wrote, "To my last day I will not forget their brutal appearance." Months later she recalled, "They came up brandishing their guns with an air of wildness … it was awful to hear the screams of the cattle and hogs as they were chased and bayoneted, and the scatter and terror of the sheep was terrible to see."[287]

Some of the Union forces commandeered two steam locomotives to shuttle rail cars with troops and supplies from Charleston into the countryside. The Confederates did not sabotage the engines, but so poorly maintained them that the usual forty-minute ride to Porcher Station from Charleston required most of the morning, with frequent delays for repairs.[288] The Northeastern Railroad made the short run from Charleston to Florence

286. Katherine Dhalle, *History of the 55th Massachusetts Volunteer Infantry* ("Lest We Forget," LWF Publications, v 3, Number 2, April, 1995). Marianne Porcher Letter to Clelia, Otranto, 3-14-1865, among the Porcher letters. The Union infantrymen sometimes carried Springfield rifle-muskets. The barrels were rifled and thus more accurate than the outdated smooth bore muskets but were just as long as the old-fashioned firearms to accommodate bayonets and strike from a five-foot distance.
287. Ford, 109-111 and see Marianne Porcher Letter to Clelia among the Porcher letters.
288. Engineers successfully cannibalized a boiler from a Northeastern Railroad engine and converted it into the torpedo boat "Little David." This wartime vessel was the forerunner of the naval submarine and torpedo. Robert S. Solomon, M.D. *The CSS David, The Story of the First Successful Torpedo Boat* (Columbia, South Carolina: The R. L. Bryan Company, 1970), 6, 7, 19. At the commencement of war, the northeastern railroad employed 14 freight engines and 156 cars including passenger, box, platform and stock cars. The engine named, St. John's Berkeley, was a typical 4x4x0 wheel configuration. The company put it to service in October 1855. G. T. Beauregard wrote James A Seddon, Secretary of State on January 2, 1863 stating that the Northeastern Railroad was in "wretched condition." The following day Brigadier General R. S. Gist, Commanding, Charleston, wrote, "I am convinced that no reliance can be placed upon the railroads for the transportation of troops." Beginning in 1864, A.F. Ravenel, President of the railroad company complained frequently of the military drain upon his company and the lack of raw materials and skilled engineers to keep the trains operating.

for only three years before the conflict began. However, by 1865 the moving stock was so overworked and cannibalized that the remaining two engines barely mustered sufficient steam to move. Nonetheless, by rail or road, men and horses eventually assembled on the banks of Goose Creek.

Figure 6.4: The map shows Berkeley County in the 1895 *South Carolina Atlas* published by the Rand McNally Company. The map shows the Atlantic Coastline Railroad as well as Mount Holly Station.

On the western bank of the creek, General Potter and his entourage settled into the Otranto House, employing the parlor as a staff room. The general ordered a few men under the command of Major [no first name] Place to guard the smoldering Goose Creek Bridge and directed Lieutenant Colonel [no first name] Fox, a civil engineer, and his Fifty-fifth Massachusetts Volunteers to rebuild it.[289] The men quickly felled, cut and lashed together loblolly pines to span the rain-swollen waterway.

Soon long blue lines of men marched across the wobbly flyover while loud, wet and unhappy hostlers forced horses through the frigid chest-deep water. The withdrawing Confederates did not sabotage Porcher, Mount Holly or Strawberry Railroad Stations, nor did they take up the tracks

---

289. Letter from General E.E. Potter at Otranto to Major General John Porter Hatch in the field at St. Stephens, 2-28-1865, the correspondence is among the Union Official Records, Series 1, volume 47, part 2 (Columbia), Chapter LIX, 617. Also see Ford, 109-112.

above the Goose Creek trestle, allowing easy passage by the Union forces after a brief delay at the creek.

The sacred places, including the old St. James, Goose Creek Church, survived the marauding army unsullied, even as the raiders occupied nearby farmhouses and barns as temporary quarters in February and March of 1865. Most of the Union soldiers slugged along the muddy State Road toward Columbia, but others followed the Moncks Corner Road fifteen miles past Mount Holly Station to Moncks Corner. There, the volunteers from Massachusetts engaged retreating Confederates at Biggin Creek before pushing on to St. Stephens. Some units remained behind in Goose Creek to guard the strategic bridge and the rail stations in support of the logistical string of people and supplies reaching farther every hour.

On the eastern side of the creek, foot soldiers bedded in abandoned tenant shanties scattered on the overgrown glebe. Others built a campfire under the circle of five spreading oaks near the fallen brick academy. More hunkered in tents pitched in the tall dead grass on "old fields" spanning both sides of State Road. The winter of 1865 was wet and icy in South Carolina and the chilled warriors found it "impossible" to stay warm. However, some soldiers discovered great stacks of dry hay in a barn, piled it high in their tents and slept comfortably on top. In addition, most of the infantrymen supplemented their monotonous rations with roasted pork and poultry pilfered from nearby farmyards. They bribed idle slaves with tobacco and coffee to divulge the whereabouts of hidden larders, and during their brief stay, many young men feasted under the gallant trees leading to the Oaks Plantation main house. Arthur Middleton, the immigrant, planted that double row of trees two-hundred and twenty years before. Young men in red coats from Britain slept under them during the Revolutionary War. Now, eighty years hence, men in blue uniforms hoisted canvas and spread bedrolls beneath the leafy branches arching overhead and filtering the camp smoke before it filled the cold, dank sky.

CAPTAIN HENRY ORLANDO MARCY

On the evening of February 27, 1865, Captain Henry Orlando Marcy, a twenty-eight year old Union Army Surgeon, with the fifty-sixth United States Corps and other white officers of that unit enjoyed dry mattresses in the one-story brick farmhouse at the terminus of the Middleton avenue.[290]

---

290. Henry Orlando Marcy, *Diary of a Surgeon, US Army, 1864-1892*, November 25, 1864

While Marcy waited for horses and supplies to "come up," he depended on meager personal effects totted in a saddlebag slung over his shoulder. His bag contained "one change of underclothes, two rolls of blankets... a good supply of medicine," and his medical instruments. He was in no immediate need of his tools of trade because his unit encountered no enemy resistance for more than a week. Consequently, when the quartermaster assigned a spirited black Morgan mount to him, he commenced regular patrols into the countryside, as did most of the other officers.[291]

On March 1, as hundreds of soldiers reconnoitered the parish, Marcy, warmly dressed but lightly armed, embarked ahead of six mounted men. He carried only a belt and pistol but the others brandished swords in sheaths, side arms, and short Enfield rifles in black leather saddle holsters. The well-armed company set out to liberate the bound souls at Medway Plantation, six miles distant, as part of the strategy of occupation employed by General William Tecumseh Sherman.

When Sherman's soldiers moved into South Carolina from subjugated Savannah, Georgia, they arrived in pursuit of Confederate General Joseph Hardee. Hardee reluctantly evacuated Savannah with more than 10,000 men, abandoning precious resources including 180 rail cars. Union forces, supported with gunboats, rail engines and an intact logistical system acquired the rail cars and other materials of war and persisted steadily north, encountering little or no resistance, thus allowing small cadres of armed men to visit each home, farm, and plantation to liberate the slaves through force or persuasion.[292]

---

to March 3, 1865. The Diary is among the collections of the SCHS, 34/0496. Henry Orlando Marcy diary entry, Goose Creek, South Carolina, 2- 28-1865, "We quarter in the house and get a good supper. The Colonel furnishes music...,""...Colonel and myself sleep in the house. Lt. Col. W. with the men. Rainy night." Henry O. Marcy, surgeon and gynecologist, was born in Otis, Massachusetts. He received a M.D. degree from Harvard Medical School, became assistant surgeon of the 43rd Massachusetts Volunteers in the spring of 1863 and soon after served as surgeon of the first regiment of Negro troops recruited in North Carolina. The following year he served as medical director of Florida and on Sherman's staff in the Carolina campaign. A prominent surgeon and author after the war, he sat as President of the American Academy of Medicine and the American Medical Association. Hereinafter cited as Marcy Diary.

291. Marcy Diary, Goose Creek, South Carolina, 3- 1-1865, "Spring opens with plenty of rain...our men are almost afloat."

292. Marcy Diary, Headquarters, Pocotaligo South Carolina, 11- 26- 1864.

Figure 6.5: The photograph shows a driver upon a one-horse carriage and pedestrian approaching the entrance gate at the Oaks Plantation. The iron gates are missing and likely converted to weaponry. Retreating Confederate and pursuing Union soldiers camped under the spreading oaks. A Confederate soldier wrote, "...it rained and froze constantly. Not a particle of shelter did we have day or night, (Ford, 42). A week later, a Union officer at the Oaks wrote, "...it is impossible to stay dry..." (Marcy, Goose Creek, February 28, 1865). The image is in the Johnson Scrapbook among the collections of the South Carolina Historical Society.

Union patrols found overjoyed servants at every stop and received prayers of thanksgiving. Marcy recalled, "...they thank God, and say they have long prayed for freedom...and ...they don't want Massa anymore."[293] Hundreds of visitations ensued and each scene of personal emancipation supplanted the prevailing southern order based on slavery, with a new untested arrangement, exhilarating the emancipated slaves, but anguishing the stunned and subjugated landowners. Applying Sherman's strategy,

293. Marcy Diary, Savannah, Georgia, Saturday, 12-24-1864, "We find 5000 bales of cotton and 18 engines, 180 cars in Savannah." Marcy, Charleston, Monday, 2- 27-1865, "A.M. rainy. Moved baggage to depot and placed it in store. Rode through King Street. The damage done by our bombardment has not been exaggerated. Half the houses are injured and long since deserted... train engine a poor one. Gave out several times..."

Marcy and his comrades departed in search of Medway Plantation on a gloomy March morning.

The riders left the Oaks Plantation by way of the utility trail egressing onto State Road near the Seventeen-Mile House Tavern. A fire of unknown origin severely damaged the old hostelry months or perhaps years before, and it tottered obscenely in want of strong hands to raze it and build anew. However, all capable men and many boys departed the parish years before to supply the Confederate Army with lifeblood. The under-manned and poorly supplied home guard under the command of Confederate Captain Philip J. Porcher possessed few resources with which to repair failing infrastructure and for four years, the war consumed their meager supplies. Nonetheless, the captain worked resolutely to lead the four companies of the 18th Regiment of South Carolina Militia and protect his sacred land until he possessed few options.[294]

Steadfast to his duties, fifty-eight year old Captain Porcher persisted in command of a shrinking body of men, too old, too young or too feeble for the front line. His neighbors relied upon him to impart civil justice, secure the peace and keep the Africans at work. Slave labor supplied food, fuel, and patched the dilapidated rail system upon which all depended for imports, exports and precious news from the war. Nonetheless, the front lines sapped the waning energy of the home guard until the exhausted men joined the evacuating Confederate forces shrinking from the parish in February 1865. Desperately, the retreating home guard consigned the bound servants to the disposition of the Union forces and the white women and children to the mercy of both.

Henry Orlando Marcy learned of his mission to Charleston from a staff officer for General Sherman in Pocotaligo, South Carolina thirty days before. That morning Colonel Charles Van Wyck of the fifty-sixth New York Volunteers acquired command of Marcy's brigade and announced his intention to occupy Charleston. Marcy felt optimistic when he learned the rebels were fleeing and when Sherman announced, "...the way to Charleston

---

294. *Return of Men Liable Under the Recent Call, for each of the four-militia companies in the St. James, Goose Creek Parish on September 12, 1864.* The record describe the 18th Regiment of South Carolina Militia. With the papers of the Adjutant and Inspector General Office, SCHS. Hereinafter the source is referred to as *Return of Men Report*. Philip J. Porcher advertised nine slaves for sale in the *Charleston Mercury* newspaper on 3--9-1855 indicating that he needed to liquidate some resources. Also, see the Ford Family of Charleston Papers, 5-21-1810 to 7- 28-1907, among the manuscripts in the collections of the University of South Caroliniana Library, Columbia, South Carolina. Lieutenant Philip Porcher, son of Captain Porcher drowned at sea off the coast of South Carolina, 3-10-1864.

is through Columbia," Marcy celebrated, expecting that bold strategy to awaken all of them from a fitful nightmare. Nevertheless, the war persisted additional months, propelling the surgeon deeper into rebellious Carolina, but unlike frantic alarm riders galloping across the Goose Creek Bridge with news from the hostile Yamassee village at Pocotaligo one hundred and fifty years before, Marcy simply stepped aboard a train at Pocotaligo with his saddlebag and orders to "...take the cars for Goose Creek."[295] Now, a month later, he and six riders carefully picked their way along Back River Upper Road toward Medway Plantation, the ancient manor of the Peter Gaillard Stoney family.

Back River Upper Road was a road in name only. Rice planters of the colonial era depended upon the route to reach deep water on Back River, but locals long avoided it and allowed it to overgrow until it resembled the ancient packhorse trail that once carried Indian trader, James Moore to his door. Thus, after accessing the abandoned pathway, Captain Henry Marcy ordered three lengths between the riders to reduce the amount of injury if an unlikely assault occurred from the opaque undergrowth.

The previous week, before arriving in Goose Creek, he heard a sharp click of gunlocks in a similarly dense bush and instantly saw two rifle barrels protrude from thickets toward his chest. Nearly fainting but frantically holding fast to his leather reigns, he heard shouts not shots from the undergrowth when two alert African- American Federal sharpshooters "almost overcome with their emotions..."[296] instantly pulled up their heavy rifles barrels and yelled out to spare him from mortal wounds. Now Marcy keenly assayed the thicket along the first mile of Back River Upper Road until it opened onto five or six acres of abandoned high ground on the western side. Boochawee Hall once stood upon that slight rise, under a grand canopy of oaks, but the northern horsemen did not recognize the remnants of the brick house and though they suspected that it was once an important place, fallen pine needles and wet litter from the unkempt forest shrouded the ghostly footprint.

Pressing on another careful mile, the riders navigated clinging vines and naked foliage that obscured their way as they crossed the eastern boundary of the once elegant Springfield Plantation and within ten minutes approached its wasted manor. Dr. J. Keith Irving owned the ancient place since 1858, but he resided in Charleston and the previous white tenant

295. Marcy Diary, Pocotaligo, South Carolina 2-1-1865.
296. Marcy Diary, near Charleston, South Carolina, Monday, 2- 20-1864.

abandoned Springfield long before Dr. Keith purchased it, relegating its care to black families.

Natural forces persistently devolved all of the structures at Springfield, and men and boys carried off many of the clay blocks decades before. Brick and mortar ruins marked the place of the two-story home, the bathhouse, the garden walls and the paved paths that once led guests through elegant pleasure grounds. Now some of those bricks supported floor joists to a half dozen homes and framed the crooked chimneys where no white families dwelled. Bound workers, tied to the soil, erected tiny clapboard hovels in an unrecognizable pattern all around the old manor, using saplings or split rails to fence gardens and pens. However, in service to some unseen master, all of the villagers deserted the place in pursuit of an unfathomable destination, taking most of their livestock with them. Eerily, the random chimneys emitted faint whiffs of gray smoke from dying fires broadcasting the time of the exodus, shortly after sunrise. Pressing on, the seven riders skirted the silent settlement without pausing and persisted two more miles until the higher pine woods descended into a mixed grove. There, great swathes of palmetto understory spanned beyond their sight to the rice bottoms of Medway.

The last quarter mile rose markedly, requiring a slight spur to encourage the beasts forward toward the intersection of the trail with the southern shoulder of the main avenue to the Medway House. The softer surfaces surrendered to a firmer, slightly crowned wagon road that allowed the riders to canter east in two columns through the thinned and managed woodland. A collection of minor clapboard slave quarters came into view aside barren fields, several large utility structures punctuated the tree line to the north and partitioned rice lands and water reserves spanned to the southern horizon all along the way until an ancient dwelling materialized a quarter of a mile distant.

MEDWAY HOUSE

Medway House, the oldest abode in the Charleston hinterland, appeared at the terminus of the long, wide drive that split a hundred yards before it, pursuing a circular route onto the façade. In the closing distance, the riders saw people moving near a tiny portico, assembling into a tight cluster as if drawing confidence from each other. The riders, sitting tall but keeping firearms holstered, neared the cohort of eighteen women and children, and one disabled male, when as a precaution, Marcy signaled his troopers to scout the perimeter of the large messuage while he approached the lone man, propped on crutches in front of the stiff and silent assembly.

Collectively, the "intelligent, but bitter rebels" personified the ancient Medway House looming behind them in tribute to the fading Confederacy. The aging structure stood proud but tired and poorly kept; with the fifty-five-year old patriarch, Peter Gaillard Stoney serving in the home guard[297] and his five sons on the front lines, the family was the epitome of the southern cause.[298] The matriarch, Mrs. Anna Maria Stoney stepped forward to confront the marauders with "sharp talk." She "plainly spoke ... glorified in their [her] struggle,"[299] and vigorously confronted the northern interloper. Marcy, unimpressed by her rude boasts, waited patiently in deference to her, and as she railed, he assayed the Medway house moldering at her back. Long ago, that ancient abode reigned as the "best brick house in all the country..." but now it tottered pitifully at attention like a tired old soldier in a threadbare uniform.

When the six Union scouts reported from the perimeter, followed by gaggles of curious workers, Anna Stoney abruptly ended her lecture, changed her tone markedly and invited the riders to dine with the family. An hour before noon, suspecting no danger, and ill inclined to confront the "attractive women," Marcy accepted the invitation on behalf of his men and followed Mrs. Stoney through the parlor door unsuspecting her ulterior motive.[300]

The Stoneys sought common ground with the intruders because throughout the countryside, as Union Troops raided one plantation after another, slaves walked away in the wake of their liberators creating chaos and leaving the fields unplanted. Union soldiers harbored no desire to lead hordes of dependent people. When Mrs. Stoney informed Marcy that Union gunboats fired rounds into their forest from Back River a day before and her workers were becoming increasingly "unruly." She "feared [more] trouble..."[301] if Marcy did not convince her, "servants" to "take up"

297. *Return of Men...Report:* "Men over fifty," 461
298. Marcy Diary, Goose Creek, 3-1- 1865.
299. Marcy Diary, Goose Creek, 3- 1-1865. P.G. Stoney, age 55 is listed on the 18th Regiment South Carolina Militia (Home Guard) commanded by Captain Philip Porcher. See *Return of Men Liable Under the Recent Call...*
300. Marcy, Goose Creek, 3- 1-1865. Additionally see Virginia Christian Beach, *Medway*, (Charleston, South Carolina: Wyrick and Company, 1996), 10.
301. Marcy, Goose Creek, 3- 1-1865.

spring planting. Marcy agreed to try, and waited as she called all of the 150 workers to assemble before the little veranda.

Figure 6.6: The image shows the back view of Medway House prior to twentieth century renovations. Captain Henry Orlando Marcy delivered a fifteen-minute oration from the low portico overlooking the circular entrance avenue in the front of the structure. The image is among the collections of the Library of Congress, 308417.

The souls standing in front of the surgeon from Massachusetts chilled him deeper than the damp March clouds hanging low over the old brick and rice plantation. Black people of all ages and sizes stood within arms reach, starring up at him atop the steps. They wore all sorts of clothing, from typical homespun shirts and pants, to "whole suits" made of old carpets and blankets. Almost all the laboring souls arrived without hats or shoes and none dressed appropriately "to prevent them from suffering."[302] Notwithstanding his uncertainty before the pathetic throng, Marcy diligently explained the benefits of remaining with the land during the important months ahead, and with professional confidence he spoke of smallpox and other dreaded ailments that awaited careless and unclean workers. However, the slaves knew the words of "Massa Linkin," and

---

302. Marcy Diary, Goose Creek, 3-1-1865.

"couldn't exactly see how they were free if they must do as before...."[303] Nevertheless, the huddled multitude politely listened as he spoke and after the fifteen-minute oration each man, woman and child passed before the little stage. Each reached up to touch Marcy's woolen uniform, as if to test the reality of the moment, and shook his hand, "...as was their particular custom."[304]

Figure 6.7: The undated photograph entitled "David's House" shows an African -American family and home at Medway Plantation. This photograph, 1001.15 is among the Berkeley County Collection at the Caroliniana Library, University of South Carolina, Columbia, SC. The image is courtesy of Caroliniana Library.

Marcy harbored grave doubts that his words reversed those of the Emancipation Proclamation recently signed by President Abraham Lincoln and the stark expression on the dour face of his host convinced him that he did not abate her fears. She rued the uncertain future and feared the retribution that haunted every white resident since the earliest years of human bondage in Carolina.

A somber mood descended upon the riders as the Stoney family waved farewell, prompting Marcy to forsake the return route along the dismal

303. Marcy Diary, Goose Creek, 3-1-1865.
304. Marcy Diary, Goose Creek, 3-1-1865.

Back River Upper Road for a longer but safer course. Thus, the returning posse pursued the four-mile long Medway allee to its intersection with the deeply rutted Road to Moncks Corner, one-tenth mile above Mount Holly Station.

That afternoon the station hummed with an emancipated humanity shuttling to feeding centers in increasingly overwhelmed Charleston and with soldiers moving north. Sentries kept the loading platform clear, but an absurd mountain of bedclothes and luggage rolled from blankets, quilts, curtains and homespun cloth flanked the little station house and lined the tracks in both directions. Exhausted men, women, and children excitedly milled about, watching carloads of soldiers stream north seeking Florence and points beyond on cars of all descriptions behind engines brought up from Savannah, Georgia. Within a year, most of the local Africans who assembled at the Mount Holly Station that day returned to the lands they knew and some of the soldiers disembarked at the same depot to take up the task of "reconstructing," the recalcitrant South.

Figure 6.8: The South Carolina Rail Road Company ran from Charleston north through Ladson and Summerville. The ticket issued April 1, 1864, depicts a steam locomotive and cars.

Within two miles of warm beds, Marcy approached the re-established livery at the Nineteen-Mile House, busy with a portable blacksmith wagon and federally issued horses in need of various types of maintenance. Less than a half mile farther, he approached another congested scene at the Eighteen-Mile House. There, African-American soldiers claimed the dry quarter and patrolled from it in search of bound workers. Carsten Vose, and his wife departed for Summerville days before, leaving their home to the mercy of hundreds of displaced people. Within days of their departure during the confusion of retreat and occupation, someone thoroughly ransacked the old structure for firewood, doors, window glass and sashes. Moreover, long neglect degraded the intersecting Road to Dorchester, now greatly overgrown and barely discernable. Nevertheless, the Eighteen-Mile House store like the ancient tavern was alive again. Youthful boys in blue cooked, ate, slept and shouted orders from the meetinghouse to small clusters of obedient, barefoot and liberated souls mulling about. Long ago, that place resounded with talk of deerskins, furs, horses, rice, thrashing machines and politics and much more recently flew a banner against the "northern fanatics."

When all able-bodied white males rushed to volunteer for Confederate service, Carsten William Vose, Captain of the Goose Creek Company attached to the 18th Regiment was no exception. As proprietor of the Eighteen-Mile House, he heard all of the prevailing political arguments and wished to enlist in the Confederate army until he learned that his advanced age disqualified him. Not deterred, the fifty-nine-year old warrior joined the home guard for the duration of the war, while his son, John George Vose, marched off with the "rebs."[305]

Young Vose recalled the excitement after couriers brought news of the Proclamation of Secession, shouting and plastering the words, "The Union is dissolved," along every street in Charleston. His entire family stayed awake all night making a flag with a "Palmetto tree and the words 'Southern Republic' sewed on under the tree."[306] Vose recalled, "...someone hung it from a pole across the road from Pa's store...I expect it was one of the first flags of the Confederate States."[307]

---

305. Dordal Family Papers, Carsten William Vose does not appear on the roster of the home guard. The guard captain may have excluded him from service due to some extenuating circumstance.

306. Dordal Family Papers.

307. Dordal Family Papers and Marcy, Thursday, 3-2-1865, "...the rain has caused considerable suffering...Shall march for Moncks Corner tomorrow morning."

No such banners greeted the seven riders returning from Medway. Instead, the riders passed exhausted souls of all ages, liberated from places called Cherry Hill, Crowfield, Bloomfield, Fredericks, Button Hall, and Mount Holly Plantations. Marcy assumed that the vanished Springfield workers found their way to Mount Holly Station or the inn, as did many in subsequent days. That cold night, black soldiers slept on the floor before the roaring hearth of the Eighteen-Mile House. All week they witnessed the passing of an era, and all night and until their dying days, some harbored dream images of joyful souls in a rebellious place called "Goose Creek," South Carolina.

On Thursday, March 2, rations arrived at Porcher Station, some assigned to Henry Orlando Marcy with orders for him to depart. He joined a steady blue line streaming along the Road to Moncks Corner past the St. James Baptist Church (Bethlehem Baptist Church). Fifty-three year old farmer John McCuller assumed ownership of the church land from his father, the preacher. Too old to march to the front lines, John McCuller served with his neighbors George Lynes (Minister of the Gospel), Henry Hough (Huff), Benjamin and John Donnelly and others in the home guard and evacuated with them, while their wives and other loved- ones sequestered at Foxbank Plantation.[308]

Strawberry seemed devoid of humanity when the first Union soldiers disembarked at the station and fanned along the old highway, but the countryside enlivened as curious Africans lined the Road to Moncks Corner to see black men with rifles and uniforms. The soldiers ignored the nondescript and deserted St. James Baptist Church sanctuary at Chicken's old camp, but others traversed the State Road and some stopped to stoke the cast iron parlor stove in the larger Wassamassaw Baptist Church. They staved off the persistent chill overnight and left several sick and injured comrades to convalesce on the dry floor of the improvised hospital. Within three weeks, most of the intruders departed the denuded countryside and soon celebrated the stunning surrender at Appomattox Courthouse, Virginia.

---

308. *Report of the Men Liable*, 462. See the last will and testament of George Lynes, 12-10-1866 among the Lynes Family Papers. George and Elizabeth Lynes owned Foxbank Plantation north of the camp. George served in the home guard while their son Samuel served in the Confederate army. See the last will and testament of John Donnely, proved 9-5-1865. John and Benjamin Donnely served in the home guard while John's son, Samuel served on the front lines. These men worked less than eight slaves each on subsistence farms (approximately 100 acres) near Mount Holly and Strawberry Stations.

CHAPTER 7

Preludes to Reconstruction

The liberated workers at Medway walked off the plantation during the last days of winter, 1865, and joined the exodus from Mount Holly Station. Other emancipated African-American families departed Strawberry Depot or walked along the pine sapling bridge over Goose Creek to Porcher Station where they boarded carriage cars or mounted box or flat cars bound for the federal commissaries in Charleston. At first, most of the white women and children in Goose Creek self-sequestered in their weathered homes, too stunned to venture far. However, hunger and fear eventually forced them to chance the trip to town on the heels of their emancipated workers. Marianne Porcher, her mother, three aunts and two house-servants huddled on the second floor of the Otranto home near the destroyed Goose Creek Bridge for three days before boarding a "dirty" boxcar for Charleston. The women were "...much afraid" that they would find their town house occupied by some authority, but that was not the case.[309] Soon, they and most of the white families, including all of them dwelling along Back River, found the relative safety of the Union controlled city.

The federal occupation forces kept a modicum of calm in Charleston, but naval gunboats steamed up and down Back River wantonly lobbing cannon balls into the forests to flush out the white residents from hiding, and support the foot soldiers canvassing the rural homes and outbuildings.

---

309. Marianne Porcher letter to Clelia, Charleston, 5- 25- 1865, and Ford, 115, 118. "Our servants behaved admirably...and served our meals with unfailing regularity, and managed to give us many little treats, which we suspected came from the United States commissariat. After the war, fewer used the "Porcher" moniker in reference to the railroad depot, tagging it "Otranto Station" instead.

In this manner, all winter and into spring, the southern social order dissolved one plantation at a time, like a castle of sand, until on Palm Sunday, April 9, Confederate General Robert E. Lee surrendered at Appomattox, Virginia. That news sent the final retort to the fading hopes of all but the most intractable white southerners, and many of the disheartened souls sought spiritual strengthening. However, the sacred places remained deserted and the St. James, Goose Creek Church stayed shuttered against the dreaded news from Appomattox as well as the Union forces camping on its glebe.

Figure 7.1: The image entitled, "Marching on!" shows the Fifty-fifth Massachusetts Colored Regiment singing John Brown's March in the streets of Charleston, February 21, 1865. The image is among the collections of the Library of Congress Prints and Photographs Division Washington, D.C.

Three days after the surrender at Appomattox Courthouse, a ceremony marked the disbandment of the Army of Northern Virginia and the parole of its officers and men, effectively sending the soldiers home. The formal event signaled the end of the attempt by southern states to create a separate nation and virtually every lucid black and white Carolina family, including the Stoneys of Medway Plantation, struggled in the confusing aftermath to conjure a satisfactory arrangement for racial co-survival.

The deep Back River channel to Medway facilitated heavy ship transport, and for many decades before the Civil War, workers extracted clay deposits along its banks for profitable brick manufacture and export. From an early date, many builders preferred Medway brick. Slaves pulled narrow shallow draft pirogues with low stacks of the heavy blocks along the Back River/ Cedar Grove canal to shore the walls of the cruciform chapel of ease early in the 18th century. A hundred years later, Peter Gaillard Stoney improved the baking process, until his highly touted "Carolina gray" blocks blanketed and filled the thick walls of Fort Sumter in Charleston Harbor.[310] Additionally, he and his sons successfully planted rice and raised thoroughbred horses until the men reported to duty in the Confederate Army. When the second oldest son, John Stafford Stoney arrived home to Medway in the summer of 1865 from the front line, he discovered all of the workers scattered, his home burned to the ground,[311] and his family missing. In anguish, he hurried to Charleston where he found his loved ones safe at a neighbor's townhome. His wife and children, fearful of restless slaves and Yankee gunboats, sailed their brick sloop to town with two neighboring clans, the Fitzsimmons and the Balls.[312] They joined many other Goose Creek families, such as the Porchers, Tennents and the Keckleys in the crowded port city.

In addition to the frightened white families, Colonel William Gurney, Union post commander, warned, "…thousands of freedmen are pouring into Charleston, threatening famine in the city and desolation in the country."[313] Janie Mitchell, a newly emancipated servant recalled, "At freedom, we were turned loose like wild animals, not capable of doing for ourselves." Nonetheless, she recalled, "it was a glorious morning…"[314]

The southern whites recoiled from the loud black crowds on the city streets. Edward Keckley, patriarch of Spring Grove Plantation in Ladson, sought refuge in Charleston but lamented its hostile conditions. He complained that, "Everything is done to infuriate the [N]negroes against the whites." Such widely held suspicions fed the long-standing fear of "Negro" rebellion, and the southern whites in Charleston clustered tightly against a black uprising they expected to erupt on July 4, 1865. Fortunately, no riots occurred that day or afterwards, prompting Keckley to reason that

---

310. John Beaufain Irving, *A Day on Cooper River* (Charleston: Enlarged and ed., Louisa Cheves Stoney, R.L. Bryan Co, 1932), 48. Also see, Samuel Gaillard Stoney, Stoney Family Documents, 1775-1935, 1209.01 and Plantation Journal of Medway 1852-1853, 1202.01, SCHS.
311. The destroyed home was not the Medway main house.
312. SCHM 60: 218.
313. "Colonel William Gurney letter," *Charleston Daily Courier*, 4- 5-1865.
314. Lisa Foster, *Janie Mitchell, Reliable Cook, An ex-slave's recipe for living, 1862-1931* (Charleston: Evening Post Publishing Company, 2011), 39, 47.

the unarmed but uniformed Confederate units in town managed by their mere presence to, "...keep the [N]negroes down."[315] Nonetheless, the social circumstances remained unsettling through summer when the daughter of another Goose Creek planter expressed surprise stating, "...so far the poor wretches [emancipated African-Americans] have behaved better than might be expected, that is, they have not attempted to cut our throats yet." Soon again, she objected, "They [African-Americans] are very insolent in the streets and try to squeeze themselves in the inside & say 'Look at dat [that] rebel!'" She continued, "[They] sing their favorite songs shouted in your face, 'Hang Jeff Davis on the sour apple tree!'"[316]

The unsettled conditions prompted many whites to seek the protection of the Union Army and take an oath of allegiance to the United States of America, but the Porcher women refused. Instead, Captain Thomas L. Appleton, Provost Marshal, administered an "oath of neutrality" to the women on March 15.[317] The pledge permitted them to return to their home in the countryside and elude circumstances in town where people of all stripes tested the newest forms of racial segregation.

SEGREGATION

As the chaos of war ebbed and old planting families returned to familiar lands, the Otranto, Mount Holly, and Strawberry Railroad Stations transformed into sanctuaries for the European-Americans while liberated

315. Edward Keckley letter to his daughter, Charleston, 7-4-1865. The Keckley brothers owned two plantations named Spring Grove. Edward Keckley owned one in Ladson and William owned another contiguous to Cedar Grove on Back River. The 7-4- 1865 letter is with the Keckley family papers, 43/2073, SCHS.
316. Marianne Porcher letter to Clelia, Charleston, 5- 25-1865 with the Porcher papers. Marianne Porcher traveled to the family town house at #3 Legare Street in Charleston. Mary Simons, a free person of color managed the Porcher town house during the war. Marianne returned to Otranto to endure the post war transitions in the countryside. Also, see Ford, 108. Several letters to Clelia Missroon from Marion ("Min") J. Porcher (later Marion Ford) concerning U.S. "colored" troops occupying and plundering Otranto Plantation in February 1865. She wrote that "Gen. P" (General E.E. Potter) used the house as his headquarters. She commented on the defiant attitude of her mother Louise P. Porcher, and the loyalty of some servants.
317. Ford, 108, Marion (Marianne) Porcher Johnstone Ford wrote, "I give you a copy of the oath of neutrality I had to take; it is such a farce." In June 1865, the Porcher family was on a "suspected list." She reported the authority arrested some "ladies for not testifying any grief" at Lincoln's assassination and her hatred for northerners stating, "It seems as though Satan was let loose when such a people triumph."

African-Americans worked the greater part of the parish subdivided into small farms. Many worried white families possessed scant options except to cluster with other white families for mutual support near rail stops, where they jointly engaged a world plagued by distrust and despair. Understandably, they drew spiritual strength from familiar sanctuaries. They prayed at the St. James and Wassamassaw Baptist Churches and interred departed loved ones on the grounds of the ancient chapel of ease cemeteries. The remains of twenty-two Confederate veterans lay at the Wassamassaw Baptist Cemetery and an unknown number repose at the St. James Baptist Cemetery, one mile south of Strawberry Railroad Station at George Chicken's ancient bastion.

Forces similar to those buffeting the white families challenged the African-Americans celebrating freedom in tiny cabins throughout the parish. Private Harry Porcher and his manservant, Kent survived the front lines together in Virginia and Tennessee until illness separated them. Harry evaded capture and recuperated several weeks at Otranto before returning to his regiment. Kent, wracked with pneumonia, lay in a Union hospital until he strengthened sufficiently to work as a camp servant. Determinedly, he kept his promise to "Mama" when he and Harry returned safely to Otranto. Kent wed Affy, his longtime sweetheart, and settled with her into a familiar cabin on a particularly "pretty part of the plantation," where they lived together in freedom the "remainder of their lives."

John Vose returned to the remnants of the Eighteen-Mile House and found "Alex." Vose ruefully recounted, "I owned Alex all his life, [we] grew up together and trusted and loved each other. ...he remained with me for quite a while [after emancipation] just as if he did not know he was free." Alex finally walked away and never returned, as did many black Goose Creekers, but most emancipated African-Americans returned to the places they knew.[318] They built homes near whitewashed houses of worship where liberated souls assembled in prayer and jubilation, and where they buried loved ones in expanding churchyards. Although far outnumbering the white residents of the parish, black families remained sequestered from the busy train depots. Additionally, impassable roads and washed out bridges restricted travel for everybody.

The Union Army engineers lashed pine logs together to replace the

---

318 Ford, 86. 316. A list of interred Confederate soldiers are found in the General Ellison Capers Camp #1212, Cemetery Listing, http://camp1212.scv.org/cems/wass.html. See the Dordal Papers for comments about Freedman Alex and see the S.C. Historical Society maps and Plats 33-40-55a, Plat of a tract of 260 acres on Back River Road in St. James, Goose Creek Parish "property of Mr. Beiling [Behling] now C. Voses [Vose] to be conveyed to Henry A. Middleton, 1871.

burned road conveyance over Goose Creek, but it decayed rapidly and soon became too unstable for wagons or horses. No state commission convened to undertake public projects, and Federal authorities allocated no financial aid to repair the crossing, leaving it usable by pedestrians only, for more than a year. After the war, federal assistance in the northern states stimulated agricultural production by improving vital road and rail links between farms and markets. Little help arrived in South Carolina and the economy degraded to inefficient "sharecropping" and "crop lien" arrangements that suppressed the workers and leached the soils. Furthermore, John F. Poppenheim, Chairman of the St. James, Goose Creek Road Commission offered disturbing details when he submitted his annual report within a year of the surrender at Appomattox Court House.

John F. Poppenheim reported all of the major bridges along the State Road, including the overpasses through Wassamassaw Swamp, needed extensive repair or replacement. He further explained that the great majority of the white population either immigrated beyond the parish or settled near rail stops, leaving scant households along the roads, incapable of contributing sufficient labor for road or bridgework. Additionally because the rail lines were the only reliable connection for rural families and the marketplace, fewer travelers attempted to use the roadways further relegating the anachronistic road toll system, "unproductive."[319]

Within this post war context, the Mount Holly Railroad Station became the loci of the most important white community in the parish, carrying mail, bringing commerce to the stores, smiths, grist and sawmills, and connecting the fragile farm families to the markets. A racially segregated village of white families consisting of more than a dozen homes emerged proximate to the station and persisted as the only place in the parish with a widely recognized name, "Mount Holly." Consequently, Charleston newspapers soon referenced much of the eastern section of the St. James, Goose Creek Parish as "Mount Holly," and that moniker attached to the official records as well, ignoring nearby black neighborhoods tagged "Casey," "Howe Hall," "Bowen's Corner," "Liberty Hall," and others. Consequently, the minority white population kept the majority black demography sequestered, dependent, and as much out of mind as possible, although the majority race

---

319. SCDAH, Petition to the General Assembly, S165015, 1865, Number 22. Also, see a Receipt for Payment of $1000 for the repair of the Goose Creek Bridge. The receipt states "Received Charleston Sept. 3, 1866 of Dr. John F. Poppenhein...the sum of one thousand dollars being in full demands [sic] for bridge building- Goose Creek Bridge ..."The receipt is among the Lynes Family Papers.

represented nearly ninety percent of the population in most sections, and more than seventy percent of the entire parish.

The people of the post-war parish segregated for many reasons including resentment, fear, and members of both races generally complied with strict segregation when the prevailing norms of slavery transitioned to hourly wages. Immediately after Union forces occupied the parish, General John Porter Hatch granted freed persons, "David and his friend, Cesar, his wife and two children and an elderly women…" permission to remain [unmolested]…" on land of their previous master. Similarly, a contract between freedmen and their previous owner commenced within a year of the termination of war, when freedmen Caesar Manigault and William Zorn contracted separate written rental agreements with "Mrs. [Gracia M.] Turnbull." The contracts specified conditions of work, payment of crops or taxes, use of the untilled forests and required time-periods before lawful termination of the arrangement.[320] Fortunately, the great percentage of racial mixing remained peaceful, and written contracts helped many individuals successfully adjust to the labor arrangement. However predictably, racial problems erupted when hunger, disease and poverty caused desperation, blame and resentment. Thus, persistent discord after the war prompted the federal government to assert more than a decade of civil authority over the defeated but recalcitrant south in an attempt to reorder the prostrate states according to the legislative designs of the Congressional Reconstruction Act.

CAPTAIN FREDERICK W. LIEDTKE

In the aftermath of the Civil War (1861-65), the United States Government followed a course of "reconstruction" that imparted federal intervention to overhaul the political and social structures of the south and ensure equality for the emancipated African-Americans. The Assistant Commissioner for the State of South Carolina, Bureau of Refugees, Freedmen and Abandoned Lands, assigned Frederick W. Liedtke to assist the people of Mount Holly District during the transition from a slave state to a free state.

---

320. Union General John Porter Hatch granted permission for selected "married negroes" to remain unmolested on specified land by order number 204, Head Quarters, Northern District, Department South, Provost Marshall Office, 35 King Street, 4-18- 1865. Also see sharecropping agreements in Goose Creek, one dated 4-17-1865 and another dated 9- 20-1865 that contract work arrangements between freedmen and members of the Turnbull family. The Hatch order and contracts are with the Turnbull family legal papers, 1856-1865, SCHS call number 0431.02 (T) 11. SCDAH Series L10005 Reel 3, plats 1597, 1685 and reel 8, plats 4265, 4270. See the 1870 and 1880 Enumeration Census.

Figure 7.2: The photograph is entitled "Charleston, S.C. Ruins of the North Eastern Railroad Depot, 1865." The United States Engineer Corps created temporary terminals to tie Charleston by rail to its hinterland including Mount Holly Station eighteen miles north. The image is among the photographs of the "Federal Navy, and Seaborne expeditions against the Atlantic Coast of the Confederacy -- specifically of Charleston, S.C., 1863-1865." It is courtesy of the United States Library of Congress. Reproduction Number LCB 8171-3082.

Frederick W. Liedtke arrived in Charleston in July 1865, merely three months after the surrender at Appomattox. A Prussian-born military officer, he enlisted as a private in the Ninety-seventh Pennsylvania Infantry in 1862 and rose to the rank of captain by March 1865. Arriving from

New York City, he wore a blue Union Officer uniform and carried a belt, holster and pistol but he intended to wage peace in lieu of war. He was one of hundreds of army officers sent south to enforce the new labor agreements over an unhappy, sick, hungry and dispirited population.[321]

The thirty-year old Liedtke reported to Major H. W. Smith, Assistant to the Adjutant General assigned to Charleston. The major obligated a huge zone of responsibility to Liedtke that included St. Johns Berkeley, St. Stephens and St. James, Goose Creek Parishes and "land along the Cooper River." The territory size was as expansive as the largest counties in South Carolina and the vastness as well as the complexities of human suffering lent greatly to the enormity of the captain's responsibilities.

Liedtke dutifully rented a room in Moncks Corner within a short walk of the North Eastern Railroad Depot, and commenced visiting nearby plantations to assess the work contracts between the owners and the laborers. The Moncks Corner Station connected him by rail to much of his district reaching south to Saxon Depot near the twelve-mile marker and north to the train depot at the Town of St. Stephens near the Santee River. At each stop, he rented horses from nearby liveries to access much of the breadth of his demesne. Thus, the rail and livery arrangement facilitated the execution of his duties by putting a large part of his territory within a daily commute. His first visitation required a morning horseback ride from his Moncks Corner quarters to an isolated farm.

Captain Liedtke rode along the bank of the western branch of the Cooper River in search of the home of "Mr. Ben Ville Ponteaux [Benjamin Villeponteaux]...at the 36-mile on the Northeastern Railroad." The captain's primary responsibility involved assessing work contracts between landowners and farm workers to ensure the employer/employee relationship complied with recently enacted state laws. During his tenure, the new South Carolina Constitution established a progressive labor contract system under the influence of the Reconstruction Government, the South Carolina Land Commission and the Freedmen's Bureau. This arrangement allowed African- Americans to

321. Paul A. Cimbala and Randall M. Miller, ed., *The Freedmen's Bureau and Reconstruction, Reconsiderations* (New York: Fordham University Press, 1999), 237-239, 243 for an overview of Liedtke and his work in South Carolina. Frederick W. Liedtke, Twelfth Census of the United States, 1900, Paducah Town, Cottle, Texas. Frederick W. Liedtke was born in Germany (Prussia) in 1836. He and his spouse Annie (Anna) listed five children in the household. For his service in South Carolina, see the records of the Bureau of Refugees, Freedmen and Abandoned Lands (BRFAL), National Archives, Microfim Publication M869, reel 34. Excerpts of more cases involving Liedtke are available in letters from R. Scott to O.O. Howard, 1-23-1867, reel 1, Moncks Corner, SC, Vol. 1:4, 162-63, 164-5, 176-7, and vol. 2: 4-5.

"have land, and turn it and till it by their own hands." Additionally, African-Americans gained the right to end contracts and establish new agreements with other employers. As a result, African-Americans in South Carolina enjoyed more freedom than ever, which greatly disturbed the white population. Additionally, federal lawmakers felt little sympathy for the defeated "rebels," and most enforced vigorously the new rights and freedoms.

Figure 7.3: The image shows a section of the South Carolina Railroad Map in the United States Atlas, South Carolina, Rand McNally and Co. 1900.

Within the context of the new labor laws, Liedtke responded forthrightly when the father of a twelve-year-old black boy complained that Benjamin Villeponteaux enslaved his son, brandished a rifle, and threatened to shoot. Predictably, the captain discovered that the complaint did not entirely match the circumstances when he briefly questioned the boy at the farm. The lad informed Liedtke that he willingly reported to Benjamin Villeponteaux, he wished to remain his employee and did not desire to return to his father's house. To resolve the dispute, the captain delivered the minor to his father, confiscated the rifle from the farmer and chastened all parties to end the consternation and threats. Thus, Liedtke, on his first assignment, successfully served as investigator, sheriff, judge, jury, counselor and executioner of the law, a formula he employed many times during his eighteen-month tour of duty in South Carolina.

He returned from the farm to his boarding house in time for dinner on the portico, where he avoided the stifling dining room and filed his first report before turning off the oil lamp on the wall above his writing desk. On a subsequent morning, he traveled by rail eight miles to Strawberry.

Frederick Liedtke disembarked at Strawberry Depot near Groomsville, a sullen community of white families residing in small rental cottages, and a main house called "Travelers Home." From the station, he trotted on horseback two miles south along the Road to Moncks Corner.[322] Dozens of small cabins and flimsy shacks tottered aside the old "Indian Trail" where each family planted small plots accessing one or more of the numerous shallow ponds and creeks that characterized the monotonous landscape. Beyond Groomsville, no commercial or social convenience served the populace except the St. James Baptist Church, offering Sunday services at the sacred site of the St. James, Goose Creek Chapel of Ease. Owners of the social halls that once flourished, such as Reidheimer's, Reardon's and the Twenty-three Mile House Taverns shuttered their businesses long before. Also, once prosperous plantations that employed the important roadway, such as Cedar Grove, Thorogood, Spring Grove, Cypress Grove and others devolved steadily during and after the war until the once bursting fields spanning the full breadth of the road, degraded to scrub pine forests and wild grasses. In addition, pathetic tenant farms with skinny hogs, chickens and stunted cornfields checkered the pastures of the grand old places as far as one could see.

---

322. BRFAL letter from "F.W. [Frederick William] Liedtke, Office Sub. Asst. Comr. [Sub-Assistant Commander] 43rd Infantry, Moncks Corner, S.C. April 30.1866 to Major H.W. Smith, Asst. Adjt. General Hd. Qrts. Asst. Comr. Bureau R. F. [Refugees and Freedmen], Charleston, South Carolina." Liedtke states, "I have the honor to render herewith my report of business transactions during the month of April 1866." Additional reports further explain actions taken by Liedtke to enforce labor laws. See report from Liedtke, November 1866, reel 34 and excerpt in R. Scott to O.O. Howard, 1-23-1867, and Edward L. Deane to F.W. Liedtke, 3-31-1867, reel 1, BRFAL-SC (M869). Travelers' home and Grumesville [sic] are described in the Last Will and Testament of George Grooms, proven 11-24-1848, Charleston County Will Book K, 1848-1851, 220.

Figure 7.4: Small farms and clapboard structures characterized the Mount Holly District after the Civil War and far into the 20th century. The image is among the collections of the Library of Congress, 8536, USF34-505-09-D.

Strawberry Station stood three and a half rail miles north of Mount Holly Station; the rail connection generally paralleled the Road to Moncks Corner and all of the dwellings appeared occupied. However, great disparities between the homesteads struck the captain. Successful families with warm hearths and boiling stew pots survived side by side with people of all ages weakening from pellagra[323] or suffering more severe ailments, such as the dreaded smallpox. Captain Liedtke observed individuals with fresh smallpox scars who were "so unclean" and "careless in their habits," that he expected, "great mortality"[324] to descend upon those sad places.

During the colonial era, smallpox killed and maimed many and

---

323. Severe niacin deficiency caused pellagra, a disease characterized by mouth sores, skin rashes, diarrhea, and dementia. The cause and simple cure eluded experts for five more decades. Liedtke decried the, "very low class of white people ...unwilling to work..." BRFAL, July 1866, reel 34 and R. Scott to I.O. Howard June 20, 1866, reel 1.

324. BRFAL, Report of F.W. Liedtke, April 30, 1866, August 31, 1866, Annual Report of F.W. Liedtke, November 1, 1866.

returned with vengeance when the Union Army invaded. In response to the great lawlessness sweeping the land in 1865, some Goose Creek landowners perpetuated rumors of the prevalence of the killer disease to thwart interlopers and poachers from their abandoned settlements. Notwithstanding the sweeping exaggerations, the dirge returned in brutal reality at the Back River Plantations when slave settlements degraded to chaos.

After the gunboats passed and the Federal Units liberated the villages, a brief period of celebration ended when most of the workers wandered away. Some, however, fell too ill to travel and lay in their chilled cabins with raging fevers for days and weeks until they perished from dehydration and starvation. William Tennent, oldest son of the Parnassus Plantation family, returned after the war to find the slave village on Back River deserted except the remains of one elderly man left behind to die. His body, wasted by smallpox, lay in the empty "potato house," decimated from starvation. In his hands were a "few stringy roots he had gnawed at."[325] Liedtke investigated such horrid scenes from time to time and helped on occasions, but he bemoaned the plight of "...some [who] have more or less lost their eyesight," and others who "...contract[ed] permanent diseases, such as sores, rheumatism, etc." The smallpox scourge persisted during the captain's tenure, disturbing him more than other challenges. He found the disease so prevalent in the neighborhood below Strawberry Station that he feared famine due to the suffering, disability and mortality that "...interfere with planting..."

Homelessness and starvation also hampered recovery of the moribund society. The captain counted "...several crippled freed people in my neighborhood [who are] homeless... [because] these people left their homes last year when freed and have now no one to see to them."[326] Sadly,

---

325. John Beaufain Irving, *A Day on Cooper River,* enlarged and edited by Louisa Cheves Stoney (Charleston: R.L. Bryan Co., 1932), 20. In 1867, the main house at Parnassus, built prior to the Revolutionary War, burned to the ground. See Tennent family legal papers, 1835-1875 and SCHS Tennent Family papers, 431.02T. 04.

326. BRFAL, Frederick Lietke, Moncks Corner, 4-30-1866, letter to Major, H.M. Smith, Charleston. Liedtke declared one man to be a "mean fellow." He directed half of his crop given to "freed people." and excerpt in R. Scott to O.O. Howard, 1- 23-1867, Edward L. Deane to F.W. Liedtke, 3-31-1867, and 6- 20-1867. Liedtke arrested one planter for "refusing to make [a] contract," and another for "breach of contract." Other relevant documents include letters: R.Y. Dwight to Captain F.W. Liedtke, 7- 24- 1866, Captain F.W. Liedtke to Major [?] 8-31-1866, as well as two letters from Olney Harleston to F.W. Liedtke, March 6 and August 23, 1866. His *command* promoted Lieutenant Frederick Liedtke to Captain.

both groups suffered severe consequences when the emancipated black worker and the white landowner refused to agree upon some sort of labor arrangement, and sometimes Liedtke ordered crop divisions when farmers and workers refused to settle disagreements from labor disputes.

Under these stressful circumstances, bitterness sometimes spun into lawless behavior causing the perceptive Union officer to deduce that most of the ills plaguing his district spawned from desperation. Consequently, Liedtke solicited aid from surviving white families, and sought rations from government larders in Charleston by arranging delivery to selected train stations where he distributed sacks of rice, beans, whole corn and grits.[327]

As his tour of duty in South Carolina extended from weeks to months and approached a year, word of his authority broadcasted. As a result, complaints arrived more frequently at his boarding house door, as well as every rail and livery stop. In response to one such note, and to receive supplies at a distant depot, the captain disembarked at Otranto Station in search of Ladson, a small community four miles west of the depot.

Near Otranto Station, Liedtke acquired a mount at Vance's Tavern. The tavern stood at the center of Deer Town (Deer Park), a newly emerging white community of marginally successful artisans. These families persevered as carpenters, innkeepers, blacksmiths, shoemakers, tailors, and other professions, where the State Road and Ladson Road converged near the rail stop and the Goose Creek Bridge creating the busiest intersection in South Carolina. Some Deer Town residents traveled by train every workday to Charleston and represented the first South Carolina suburbanite commuters. Deer Town shone as a rare prospect for optimism in Liedtke's depressed district and with the sun on his back, he trotted west onto the highway toward Ladson.

After a peaceful mile, Liedtke drew his reigns and pulled up his mount to peer deeply for a full minute along an inviting avenue that penetrated the mixed forest. The long, crowned allee persisted more than a quarter of a mile before it vanished in the under story of dogwood, magnolia and wax myrtles, all mature but past bloom beneath towering elms. Thus,

---

327. James D. Schmidt, *Free to Work, Labor Law, Emancipation and Reconstruction, 1815-1880* (Athens and London : University of Georgia Press,1998), 158, 159. Liedtke stated that it was "unjust to take from any freedman his whole year's work, for absence without leave for three days." BRFAL, Liedtke Report, 4- 30-1866. Walter Edgar, *South Carolina: A History* (Columbia: University of South Carolina Press, 1998), 396. More than 20,000 people received rations in the Charleston District in 1865.

the captain did not see the destination through the thick foliage but he correctly assumed the avenue terminated at some grand place.

Since the earliest colonial era, many stopped to marvel at the Avenue of Elms and some followed it to the countryseat of Ralph Izard, one of the richest men in the southern republic. Almost fifty years before Liedtke paused to enjoy the vista, Abiel Abbot, a tourist atop a fast coach penned a memorable description:

> Half the distance we pranced on a fine turnpike built road-and then entered a handsome gate & at the same time an avenue of lofty elms & of loftier live oaks, wh [which] reached their branch and limbs high over our heads, almost touching each other in fellowship, while their trunks are by admeasurement [sic] 60 feet apart.[328]

Ralph Izard and his descendents successfully worked the grand plantation for more than one hundred and fifty years until the war abruptly halted their enterprise. During the harrowing winter of 1865, Mrs. Henry Izard, matriarch of the proud family sent for a Union officer to chasten her "negroes," for looting in celebration of their freedom. The insolent soldier blurted, "I am here to liberate Negroes madam, not enforce your will." Stunned and with few options, the despondent Izard women and children departed immediately, forever abandoning their ancestral Elms.[329]

Soon after passing the entryway to the Elms Plantation, Liedtke descended abruptly into a wide, thickly forested wetland riding upon a double corduroy conveyance that lifted him in some places two feet above the swampy grade. Here the Road to Ladson crossed the headwaters of Goose Creek as a broken series of low log bridges. During the colonial era that wet expanse produced great bounties of rice for Woodstock Plantation, but by 1866, the untended fields reverted to wetland forests. The earthen dikes eroded beneath the incessant summer floods, the ditches and drains filled with alluvial silt and the heavy wooden gates that once reserved irrigation water long ago opened and fell, allowing the inundations to wash wantonly across the desuetude.

Beyond those wetlands, a collection of recently erected white occupied hovels nestled near Ladson Station on the South Carolina Railway within

---

328. Abiel Abbot, 1770-1828, *A Journal of a Voyage to South Carolina, 1818*, Abiel Abbot papers, 34/0043, 62, SCHS.
329. George C. Rogers, *Charleston in the Age of the Pinckneys* (Norman, Oklahoma: University of Oklahoma Press, 1969), 117.

sight of the intersection of the Road to Ladson and the Road to Dorchester. These "poor whites," struggled pitifully against starvation, and an African-American group assembled in equal squalor east of the roadway in a camp arranged by Freedmen's Bureau agents. Both races huddled near the depot where rations arrived predictably and a modicum of order prevailed. Also nearby, agents prepared property to accommodate two dozen black orphans.

Shaw's Orphanage appeared as a circle of box tents arranged by agents of the Freedmen's Bureau to shelter and feed skinny black boys displaced by the recent exodus of families from scattered slave villages. There, on dry ground above a steep-banked creek, where the French Huguenot Church stood almost two centuries before, displaced children from defunct plantations worked the fields, tended livestock and cut firewood for the ever-smoldering cooking pit. The boys survived day-by-day, always fearful of uncertain destinies, and oddly, some longed for their obsolete but familiar slave villages. Yet, within that disturbing context, two personalities emerged, one old and one young, who shone as beacons of hope among the squalid humankind.

Lamb Stevens, an aged patriarch and Cuffy Campbell, a sixteen-year-old African -American boy resided near the rail stop, within a brief walk of each other. Stevens, born into slavery in North Carolina, was an unusually resourceful African -American farmer who earned his freedom and emerged a highly successful planter and family man in Ladson.[330] Some described him as "nearly coal black," probably to dispel any indications that mulatto heritage explained his business acumen, but notwithstanding his dark skin tone, neighbors unanimously touted his work ethic and farming talents.[331]

The year the Civil War commenced, Lamb Stevens worked thirteen slaves on his 1,300- acre Cherry Hill/De La Plaine Plantation, a combined tract that reached along the headwaters of Goose Creek north of the renowned Elms Plantation. For twenty years, he worked the most improved property in the parish, but its value plummeted when war emancipated all of his bound souls.[332] Nevertheless, Stevens persevered as an important

---

330. United States Census, St. George Parish, South Carolina, 1840 Enumeration Census counted Lamb Stevens as a free non-white.
331. SCHM , v.29: 180.
332. L. (Lamb) Stevens, 11 and 12, United States Department of Commerce, Bureau of Census, Census of the United States, Schedule 4, Products of Agriculture in St. James, Goose Creek Parish, Mt. Holly Post Office, Charleston District, 1860.

benefactor after the conflict, caring for his robust multigenerational family and contributing twelve acres of his demesne for the post-war orphanage where Cuffy Campbell resided.[333]

Cuffy Campbell "grew up" on William Tennent's plantation on Back River, but when his slave village collapsed in chaos, he followed familiar faces to Charleston where he survived for months. Hungry and afraid, someone plucked him from the street and delivered him, with other black boys to Ladson Station and then to a bed at the rising orphanage. When Frederick Liedtke appeared the following summer, the liberated youth envisioned his future within the context of black and white men in dark blue uniforms imparting order to a troubled world. That summer he also studied an ancient black man - Lamb Stevens - small, thin, frail, but straight like he. Cuffy watched the African-American philanthropist, visionary and benefactor as he walked the land with Freedmen officials and Henry Lee, Superintendent of Shaw's Orphanage. Two years hence, Stevens died at his Cherry Hill home at the age of 102 and the same year, Cuffy Campbell opened a savings account with the Freedmen's Bank in Charleston. Coincidently, both Lamb and Cuffy, at opposite extremes of their lives, shared optimistic dreams. The elder Lamb Stevens donated land for the orphanage and by it invested in the future of his kinsmen, while youthful Cuffy Campbell dutifully deposited nickels as investments into his vision.[334] Both showed hope at a time when there was little, and in a place replete with despair.

Unaware of the chanced hope kindled by two of the newest citizens of the free nation, Liedtke assessed the hollow eyes and bent bones of the refugees at Ladson Station, arriving from unsupervised places. Discerning fading hope among that humankind, he lamented, "I fear that should the cholera reach this country, its ravages will be terrible." He continued, "... not a hundred people in my district ... have food enough..."[335] He also deduced that nagging hunger induced many to steal, and he was careful not to enforce the law when it interfered with wider goals, once reasoning,

---

333. Lamb Stevens owned fewer slaves as the war years approached, partially explaining the decrease in the value of his estate. He owned 13 slaves in 1860. See U.S. Census St. James, Goose Creek Parish, Charleston District, 45, 1860, 1870.

334. Record of Deposit for Cuffy Campbell, sixteen-year-old resident of Shaw's Orphan Asylum, account number 2237, 10- 9-1868, Records of Deposit, Freedmen's Bank, Charleston, on microfilm at the Charleston County Library. The records report "Cuffy Campbell was born in Goose Creek of parents William and Hetty, who brought [him] up at William Tennant's Place." Thousands lost all of their savings when the Freedmen's Bank bankrupted due to mismanagement in 1874.

335. Cimbala and Miller, 239.

"I find it injurious to the planting just now to bring them [thieves] to trial at Charleston."[336] Thus, Captain Liedtke relied upon an abundance of common sense in most cases, but that winter he sought the legal assistance of the magistrate in Mount Holly.

Liedtke discerned that Ely Faulk, a white man, entered into a heated quarrel with Peter Marang, a black man, regarding two missing barrels of turpentine from a wagon at Mount Holly Railroad Station. When the black man ran from the scene, Faulk fired two shots, missing his target but violating the law and endangering the public. Consequently, Liedtke brought charges against Faulk for firing the weapon and appealed to the magistrate for enforcement.

Dutifully, the magistrate set a $500 bail until trial, but released Faulk upon the promise of his employer to pay the bond. Faulk left the area, the employer refused to pay and the case never came to trial. Disappointed and frustrated, Liedtke appealed unsuccessfully for a "thorough investigation," finding no recourse, but learning a valuable lesson about justice in the post-war south.[337]

Failed justice persisted in Goose Creek, before, throughout and beyond the Reconstruction Era, but although the captain reported "many idle and worthless" people among the freedmen, he also accepted that they were "like the white population." Nonetheless, the captain sympathetically deduced that poverty led to most transgressions and sought relief on that front as a remedy for most problems. Thus, Liedtke pleaded with the white landowners to provide food and care to the emancipated workers and encouraged the revival of some aspects of the paternalistic slave/master relationship that existed prior to emancipation. Gradually he convinced many farmers to advance food in exchange for work and by the close of his eighteen-month tour, some families agreed to support the workers on their land until harvest. Liedtke consternated that "those who are inhuman enough to let their working people suffer might properly be considered as 'rebels,' [because] they refuse to acknowledge the colored man as free."

---

336. BRFAL Reports of murders and outrages for June 1867, "Lieut. F. W. Liedtke" reported that Leslie Slawson ordered Reuben Thompson to go into the woods for certain timber. It was raining and Reuben, whose contract does not require him to work on rainy days, refused. A quarrel resulted in a physical threat. "Slawson was arrested and tried in Provost Court held by Liedtke on 6-25-1867. Liedtke fined Slawson fifty dollars in lieu of confinement at hard labor for fifty days.
337. BRFAL, Lieutenant F. W. Liedtke, Mount Holly, 5-31-1867, Report of outrages committed by whites on blacks and blacks on whites.

Liedkte met many "obstinate rebels" during his tour of duty in South Carolina, but none more dangerous than Shanghai Riggs.

During his time in South Carolina, the most risky assignment sent Liedtke to Carnes Cross Roads, four miles west of the Mount Holly Station, to investigate armed resistance at that intersection. To facilitate that responsibility, the resourceful captain combined the journey with a preliminary stop at Persimmon Hill Plantation, halfway to the destination, where he hoped to interrogate, "freed people [who] had broken into barns..."[338]

The livery near Mount Holly Station stood conveniently in sight of Mount Holly Road (Old Mount Holly Road), diverging from the Road to Moncks Corner (Old Moncks Corner Road) two hundred yards west of the depot. The captain entered Mount Holly Road and within two hundred yards descended along it onto a steep descent across a creek bed. At the bottom lay "Casey Spring," a small pond fed by a reliable stream. The captain halted upon the feeble wooden causeway to judge a jumble of items arranged in the trees shading and overhanging the shallow pool. He mistook the collection of jangling junk for some sort of African incantation, not surmising that the locals hung those strips of tin and glass to twist and clink in the breeze, frighten away animals, and deter the beasts from fouling the precious water source. The little freshwater spring was the principal potable water supply for the Casey (sometimes Caice) Community. It provided tannic, slightly bitter tasting water for a dozen clustered families who also employed the nearby ponds to wash and clean, as well as to wile away the hot summer afternoons fishing and swimming.

Casey, a neighborhood named after a freedman, was once part of Mount Holly Plantation that divided from the larger Thorogood tract. The emancipated African named, "Casey" walked to Mount Holly from the western section of the parish in 1865 and began preaching the Christian Gospel. Soon he attracted a small assembly and converted his cabin into a house of prayer and worship where a vibrant center of an African-American community emerged.[339] The Casey Community ascended as an important

---

338. Schmidt, 158, and Cimbala and Miller, 238-9, and BRFAL, Liedtke report, 5-31-1867.

339. The origin of the name, "Casey" is unknown but a European American family of that celebrity resided near the Wassamassaw wetlands. Casey may have been a liberated worker from the Casey family at Wassamassaw.

339. MCO Book L. no.15: 411, 467. A plat showing the 25-acre tract in a triangle formed

minority neighborhood. Freedmen such as Sampson Bryant and Frank Brown successfully worked post-war farms, a short walk but a world apart from the Mount Holly Station. Both farmers remained virtually invisible to the outside world and dependent upon the white controlled rail stop for essentials such as fertilizer and seed.

Euro-American Lewis Cannon held the larger part of Mount Holly Plantation until 1868, when Cannon and later Benjamin Donnelly transferred the last of it to small farmers. All of the farmers abandoned rice production long before, and allowed the wet grounds to return to tupelo and willow swamps. They converted the higher fields to subsistence farming and a few acres of cotton. Cannon and his neighbors worked shrinking estates for a few more years, until he conveyed 200 of the remaining acres for $700 to John R. Pinckney, an African-American farmer. Soon Pinckney sold 65 acres of the tract to his brother, Thomas. Cannon also conveyed 25 acres to T. W. Lewis, Trustee for the Casey Methodist Episcopal Church for $125 in 1868. This site became the religious center of a bustling community of liberated African-Americans.[340]

Captain Liedtke continued through the leafy tunnel-way and within thirty minutes came upon an avenue of oaks. That allee conveniently accessed the intersection of Mount Holly and State Road and led to the main house of John F. Poppenheim at Persimmon Hill Plantation. John F. Poppenheim was the grandson of Lewis (Ludwig) Poppenheim, a Revolutionary War era infantryman, who as a thirty-year-old "soldier of fortune," invaded with the British army during the siege of Charleston. Unlike his comrades in arms, he remained in Carolina after the occupation forces departed and the soldier-turned-farmer emerged a successful post-war landowner in the St. James, Goose Creek Parish. He sent to Germany for his thirteen-year old son, affectionately called "Wee John," whose sobriquet long attached to "Wee John Plantation," the family land in Ladson. "Wee" John Poppenheim successfully planted more than 1000 acres contiguous on the south of Elms Plantation and fathered Dr. John Frederick Poppenheim. Now, eighty-five years after the Bavarian soldier gambled his future in Carolina, Liedtke approached Persimmon Hill, the home of sixty-year-old Dr. John F. Poppenheim, grandson of the

by Thorogood Avenue and the Road to Moncks Corner includes a footprint of the church. The plat in Simon's Plat Book, 174 is with the Langdon Cheves Papers, SCHS.
340. Michael J. Heitzler, *Goose Creek, A Definitive History, Rebellion, Reconstruction and Beyond*, Volume Two, (Charleston, South Carolina: The History Press, 2006), 135-140.

German mercenary, successful physician, planter, chairman of the St. James, Goose Creek Parish Road Commission and a victim of crime.

Liedtke investigated and punished dozens of minor offenses in South Carolina and the diverse experiences honed his intuition. Thus, when his arrival at Persimmon Hill attracted little curiosity from the workers, he accurately concluded that the farm hands knew the perpetrator, but intended not to divulge his identity. Furthermore, landowners typically settled such scores with no outside assistance and Poppenheim was especially reticent because he harbored little confidence in federal authority.

John Poppenheim served in the home guard under the command of Confederate Captain Philip Porcher, but he did not retreat with his unit when the Union army arrived in Goose Creek. Instead, as the chairman of the parish road commission, he stood as the lone civilian authority in Goose Creek to meet General Edward E. Potter at the Eighteen-Mile House where he surrendered the parish. Within that disturbing context on February 23, 1865, Union General E.E. Potter granted safe passage for Poppenheim and his family to Union-occupied Charleston. General Potter also promised to safeguard his house and property, but when Poppenheim returned from Charleston, he found his land, "…stripped of everything of consequence." Union troops stole livestock, crops, and implements and vandalized sections of his house and outbuildings but Poppenheim received no compensation for the stolen items and the "injury and destruction of [the] house."[341] Nonetheless, a year hence, the aging landowner opted to involve Liedtke in the pursuit of a thief, probably with little positive expectation but perhaps wishing to re-engage federal officials and garner aid for desperately needed road and bridge repair of which he was responsible.

The crime at his farm one year after the termination of hostilities, allowed the two German kinsmen to visit briefly. Liedtke emigrated from Germany six years before, joined the Union Army soon after his arrival,

---

341. "[A] schedule of property taken from Dr. John F. Poppenheim…farm on Goose Creek…23rd day of February 1865 by United States Troops… [a total of] $2815," and a notice from Captain D.R. Haulk and Provost Marshal Captain, R. Allison, from the Office of the Acting Quartermaster…Charleston, S.C., April 25th, 1865 granting permission for Poppenheim to search barns for his livestock and other possessions. Bond and Obligation Statement 2-1-1871 explain that John F. Poppenheim purchased Marrington Plantation that year. These records are with Simons and Simons, Poppenheim Family Legal Papers, 1854-1876, 0431.02 (P) 10-02, SCHS. For a composite of information from the Enumeration and Agricultural Census, Slave Schedule, and miscellaneous land records describing Persimmon Hill, see Heitzler, volume II, 44.

and traveled to post-war South Carolina to oversee the labor contracts of liberated workers. John Poppenheim, a third generation southerner, successfully grew rice, cotton, corn and raised cattle with sixteen slaves on his 1700-acre Persimmon Hill Plantation. His estate, worth $5,000 when war commenced, depreciated to a paltry $500 by the end of the conflict. Understandably, the two met that day half a world away from their Teutonic homeland and equally detached in their perceptions of the African- American conundrum. That day Liedtke questioned a few of the hired help, filed a cursory report to the chagrin of the landowner, and departed Poppenheim's demesne to investigate multiple gunshots at Carnes Crossroads, two miles farther west along heavily traveled State Road.

A persistent scene of semi-organized resistance to northern occupation, Carnes Cross Roads, twenty-three miles from Charleston, marked the intersection of the State Road with a lesser connector from Moncks Corner to Summerville (State Highway 17A). A longstanding tollbooth pronounced the crossing and Union Army personnel frequented a temporary campsite under a grove of tall pine trees. The popular stopover lost its appeal several months after the surrender at Appomattox, when Union soldiers camping at the cross roads complained of nightly harassment.

When U.S. troops encamped in the field by the tollgate, occasional rifle shots sent rounds through their tents from multiple directions all night, unnerving the soldiers. Rumors identified Shanghai Riggs as the responsible party, although his family farm lay near Wassamassaw, ten miles farther west. Riggs stood 6 feet, 8 inches tall and reportedly, "you could not get him into the Confederacy, but after he was captured and conscripted (Shanghaied), you could not get him out of the Confederacy."[342] The tollgate keeper denied knowledge of the culprit, as did all others in the vicinity and the Riggs family farm lay beyond the limited means of Liedtke to chance a solo visit. Consequently, the harassment persisted as long as men in blue traveled that byway.

Captain Liedtke dutifully served his nation in South Carolina into 1867, and notwithstanding the enormity of the task and few signs of permanent improvement, his final submittal optimistically explained, "… the people generally work well …" and he expected a good harvest. More realistically, he expressed his immense concerns for the freed workers who struggled mightily against great odds. He doubted that the tiny

342. William Henry Johnson Scrapbook, Volume I, 34/293, SCHS. Notations accompany photographs near Carnes Cross Roads. See Records of the 18th Regiment, SCHS.

homesteads, tentatively surviving in minority ownership, could survive in the New South.[343] Captain William F. Liedtke accepted promotions and a transfer to North Carolina before he turned his back on the angry South to farm his own land in Texas, where he reared a large, healthy family, and eventually retired.

343. BFRAL, Lieutenant F.W. Liedtke reported that F.B. Leslie Slawson tried to shoot Reuben Thompson near the Mount Holly Depot in June 1867 and the next month, John Hamlin viciously kicked Hickory Foster. For a summary of the work of F.W Liedtke see, Schmidt, *Free to Work, Labor, Law, Emancipation and Reconstruction 1865-1880*, and Paul A. Cimbala and Randall M. Miller, editors "A Full-fledged Government of Men:" Freedmen's Bureau Labor Policy in South Carolina, 1865-1868, in The Freedmen's Bureau and Reconstruction, Reconsiderations, Fordham University Press, 1999. Liedtke served from December 1866 to April 1868 in the South Carolina Freedmens' Bureau and as Provost Marshal and Judge of Provost Court for the South Carolina Parishes from June 1867 to March 1868. He transferred to Sub-assistant to the Commander of the Freedmens' Bureau for North Carolina in April 1868.

CHAPTER 8

Reconstruction and Beyond

The Confederate States reintegrated into the United States of America during the Reconstruction Period, an era characterized by furious debates that thrust the American people into a caustic post war political environment. Well before the surrender at Appomattox Courthouse, Virginia, disputes raged in the United States Congress concerning the terms of re-admittance of the secessionist states. After the Civil War, moderates prevailed for a time sending agents such as Captain Frederick W. Liedtke to lend essential aide, improve work arrangements, and moderate opposing political views. However, a sweeping Republican victory in the 1866 Congressional elections gave the so-called "Radical Republicans," enough control of Congress to override the moderates and initiate harsh new arrangements for the "traitorous" Confederacy. Under the provisions of the Congressional Reconstruction Act, signed March 2, 1867, authorities arranged the defeated southern states into five military districts. They assigned South Carolina to District 2 under the command of General Daniel E. Sickles. In compliance with the new policies, the general removed white political power brokers, disenfranchised leading white males, and established new governments elected by an overwhelming freedmen franchise. In response, the marginalized white South Carolinians almost universally rejected the new state authorities and put shadow governments in place until the Reconstruction Era ended more than a decade later (1877).

Always at the center of the war of words was the defunct institution of slavery and the social/political arrangement that replaced it. Within a few years of the war, most emancipated families in Goose Creek, owned small farms and lived somewhat independently. However, many liberated souls worked as tenants or sharecrop farmers on white-owned lands in environments resembling slavery, and more debilitating systems of servitude arose in some settings when planters advanced food and shelter to distressed workers in exchange for unpaid labor. Furthermore, some desperate freedmen joined work crews resembling slave gangs from the past. One such crew razed the relics of the derelict Goose Creek Bridge and replaced it in 1866.

Within a year after the war, a durable structure again bridged the waters of Goose Creek, conveying travelers to the sacred neighborhood near the St. James, Goose Creek Church. Engineers bypassed the brick abutments that anchored the previous 200-foot long covered bridge and in its place erected an overpass with structural integrity that evolved from decades of railroad construction and honed by the lessons of war. Workers laid long creosoted posts on flat railcars in an industrial yard on Charleston neck and shuttled them to Otranto Station. There, men transferred the posts one by one onto mule wagons and hauled the long pointed stanchions to the nearby waterway where labor gangs erected tall derricks. Atop and along the boring structures, workers applied muscle power, block and tackle, and gravity to hammer pilings deep into the clay creek bottom. Once embedded, men stabilized the underpinnings by drilling holes through each piling and bolting crossbeams from one to another creating a quay that traversed the waterway. In this fashion, they built a rugged superstructure similar to a railroad trestle sufficiently sturdy to hold a train engine. However, four-inch thick floorboards spanned the cross beams in lieu of steel rails, and the wooden floor planks similarly treated with tar-based creosote connected the two approaching causeways by spanning the two hundred-foot wide channel. Finally, four-foot tall guardrails guided the riders and pedestrians across the low and stout flyover onto a tar and gravel mixture that filled the gap between the wooden bridge floor and the rutted dirt roadway.

Notwithstanding public works victories such as the "reconstructed" bridge, most white residents rejected the post-war state government that advocated a new social order based upon racial equity, male suffrage and equal protection of the law. Many whites in Goose Creek perceived the newly enacted tax laws to be unfair. For example, the state supply bill in 1866 exempted freedmen bureau property from the ad valorem assessment and increased the commission for tax collections in the St. James, Goose Creek Parish to ten-percent of the take-in. That rate, three percent higher than almost all districts in the state, encouraged robust collections that infuriated many. One farmer residing near the bridge resented all state taxes and explained further that, "...the whole moral character of the people has changed." He blamed the malaise upon "lazy Negroes [who] loiter[ed] along the road," as well as members of his Caucasian race. He decried the "old fogeys [fogies] crowing..." and hurled the vilest accusation of that day when he faulted his neighbors as "...worse than Yankees..."[344] Such reticence prevailed throughout the ancient parish instigating white citizens to support vigilantes (night riders) enforcing their will on both sides of the creosoted overpass.

NIGHT RIDERS

The night riders emerged immediately after the war and railed as "deconstructionists" well into the 20th century. The riders enforced the quasi-laws of unauthorized white local governments by raiding non-compliant individuals and their families under cover of darkness and suppressed supporters of the so-called "radical" government. Moreover, the night riders underpinned the conservative moralities emanating from church councils who intended to keep the racial groups socially separated.

Virulent resistance to reconstruction policies and support of the night riders stemmed from widespread fury felt by leaders statewide, when the federal government forced emancipation upon the white dominated labor force and enfranchised the adult African-American males. The resentment led to hotbeds of anger and converted into armed political resistance when men, such as Shanghai Riggs, shifted his intense fury against "blue bellies," toward "Radical Republicans" and organized secret white vigilante-type cadres. Most white residents in Goose Creek encouraged the vigilante response and one grateful family man testified "...by his (Riggs) terror to the Negroes, he saved many-a-white family from destruction during the reconstruction period."[345] Such resistance spread statewide, but no people exemplified the movement more than did the residents of Wassamassaw.

The ancient sanctuary at Wassamassaw remained the center of a robust

344. Edward Keckley letter to his daughter, Charleston, December 10, 1868, Keckley family papers, 43/2073, SCHS. Also see, *Acts of the Legislature, An Act to Raise Supplies, 1866, Keowee Courier*, Pickens Court House (Pickens, South Carolina: R.A. Thompson and Company Publisher), University of South Carolina Library.
345. William Henry Johnson, *William Henry Johnson Scrapbook, ca. 1920-1933*. v.I: 150, 34/293, SCHS. Notations accompany photographs.

farming community, long prospering along the State Road near the well-known floodplain. A church, school, general store, blacksmith and other shops, mills, and an office for the sheriff and magistrate marked the most dynamic neighborhood beyond Mount Holly. There, a formidable body of resistance to radical rule, deeply rooted in the moral fiber of the Baptist Church, emerged immediately after the end of the Civil War.

The Wassamassaw Baptist Church council convened November 12, 1865, within seven months of Appomattox and after a four-year lull due to "all male members being off in service."[346] The council reconvened with twenty congregants, including loyal black attendees, to express support for each other and their "ordinance of God," that superseded all laws of man, including the new federally imposed State Constitution.[347] Membership more than doubled during the ten years of Reconstruction as the congregation navigated through a maze of emotions. Within their sincere expressions of faith, hope, and charity persisted a universal resistance to federally imposed rules. As a result, and sadly, during that bitter decade, some innocent African-Americans, such as John Wesley felt the blunt of the brooding rage.

In late May 1867, John Wesley, a freedman drove his heavily loaded "timber cart" along the "Wagon Road" that paralleled Wassamassaw Swamp. Atop the byway, he met Ann Fielder, a young white woman driving a much lighter buggy on a narrow section of the path. Soft shoulders prevented either from easily diverging from the harder crowned surface and the stubborn drivers refused to let the other pass. By the time the deputy sheriff arrived to settle the rising shrill, the enraged woman was in tears and demanded "justice." As a result, law enforcement officers brought the wagon driver to the general store in Wassamassaw to appear before P.M.C. Earnest, magistrate for the central parish.

P.M.C. Earnest, older brother of the female buggy driver, perceived no justification to recuse him from the hearing, but immediately ordered the sheriff to bind over stubborn John Wesley until trial. Neither the sheriff nor the magistrate called the freedman to court, causing him to languish for ten weeks in a tiny cell. Finally, Magistrate Earnest dismissed the case and released Wesley, effectively imprisoning him without indictment or conviction. Resentful white officials taught many such lessons to innocent

---

346. George H. Ballentine, ed. *Church Record Book of the Wassamassaw Baptist Church, Wassamassaw Section, Berkeley County South Carolina 1875-1919* (Copperas Cove, Texas: 2001), 2. Hereinafter cited as "Wassamassaw Church Records."
347. Wassamassaw Church Records, 2.

African-Americans in Wassamassaw and throughout the St. James, Goose Creek Parish, and that pattern of inequity paralyzed many little southern communities until modern times.[348] Such unfairness throughout South Carolina prompted the Republican Congress to refashion government on all levels, including a new state constitution in 1868.

White Goose Creekers almost unanimously refused to legitimatize the government of South Carolina based upon the 1868 State Constitution, and after Congress readmitted South Carolina to the Union that year, hotbeds of political reticence heightened, pitting the agenda of the Democrats (mostly white) against the Republicans (mostly black) and causing violence at political rallies. The Republicans depended upon state militias to advance their will, while the Democrats organized "Democratic Clubs," and relied upon armed support in the guise of social, hunting, riding or rifle "clubs." Mercifully, the anger fell short of all-out internecine warfare, but violence erupted throughout the state in 1876 and that fury penetrated deeply into the St. James, Goose Creek Parish.

WADE HAMPTON III

In 1876, Reverend John Grimke Drayton concluded his sermon for the 165th anniversary service and rededication of the St. James, Goose Creek Church, beseeching "Long may it remain a monument to the refinement and piety of an age and a generation that have long passed away." The priest reopened the sanctuary after "…it fell into the hands of the Negroes after the Confederate War," and that summer, President Ulysses S. Grant sent Federal troops to suppress riots in Charleston resulting from black enfranchisement for the presidential election of 1876. That year was a pivotal time for South Carolinians and the Confederate General Wade Hampton III (1818 -1902) provided indispensable leadership.

Wade Hampton III, a wise postwar politician refused the nomination of governor when Democrat Party supporters offered it to him immediately after the war. He believed too many victorious federal officials resented Confederate Generals such as he, and their reticence precluded his successful service so early after the conflict. The same thinking prompted him to refuse a role in the new unpopular state government fashioned in 1868, but he accepted the chair of the State Democratic Party Central

---

348. BRFAL, May 1867. Liedtke reported the case to the Headquarters of the Freedmen's Bureau for the District of Charleston on August 29, 1867.

Committee. In that position, Hampton advocated a conciliatory vision underpinned by political participation, land ownership, and office holding for black and white adult male citizens, a peaceful prophecy that vaulted him amidst acts of violence toward statewide service.

Democrats created political clubs in most white communities, and Wassamassaw was no exception. The Wassamassaw Mounted Club enforced the will of the Centennial Democratic Club of St. James, Goose Creek Parish. The mounted group first met in September 1876 at the Wassamassaw General Store with C.W. Sanders as Secretary of the political arm and T.S. Browning as captain of the armed enforcers.[349] The riders drilled as a quasi-militia on old fields near the Wassamassaw Baptist Church where they practiced mounted and dismounted maneuvers, and drew from nearby hidden armories where they stored rifles, pistols, sabers and bayonets. As the sole armed force in the center of the parish, the Wassamassaw Mounted Club diligently policed the countryside, patrolling the roads and intersections during the day, visiting perceived offenders at night and banishing the non-compliant. The threat of violence sufficiently compelled most to comply, but nonviolent means also proved effective when all landowners denied employment to persons associated with the "radical" government forcing those offenders to walk away with no jobs, no support and no options. Predictably, in 1876, the people of Wassamassaw enthusiastically backed General Wade Hampton III, the Democratic nominee for governor and attended loud rallies that drumbeat voters to the polls.

Large numbers of Republicans and Democrats met for political demonstrations in September of 1876 at Strawberry Landing on the western branch of the Cooper River, six miles east of the Strawberry Railroad Depot.[350] Cheering Democrats steamed up the Cooper River from Charleston on the ship, M.S. Allison, while others arrived on horseback. Members of the Hampton Social Mounted Club of Goose Creek, consisting of thirty men under the command of Captain George M. Tharin, assembled at Deer Town. They rode most of the day, arriving at Strawberry Ferry during the late afternoon. Major Jacob Barker led the Goose Creek Cavalry from an assembly point on Ararat (once Boochawee Plantation), where they typically drilled in the pinelands along Red Bank Road. Finally, Major Thomas A. Huguenin, ahead of twenty-five men from the Mt. Pleasant Mounted Club, joined the others.

---

349. Orvin, 180.
350. *Charleston News and Courier*, 10-17-1876 and 10-18-1876.

Figure 8.1: The undated image shows Strawberry Ferry near the end of the nineteenth century. The ferry connected St. Johns Berkeley Parish on the north shore with St. James, Goose Creek Parish on the south shore of the Cooper River. Notations, "First operated in 1707," and "Going to Church" appears on the back of the image. The photograph, 1001.22 is among the Berkeley Collection of the Caroliniana Library, University of South Carolina, Columbia. The image is courtesy of Caroliniana Library.

Essentially everyone at the rally carried a weapon of some type, ranging from old single shot muskets and obsolete sabers to the latest revolving pistols, and repeating rifles with bayonets, but no violence erupted. Reportedly, the peacekeeping acumen of Major Barker and his disciplined equestrians from Goose Creek kept the peace all day as they protected the "colored" Democrats from being intimidated.[351] According to the print media of that time, the Republicans persistently threatened black citizens attempting to join the Democrats, but Major Barker skillfully prevented violence from erupting throughout the noisy day. The biased media supported the Democrats and meted no credit to the Republicans in any of the news reports in Charleston. It is more likely, that peace prevailed that day because Major Barker purchased 25 navy revolvers for his mounted troupe,

---

351. *Charleston News and Courier*, 9-1-1876 and 9-7-1876.

effectively emerging the best-armed and most formidable force at the rally, tipping the balance of power to the Hampton supporters.[352]

Governor Wade Hampton III led the opposition to Reconstruction policies as the first southern gubernatorial candidate to run on a platform opposing it. He challenged the Radical Republican incumbent Governor Daniel Henry Chamberlain, whom most black residents favored, and whose militia earned a tarnished reputation due to their violent behaviors. Similarly, Hampton devotees earned equally harsh celebrity and their Democrat Club members, tagged "Red Shirts," behaved brutally at times. Consequently, the 1876 governor campaign raged as the bloodiest in the history of the state[353] and ended when the South Carolina Supreme Court ruled Hampton the narrow victor of the disputed contest.

Governor Wade Hampton III was the first Democrat elected to state office in South Carolina after the close of the Civil War. When he immediately replaced the so-called radical trial judges with men of his liking, including posting H.H. Murray in the St. James, Goose Creek Parish, white supporters breathed a common sigh of relief.[354]

Furthermore, wider implications portended when moderate Rutherford B. Hayes ascended as President of the United States the same year, spelling the end of the Reconstruction Era.[355] Two years hence, the gubernatorial race was far more peaceful, but no less exciting, and Democrats in the St. James, Goose Creek Parish rallied at Bonneau in support of their sitting Governor Hampton. Supporters commenced the exciting daylong event boarding a train in Charleston.

DEMOCRATS RIDE THROUGH GOOSE CREEK

On October 2, 1878, several Democrat Clubs chartered a four-car train to carry members free of charge from Charleston, through the St. James, Goose Creek Parish, to a political rally at Bonneau, a small community four miles north of Moncks Corner.[356] At dawn, the caboose flagman led the train in reverse along

352. Alfred Brockenbrough Williams, *Hampton and His Red Shirts: South Carolina Deliverance* (Charleston: Walker Evans and Cogswell, 1935), 114. *Charleston News and Courier*, 8-28-1876 and September 1 and 7, 1876.

353. Cainhoy Race Riots, "Records chiefly consisting of affidavits of a disturbance at a meeting in Cainhoy, South Carolina in which several persons were killed by gunfire on 10-16-1876," 1004.04.04, SCHS.

354. *Charleston News and Courier*, 6-11-1877.

355. Alfred Brockenbrough Williams, 447. The federal troops marched out of the South Carolina State House at noon on 4-10-1877.

356. Orvin, 185, 186.

the familiar track from the 8-mile railroad "turnout" yard to the northern reaches of the city, stopping alongside upper Meeting Street. Northeastern Railroad Engineers routinely backed cars into Charleston to deliver loads too difficult to transfer or deliver other ways. For example, slave gangs from Mount Holly, Strawberry and other stops, disembarked on Meeting Street in 1861 with thirty-day rations. The slaves manually transported their provisions to the water edge where they erected harbor defenses against the impending Union Naval assault. During the next two bleak winters, volunteers unloaded donated firewood along the Meeting Street railway line to warm the hearths of stunned families huddled in the chilled bombarded city, and the train brought slaves again late in 1863 to erect defenses in preparation for a land invasion. Now, sixteen years after the end of the greatest conflagration in North America, a struggle some sublimely tagged the "Civil War," political warriors arrived in force to commence the forty-mile journey by train with Governor Wade Hampton III into an unusually optimistic countryside.

The chartered locomotive departed thirty minutes after the regular morning train, but immediately lagged farther due to frequent stops to embark cheering Democrats waving hats and red banners beyond the edge of the city. However, two miles out, the engine chugged relentlessly through the industrial zone where creosote dips, kiln pits, steam driven sawmills, and iron works and other obnoxious industrial accoutrements spilt an acrid stench into the thick morning air. Hurrying, the steam engine sped past the ugly eight-mile railroad yard before gradually slowing at the first planned stop at Ten Mile Hill.

At the bustling Ten Mile Hill neighborhood, several side paths converged onto the Road to Goose Creek where an important inn once marked the busy place. The Ten Mile Inn and tavern fell out of use before the Civil War and long since disappeared in salvage, but a copse of oaks recalled its place west of the byway. There, beneath the leafy shade, seventy-three years before, an entourage of family and friends paused on its way to the family cemetery atop Windsor Hill with the remains of General William Moultrie, iconic hero of the Revolutionary War and two-term governor of South Carolina (1785- 1787 and 1792-1794).

When Governor William Moultrie died in 1805, no one in the infant state or nation dared predict the tectonic political shifts that challenged the newest governor. In 1878, Governor Hampton rode into a transformed parish where freedmen owned most of the 800 farms, an inconceivable status seven decades before, when fewer than 90 white men possessed almost all of the land in the parish.

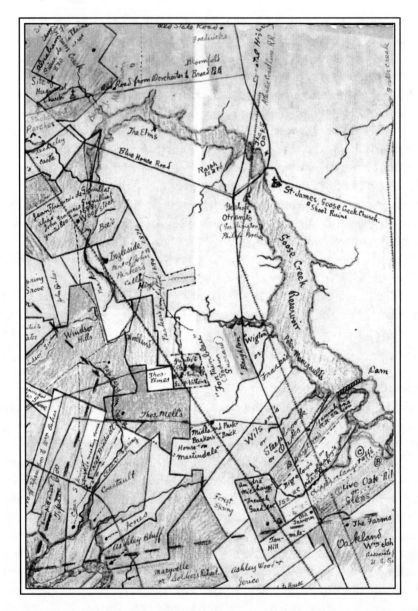

Figure 8.2: William Henry Johnson comprised the above drawing in the early 20th century from his collection of colonial era plats. The colored pencil rendering shows the boundaries of colonial plantations in the St. James, Goose Creek Parish. The drawing shows the Atlantic Coastline Railroad (assumed ownership of the Northeastern Railroad line in 1898) on the right side of the drawing. This is the route Wade Hampton III and his supporters followed in October 1878. The Southern Railroad running through Ladson runs diagonally across the center of the frame.

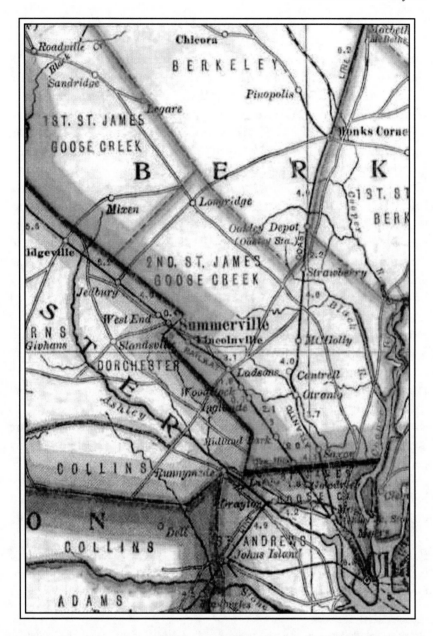

Figure 8.3: The map below shows the Southern Railway and the Atlantic Railway diverging from the Charleston Neck near the turn of the 20th century. Democrat Clubs chartered a train in 1878 that visited stops along the way. Indicated are the rail stops visited by the chartered train except Bonneau, the destination. That stop lay between Moncks Corner and McBeth.

Some descendents of the 90 land owning families tentatively held ancestral properties many years after the emancipation of bound labor, and most of those landowners rallied to shore up Hampton's promise to rid the state of Yankee interlopers. The train stopped at Saxon Station where some of those descendents worked nearby properties. Men such as Charles Manigault of Marshland Plantation and George Henry Smith of renowned Yeamans Hall oversaw tenant farmers who eked out meager incomes from leached soils on their ancient family estates. Both men supported the resilient and popular governor in hopes of retaining their gentry. Others, such as William J. Sineath, no longer relied upon agriculture to support his clan. He lost his beloved Oaks Plantation located near the 12-mile stone, immediately after the Civil War and pursued the busy Ashley Phosphate Road in search of employment at the new phosphate mines. Phosphate fertilizer mines lined the rail spurs diverging from the Southern Railway between Woodstock and Ladson Stations three miles west of the State Road. That emerging business offered supervisory opportunities to young white men who owned no land and it provided living wages to hungry black workers. However, most parish families persistently tilled and planted the ancient lowlands.

During the second term of Governor Hampton, black and white family heads in the St. James, Goose Creek Parish owned the majority (56%) of the farms. The remaining families rented land as tenant farmers (34%) or promised a share of production to the landowner (10%) as sharecroppers. The percentage of holdings compared similarly to the state average, but statistics failed to express the great heartbreak befalling many people in places such as Carnes Cross Roads, where drought or infertile soils caused frequent financial failures, forcing farmers to lose titles to their holdings. During the second Hampton term, South Carolina seized 180 Goose Creek farms for non-payment of taxes, thus relegating the family members homeless, or as menial laborers at more successful destinations.[357] Furthermore, during his second gubernatorial term, the average size of land holdings steadily shrank until half of the farms in the St. James, Goose Creek Parish measured less than ten acres,[358] considerably less than

357. Elias Ball Bull Papers, "Poor white farmers, St. James, Goose Creek Parish." 376.02 (H)01.01.01-17 and "Forfeited Lands List, Sinking Fund Commission, Columbia, South Carolina," W.B. McDaniel (Columbia, South Carolina: General Book and Job Printers, 69 Main Street), 376.02 (H)01.01.01.18, SCHS.

358. Michael J. Heitzler, *Goose Creek, A Definitive History, Rebellion, Reconstruction and Beyond* (Charleston : The History Press, 2006), 99,100. Twenty-seven percent of farms in the St. James, Goose Creek Parish in 1880 ranged from 11 to 30 acres, 9% ranged from

the 650-acre average merely twenty years before. Notwithstanding much heartbreak, most owners of large struggling plantations as well as those with small arid parcels, embraced Hampton, listened to his promises and flocked to his popular mantra.

Many African-Americans supported Wade Hampton III. He was a moderate with an even-handed approach to race relations that lent to his popularity, moreover he chastened violence and advanced a peaceful formula for success for all, including rising black family men. Consequently, African-American men boarded the train too and sped across the mile-long avenue to the Hayes Plantation near the 14-mile stone, traversed the narrow waters of Steepbrook, and slowly entered the storied forests of Otranto.

Democrats from Deer Town, Ladson and Goose Creek boarded the train at Otranto Station. Democrats including Edward R. Miles of the Oaks, Daniel Brown from White House, and Peter Gaillard Stoney from Medway supported Hampton with words, deeds and cash. They placed their legacies in his hands, trusted his political acumen and monetarily contributed to his campaign. In return, Hampton lent credibility to the chance of redeeming the "lost cause," similar to the reemergence of the fabled phoenix.

The locomotive lurched north from Otranto and soon mounted the long causeway and trestle spanning the breadth of Goose Creek. While crossing, the governor scanned the waterway east toward the wooden road crossing and recalled the exploits of his famous grandfather during a more violent revolution almost a century before. His grandfather, Colonel Wade Hampton, the flamboyant patriot cavalryman, scoured the nearby woodlands in search of loyalists and redcoats and galloped across the Goose Creek Bridge in pursuit of immortality, but rudely the blaring train horns interrupted Governor Hampton from his musings as the steam driven leviathan breached the creek and hailed its approach to two important intersections.

Beyond the waters of Goose Creek, the train engineer yanked the horn hard and long, twice within less than thirty seconds, approaching the State Road, and a quarter mile later, at the Liberty Hall Road crossing. The State Road, like the brittle spine of the frail state, reached from Charleston to Greenville connecting South Carolinians from the "mountains to the sea." The loud horn blasts alerted Richard and Margaret Myers working near the Liberty Hall crossing.[359] The Myers family, a quarter of a mile west of the

---

31 to 49 acres, 14% of the farms were 50 acres or larger.

359. The residence of Richard Myers and his small family lay near the intersection of Back River Upper Road and Liberty Hall Road ¼ mile east of the North Eastern Rail Road.

tracks, farmed land that was once part of the Button Hall Plantation. A freedman since the age of forty, Richard worked 200 acres of fertile fields and successfully supported his wife Margaret, a nephew, Washington, his granddaughter, Comida, and a young girl named Rhail.[360] He was a self-made man, who, at the age of 49 years old, purchased land bordering Back River Upper Road from Mary A. R. Austin for $750.[361] There, he worked two horses plowing 26 acres of corn and cotton, and raised chickens, cows, and pigs. He annually gathered more than 125 bushels of potatoes, 38 bags of rice and most kinds of produce.[362] His neighbors, Josiah Green and Jonas Stephens worked 50 and 25-acre farms respectively, and all of those landowners preferred stability to chaos and optimism to uncertainty, and most such men preferred Hampton's steady hand on the helm of state.

Within minutes of Myers farm, the engineer rose atop the narrow four hundred yard long trestle to traverse the soft Button Hall wetlands, penetrate a thick mixed forest, cut the main avenue to Mount Holly House and immediately stuttered, then eased into Mount Holly Depot where another gaggle of "red shirts," including Jacob Minott, noisily greeted the lumbering behemoth.

Jacob Minott, a firm Hampton Democrat, appeared among a new class of white males emerging throughout the eastern section of the parish. Minott and dozens of landless, white men such as he managed property for absentee landowners. Unlike overseers of prewar years, Jacob Minott did not "drive" the workers, but instead he secured leases, collected rents from the successful families, and evicted the failing ones. Henry Middleton of Charleston employed Minott to protect the ancient Crowfield properties, located two miles west of the depot. Arriving a year before in 1877, Minott oversaw more than a dozen tenants and enjoyed contracted rights to "live, till the soil, cut timber for the market and make turpentine..." on the grand old estate.[363] Now, greatly outnumbered in the parish by resident freedmen, landless Minott and many jealous Caucasian men such as he, sought political

---

360. Richard Myers appears as 44-year-old "Dick Myers" with his 40-year-old wife, "Peggy," in the 1870 census. The records more formally title them, "Richard" and "Margaret" Myers on subsequent public records. He claimed $100 value of personal estate, but owned no property nor could he read or write in 1870. Five years hence, he was a landowner and 20 years later, he was literate. See US Enumeration Censuses. St. James, Goose Creek Parish, 1870, 1880, 1890.
361. Cheves Papers, 34/320, SCHS.
362. St. James, Goose Creek Parish, United States Enumeration Census and Census of Agriculture, 1870. 1880, 1890.
363. Langdon Cheves, 1848-1939, Legal papers, 1875-1932, 1167.01.03, SCHS, Cheves-Middleton Correspondence, Lease to J. Minott, 1874, file 18.

power at every level, hoping to revive white mastery over all of the little black occupied neighborhoods. Dozens of black families resided within walking distance of the depot. Some thrived and some failed, but most rented or owned pieces of subdivided plantations named Mount Holly, Howe Hall, Springfield and Liberty Hall. Minott and many more whites feared the rising black franchise and prodded Hampton to rewrite the reconstructed laws of the land and return white dominance over all of the farms and fields.

Wade Hampton was popular among the people of both races and several African-American men from Casey (Thorogood/Mount Holly Plantation), St. Paul (Springfield Plantation), and Mount Zion (Liberty Hall / Howe Hall) boarded to accompany the predominantly white Republican group on the increasingly discordant ride. Some participants carried lunch buckets, some blazed red shirts while others pinned strips of red cloth to their collars, lapels, or hatbands. Most were exceedingly raucous and many shouted and talked loudly, perhaps to embolden their presence in a parish dominated by African-American Republicans.

The train paused at Strawberry Station to embark Democratic Club President, Dr. O. C. Rhame and members of the Strawberry Democrat Club. Elder Dr. Rhame exemplified the planting era once driven by black labor. He once worked eleven slaves at his 1,300-acre Grove Hall Plantation two miles south of the depot, supplementing his medical practice by raising horses, cattle and corn. A few African -American men followed him aboard, all donning red colors, including a young black man and his wife. She, a small, shy woman picked black-eyed Susan wild flowers along the rail bed, and handed the full bouquet to her husband as he stepped up and onto the all-male train. He passed the wild flowers to Governor Hampton and said, "Look at me and my wife, there ain't no starvation where we come from."[364] The coach jerked forward, gained momentum and steadily sped toward Bonneau and victory.

Wade Hampton III returned to the Governor's Office in 1878 after many loud but non-violent rallies, signifying the ebb of bitterness growing out of the post war era. During his second term, Governor Hampton earned renown as the "Savior of South Carolina" for his efforts to recover the state from Reconstruction. Before his tenure as governor ended (1878-1879), he reported to Washington, D.C. as a United States Senator on behalf of South Carolina, one of the oldest states in the New South. Years hence and soon after the new century dawned, the dying Senator prayed, "God bless all my people, black and white."[365]

---

364. *Charleston News and Courier*, 10-7-1878, and Orvin, 185, 186.
365. Wade Hampton III died April 11, 1902, at age 84. Twenty thousand mourners fol-

CHAPTER 9
The Old Parish in the New South

African-Americans residing in the St. James, Goose Creek Parish continued to transition from servitude to freedom during the waning years of the nineteenth century and into the twentieth. Minority residents developed farms, churches and neighborhoods more independently of white control as employment opportunities expanded beyond the anachronistic plantations. As the new century dawned, European-American landowners in the parish portioned great swathes of property into more than eight-hundred smaller holdings. Some landowners sold subdivided parcels to minority farmers, but others leased properties to tenant families on large tracts resembling plantations of the old south. Each year, however more property conveyed to individuals and the "new south" characterized by small, privately owned farms and emerging commercial centers slowly supplanted the large estates.[366] During this period, the State Road over the Goose Creek Bridge continued as the busiest road passage to Charleston and the Otranto, Mount Holly and Strawberry Railroad Depots remained dominant white population centers in the parish, but dynamic changes pended. As more people acquired property and new roadways provided convenient access to distant employment, iconic features of the old south including the sacred places, faded further into the rural tapestry of an earlier era.

---

lowed his casket to Trinity Churchyard in Columbia, where the Bishop-General Ellison Capers read the services. Reportedly, Hampton's final words were "God bless all my people, black and white."

366. The 844 farms counted in the United States Census of Agriculture for the St. James, Goose Creek Parish in 1879 were almost four times greater than the 215 farms counted twenty years earlier,

AFRICAN-AMERICAN FARMERS

Black farmers regularly used the white owned and operated rail depots, mills and shops to purchase fertilizer, seed and other necessities and to sell any surplus. In addition, the general store was the only semblance of a bank where a black farmer could borrow against anticipated crops. For example, July Myers, an African-American farmer, borrowed $633.00 at 8% interest from the Mount Holly Mercantile Company near the Mount Holly Station. He secured the loan with the mortgage of his farm, paid off the debt when due, and obtained another advancement with the attachment of two mules, one mower, one broken wagon, and twenty-five acres of cleared land. Myers regularly paid toward the debt, and after six years, he settled the difference with two bales of cotton and all of his cottonseed.[367] This was a successful business experience for the minority farmer, and his transaction was one of many that brought the races together for mutual advantage as an increasing number of African-American farmers derived expendable wealth from their farmlands.

The means by which most black Goose Creekers acquired land varied widely throughout the old parish. Some blacks purchased property with savings, some parents bequeathed property to children, a few white landowners gave property to favorite freedmen and in some cases government agencies sponsored land transfers. The Bureau of Refugees, Freedmen and Abandoned Lands assisted minority farmers in acquiring property and livelihoods in South Carolina, but the agency did not transfer much land in the St. James, Goose Creek Parish. Furthermore, the state created the South Carolina Land Commission and transferred small parcels of property to 2000 farmers statewide, but inexplicably, no one in the St. James, Goose Creek Parish acquired land in this manner. Nevertheless, by the turn of the twentieth century, African -Americans owned most of the farms in the parish. Many other African-Americans found non-agricultural livelihoods.

---

367. Cheves papers, 34/320, SCHS, Tenant Records, Notes regarding July Myers, 1914. Myers owned a 30-acre farm in 1914. July Myers rented 14 acres of land in 1880, U.S. Agricultural Census, St. James, Goose Creek Parish, 1879, 71.

	Number of Farmers	Percent of Farmers
Owned the Land	473	56
Paid a fixed rent	287	34
Paid share of the crop	84	10
Total number of farmers in 1879 (1880 Census)	844	100

The above table shows farm ownership and tenancy in the St. James, Goose Creek Parish according to the 1880 United States Census of Agriculture. The count indicates 56% of the farms in private ownership, and less than half of the farmers paying a fixed rent or a share of their crops.

PHOSPHATE MINERS

The post Civil War phosphate boon tempered the raucous political era immediately following Reconstruction, and helped the segregated neighborhoods look to the future rather than dwell on the unsettled past. Phosphate was an inexpensive local source of fertilizer, greatly needed for the depleted soils. Local investors leveraged their scarce resources to open mining companies until processed ore became an important export. Entrepreneurs residing in the St. James, Goose Creek Parish owned many of the phosphate mines and fertilizer-manufacturing companies near Charleston. They sought managers from among the newly idle planters and brick manufacturers thus growing a business that was a profitable substitute for the failed plantation system. Many African- Americans near Mount Holly found employment as laborers at the E. Boddington and Company phosphate plant near the Cooper River. There, barges floated the ore to markets, and trams carried rock to rail spurs near Mount Holly Station.[368]

368. SCDAH, Series L10005 Reel 3 Plat 1653 and E. Boddington and Company Report, 1882. The St. James, Goose Creek Parish, United States Enumeration Census, 1880 and

Figure 9.1: Two unidentified men stand behind a tram rail car above an open phosphate mine in the St. James, Goose Creek Parish. This mine operated for nearly twenty years at Woodstock Plantation along the Southern Railroad line near Ladson. The phosphate ore, found in large beds in the southeastern United States, contain calcium, nitrogen and other compounds that promote plant growth and thus are useful fertilizers. The image, taken near the end of the 19th century is among the collections of the South Carolina Historical Society, Charleston, South Carolina.

Many unskilled men and boys resided in barracks near the phosphate mines for weeks or months at a time, digging innumerable tons of the mucky ore, then loading and pushing it in trams, and dumping it into open railcars that the Northeastern Railroad Company made specifically for that purpose. The men that worked with the Mount Holly Phosphate Mining Company (later the Berkeley Phosphate Company) built a three-foot-wide gauge tramway and used a Porter locomotive, familiarly named "William," to pull nearly 20,000 tons of ore each year to the spur line

---

1890 lists names of men residing at labor camps near the phosphate mines. See Mitchell & Smith records relating to the phosphate and fertilizer industry, 1869-1916, 152.06.21, SCHS.

near Mount Holly Station. From there, cars hauled the cleaned rock to processing plants at Meadville Mines (later Keowa Phosphate Works) on the old Palmetto and Oakland Plantations near the mouth of Goose Creek.[369] At those phosphate works, men used steam-powered machines to extract, haul, crush, wash, and package the crumbly rock before loading the finished fertilizer onto conveyors and bagging it for markets.

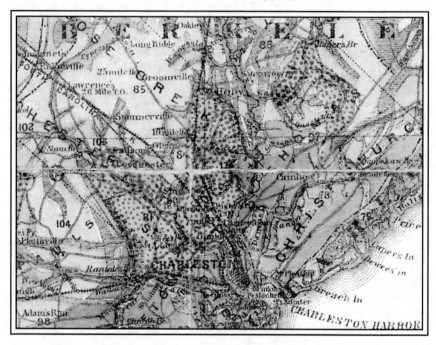

Figure 9.2: The image shows details of the *Map of State of South Carolina,* issued by the State Department of Agriculture, A.P. Butler, Commissioner, Columbia, South Carolina, 1883. A wide layer of phosphate rock, indicated by dots on light background, permeates the substrata fanning inland from the Charleston Peninsula. Agriculturalists used the sedimentary rock with naturally high phosphate concentration, as a fertilizer. The map is courtesy of the South Carolina Department of Archives and History, Columbia, South Carolina.

Toward the end of the nineteenth century, the phosphate boom slowed and residents sought work elsewhere. Some found employment at the Mount Holly Clay Products Company where they shaped and baked brick and tile

---

369. *News and Courier*, Industrial Issue 1888. The Keowa Phosphate Works used 4000 acres with four miles of rail and employed one locomotive and thirty cars to carry the rock to the drying kiln and farther to distributors.

and many hundreds of men and boys resided in barracks at lumber sites, such as Stokes Camp on the old Liberty Hall Plantation lands. Others labored with the new Atlantic Coastal Railroad that assumed ownership of the Northeastern Railroad line in 1898. They laid and repaired tracks and loaded lumber, ore or other products on rail cars backed onto rail spurs. Nonetheless, an insufficient number of jobs availed until improved roads facilitated longer commutes to employment destinations nearer Charleston.[370]

Figure 9.3: The photograph shows the dilapidated Ancrum Bridge on the Road to Dorchester circa 1920. The road connected traffic from the Eighteen-Mile Stone to Ladson. The road fell out of general use after the colonial period and was impassable by the turn of the twentieth century. The image is in the William Henry Johnson Scrapbook, circa 1920-1923, among the photographic collections of SCHS, 34/293.

370. United States Census, St. James, Goose Creek Parish, 1930, Enumeration Census and Interview with Loretta Parsons, resident of Cayce, South Carolina at Westview Elementary School, July 1, 1984.

CHAPEL OF EASE AT THE CAMP

Notwithstanding the surge of minority land ownership, European-American families retained control of the rail depots and the nearby businesses. Whites, such as Margaret Dickey, Charles Lice, and Magnus Shiver managed grocery stores, steam-powered sawmills and post offices near rail depots.[371] White farmers sought arable properties closer to the convenience of those neighborhoods. Thus, during this era, congregants relocated the Bethlehem Baptist Church, stopped using the cemetery, and officially erased the chapel of ease footprint at the camp by omitting its easement on land records after 1897.[372]

Some European-Americans residing near the St. James, Chapel of Ease at the camp, relocated closer to the Strawberry Railroad Depot. The Grooms family owned land near the Strawberry Station two miles northwest of the fallen cruciform chapel. After the Strawberry Depot commenced rail and mail service, the proximity called Groomsville, enjoyed a time of economic expansion with the construction of a school, sawmill and general store. William Bun owned the Groomsville General Store and Emil Withers clerked there during the 1880s and 1890s, while Jonathan Brogdon labored as an engineer and J. Douglas Bun served as trial justice in a tiny clapboard office aside the train-loading platform. For convenience, the Baptist minister, deacons and leading "brethren" often worshipped at the Groomsville schoolhouse and "Mr. Grooms" bequeathed partly cleared land to the congregation in 1882. Six years later, the church brethren relocated the little wooden church.[373]

The churchmen disassembled the wooden structure at the chapel of ease site, loaded the sections and boards on wagons and carried the pieces 4.5

371. United States Enumeration Census, Census of Agriculture, Social Census and Census of Industry, St. James, Goose Creek Parish, 1870, 1880, 1890.
372. The land records described in deed books: BCDB A21:147, 1897, A58:269, April 27, 1931, BCDB A70:138, July 22, 1942, and BCDB A103:62, September 3, 1956, do not indicate an easement for the chapel or its cemetery, Berkeley County Office Building, Moncks Corner. An easement for the chapel and cemetery is included in BCDB A2:86, 7-17-1972 and each conveyance since.
373. The Baptist leadership met in October 1870 at the "school house." By 1877, there were only 21 members of the St. James Baptist Church (Bethlehem Baptist Church) on the covenant roll. The church leaders met at Foxbank Plantation on 1-14-1888 and agreed to "take down," the old church building and move it to the new location. See the *Church Book of the Covenant*. Pastors serving the church during the post-war period included, J.M. Kirtin, Samuel Lynes, Wesley Bishop, and R. E. Gibson. See the Last Will and Testament of George Grooms, 9- 4-1848, Will Book K, 1845-1851, 220.

miles to its present place on Groomsville Road. John Simms, an energetic boy helped the leading men disassemble the structure and load the wagon. When finished he climbed atop the bumpy carriage and rode it to the new location. At Groomsville, the congregation reconstructed the sanctuary spending $155.00 on improvements. The reconstituted church featured rebuilt windows, sills, sashes and a new front door. The congregation sold some of the old cruciform chapel bricks garnering contributions until there was enough money to pay all of the moving and reassembly expenses, purchase hymnals for the first service at the new location and pay $9.88 to Reverend J.R. Hyatt, a traveling minister who also preached at the Wassamassaw Baptist Church. Two years later, in 1890 the assembly renamed the reconstituted sanctuary, "Groomsville Baptist Church."[374]

Figure 9.4: The photograph shows the Groomsville Baptist Church (once St. James Baptist Church and Bethlehem Baptist Church) after it was "taken down," transported to Groomsville, reassembled, and re-named. The author took this photograph on June 12, 2004.

---

374. The Baptist vestry purchased lots for a school including the "largest section" from Dr. O. C. Rhame. See the Church Book for minutes of the meeting held (no day or month given) in 1875. SCDAH L10005, Reel 8, Plat 4268. Also the congregation dedicated the new house of worship on the "...first Lord's Day in October of 1888." Rev. John R. Hyatt "preached that day from Luke:16:5, "How much owes thou my Lord." See the Church Book. Also see the assignment of J.R. Hyot (Hyatt) in the *Minutes of the Wassamassaw Baptist Church*, Second Sunday of October, 1894 in Ballentine, 109.

CHAPEL OF EASE AT WASSAMASSAW

Similar to the white families clustered near the railroad stations, others came together near general stores strung every two or three miles along the State Road through the center of the 32-mile long parish. The rail depots and general stores provided essential conduits to the outside world and a lifeline for the Caucasian residents in the stubbornly fading white dominated countryside. Most rural families relied upon rail stops and general stores for economic, social and political support, and no African-American owned or worked at a depot or store anywhere in the parish, including Wassamassaw.[375]

Though far removed from the busier eastern section of the old St. James, Goose Creek Parish, Wassamassaw persisted as an important agricultural center of trade and a watering place for cattle drivers well into the twentieth century. The cattlemen followed the State Road from remote farms to corrals at the Wassamassaw floodway where they assembled and watered the herd. Then they continued along the State Road, stopping overnight to water the beasts at Deas Swamp, before fording the creek near the Goose Creek Bridge, in route to butchers in Charleston. A religious center during the colonial era, several roads converged at Wassamassaw near the defunct site of the chapel of ease, creating a commercial nexus of stores and mills resembling a small town.

After the Revolutionary War when the Wassamassaw Chapel of Ease fell into ruin, worshippers built new churches on or near the chapel site. The new structures, as well as the ever-expanding cemetery, obscured property lines until the footprint of the colonial sanctuary vanished from sight, memory and official accounts. Church leaders obscured the old boundaries when they thrice built on the chapel site and twice failed to properly record land addendums to the tract. In 1847, Dr. S.E. Williams granted contiguous lands to the church, but trustee John J. Browning, appointed to accept the deed, never recorded the transfer. The congregation built the third church on the site in 1892, and soon after its completion, Mrs. Innis E. McKewn gave an adjoining parcel of land for a "burial ground."[376] The church leaders again failed to record the transaction. After the turn of the twentieth century, to rectify the pressing uncertainty of real estate ownership, church leaders set the boundaries of the property "pedo possessione." That is, they "stepped off" the lines, as they perceived them

---

375. Mount Holly District, United States Census Reports, 1900-1930.
376. *Minutes of the Wassamassaw Baptist Church*, 4th Sunday in April 1892, Ballentine, 102.

and registered the resulting plat. When no adjoining landowner contested the filed boundary lines, county officials accepted the deed by adverse possession. That deed included no mention of the Wassamassaw Chapel of Ease. Thus, by the turn of the twentieth century, the chapels of ease at the camp and at Wassamasaw vanished from official records as well as most memories, but the mother church prevailed in spite of natural and manmade assaults.

ST. JAMES, GOOSE CREEK CHURCH

During the Civil War, the church records and communion silver disappeared. The silver collection included a piece engraved, "The gift of Capt. Benj. Schenckingh to ye Parish of St. James, Goose Creek 1712," a goblet with the inscription, " To ye Parish of St. James, Goose Creek," and a heavy tankard inscribed, " The gift of Ralph Izard To ye Parish of St. James, Goose Creek South Carolina." The vestry locked and shuttered the sanctuary for the duration of the turbulent post-war years. The church deteriorated considerably during the Reconstruction period, but the vestry felt reinvigorated when Wade Hampton III assumed the highest office in the state in 1876. His election as governor prompted the churchmen to reopen the sacred place and raise funds to repair the wear and tear from neglect, natural elements and malicious mischief. Vandals marred the exterior and interior of the sanctuary and soon after the vestry repaired all of it, an earthquake collapsed the front gable and cracked the walls. The earthquake of 1886 stunned everyone but the vestry did not sway from its aged mission. Again, the vestry raised money, hired workers and repaired the devastation.

Figure 9.5: George L. Cook took the photograph of the St. James, Goose Creek Church after August 31, 1886. The photo is No. 47 of "Cook's Earthquake Views of Charleston and Vicinity." From the Collections of the South Carolina Historical Society.

Figure 9.6: The image is No. 48 of "Cook's Earthquake Views of Charleston and Vicinity." The image may indicate damage to the rear gable. The photographer did not identify the people in the photo, but the man standing on the far right of image 9.4 and at the far left of image 9.5 appears to be Samuel Gaillard Stoney, Churchwarden. From the Collections of the South Carolina Historical Society.

The earthquake rendered the sanctuary unusable for fourteen years, but visitors returned when the Atlantic Coast Line Railroad operated a charter service from Charleston to the old parish in April 1900, when the vestry showed the fresh repairs. More commemorative assemblies punctuated the first decade of the twentieth century. A service in April 1904 recognized the arrival of Reverend Samuel Thomas, the first missionary,[377] and the church opened in April 1906 with a special memorial service marking the 200th anniversary of the establishment of the parish.[378] For that event, more than two hundred people boarded seven train coaches and departed Union Station in Charleston.[379]

SAMUEL GAILLARD STONEY, EDWIN PARSONS AND FRANCIS HOLMES

On April 22, 1906, the two churchwardens, Francis LeJau Parker, M.D., and S. Porcher Stoney rode the train to the commemorative service at the St. James, Goose Creek Church from Charleston, but three vestrymen, Samuel Gaillard Stoney, Edwin Parsons and Francis Holmes traveled by automobile from their parish residences. All of the vestrymen shared a concern as well as the destination. Only four days before, a devastating earthquake and subsequent fires destroyed most of San Francisco, and although the event occurred a continent away, the wire reports headlined in the *Charleston News and Courier* that day, riveted the vestrymen with vivid reminders of a horrible event in South Carolina merely fourteen years before. That horror permeated conversations of all who traveled to the sanctuary as they assayed the rugged little sanctuary standing after an earthquake of similar magnitude.

The three vestrymen from the St. James, Goose Creek Parish, Samuel Gaillard Stoney, Edwin Parsons and Francis Holmes deserve much credit for working with many others, raising funds and overseeing reconstruction of the damaged sanctuary. Each of the men was forward thinking, and embraced and profited from the newest technologies of the time, but they were the last church officers to reside in the old parish.

---

377. The *Charleston News and Courier*, 4- 22-1900 and 4-17-1904. Also see, *The Life and Labors of Reverend Samuel Thomas* [pamphlet] address delivered in St. James, Goose Creek Church, Goose Creek, South Carolina, 4-17- 1904 by John Peyre Thomas (Charleston, South Carolina: Walker, Evans and Cogswell, 1904).

378. Waring, 1897, p. 22.

379. The *News and Courier*, 4-23-1906. Christians celebrated Easter on 4-15-1906.

Figure 9.7: The image shows vestryman Samuel Gaillard Stoney and Mrs. Louisa Cheves Stoney. They traveled seven miles from their Medway Plantation home to attend services at the St. James, Goose Creek Church. The image is in the William Henry Johnson (1871-1934) scrapbook, circa 1920-1923. The image is among the photographic collections of the South Carolina Historical Society (34/293), Charleston, South Carolina.

Samuel G. Stoney was the final patriarch of five generations of the family to reside at the ancient Medway House on Back River. Hurricanes during the first years of the new century washed away essential dikes and dashed all hope of growing rice again. Additionally, on higher ground above the washed-out dikes and near the forest line, lay a great boiler that once drove steam beaters for mixing clay. The Stoney family successfully grew rice and shaped and baked clay muddle into bricks for five decades, shipping all of the heavy loads on their sail powered sloop to Charleston. Now the rice fields washed wantonly and the great steam boiler tank lay near a tree line, snared by twisted vines like the carcass of an extinct beast. The dikes and boiler were ugly remnants of defunct enterprises that never resurrected. Similarly to many Goose Creek families before them, the Stoneys departed Medway for Charleston leaving the house to molder and the land to overgrow.[380]

Figure 9.8: The photograph shows Francis Holmes in his study at Ingleside Plantation (the Hayes) circa, 1875. The photograph is in the Johnson scrapbook volume 1, among the visual collections of the South Carolina Historical Society, Charleston, South Carolina.

---

380. Sidney and Gertrude Legende purchased the Medway properties in 1930 after the plantation lay abandoned for several years.

Francis Holmes purchased the venerable Hayes Plantation west of the Goose Creek Bridge in 1871, ending one hundred and sixty-nine years of Parker family tutelage. Holmes renamed the manor, "Ingleside," and founded the Ingleside Mining and Manufacturing Company where he extracted phosphate ore, processed it, and shipped the finished fertilizer to markets on rail cars from sidings near the Woodstock Railroad Depot. Most credit him with the commercial success of the phosphate fertilizer industry in South Carolina. However, by the advent of the 20th century, profits from phosphate mining, like Medway rice and brick baking vanished. The phosphate industry left scant evidence of its demise at Ingleside except deep impervious marl pits filled with stagnant water.

Figure 9.9: The photograph shows the main house at the Oaks Plantation. Edwin Parsons built the structure and surrounding gardens in 1892. Walter B. Chambers, FAIA Architect contracted the photograph circa 1894. The image is among the collections of the author.

Edwin Parsons arrived from Kennebunk, Maine to build upon the old Middleton settlement near the St. James, Goose Creek Church six years after the earthquake of 1886. The epicenter of that calamity at nearby

Woodstock Plantation was proximate to the Ingleside marl pits.[381] The powerful shockwave crumbled several principal structures at the Oaks Plantation, including a massive one-story building with three gables, "… all of wch [which] were destroyed…" and a "brick stable destroyed – all chimneys injured…"[382] Parsons cleared away the rubble and built anew upon the original Middleton manor site. He was one of the first northern entrepreneurs to seek greatly undervalued property in the south, and live the vaulted pastoral lifestyle.[383] He inherited his father's railroad fortune, resided in the rebuilt Oaks mansion, chartered the "Goose Creek Club for Preserving Game," and contributed to the parish as a vestryman. His wealth tied him to the ancient sanctuary for the remainder of his life, unlike other vestrymen who connected through heritage.

LANGDON CHEVES

Langdon Cheves, a Charleston attorney and businessman reigned as the most influential landowner in Goose Creek during the first three decades of the twentieth century.[384] He managed singularly or in partnership almost 4,000 acres of land that sprawled between the Otranto and Mount Holly Railroad Stations and eastwardly to Ladson. Tracts called Crowfield, Bloomfield, Fredericks, Greenfield, Magnolia, and Seventeen, Eighteen and Nineteen-Mile-House composed his properties as well as large sections of the Oaks and Mount Holly Plantations. He rented parcels to farmers during the time when automobiles and trucks increasingly displaced reliance on rail travel and roads extended farther into the obsolete St. James, Goose Creek Parish.

---

381. Brent Lansdell, Charles F. Philips and Ralph Bailey Jr., Brockington and Associates, Incorporated, Cultural Resources Survey and Testing of the Weber Research Tract (Charleston, South Carolina: July 2006), 34.

382. Michael Trinkley, Debi Hacker and Natalie Adama, Broom Hall: "A Good One and in a Pleasant Neighborhood," (Columbia, South Carolina: The Chicora Foundation, Inc. 861 Arbutus Drive, 1995), 68.

383. Edwin Parsons chartered the "Goose Creek Club for Preserving Game." The hunt club records nest with the Conner Family Papers, 28-235-3 among the collections of SCHS.

384. Langdon Cheves, Berkeley County Tax Records for the years, 1927, 1928, 1929 etc, Berkeley County Office Building, Moncks Corner, South Carolina and Cheves Papers, among the collections of the South Carolina Historical Society, Charleston, South Carolina, SCHS.

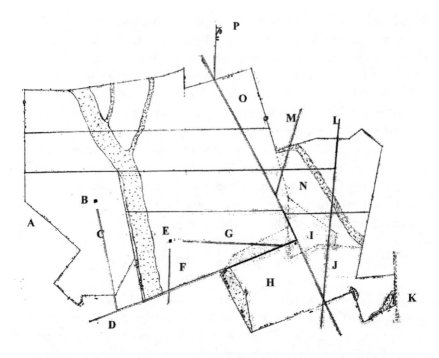

Figure 9.10: The above plat shows lands Henry A. Middleton owned and recorded May 1872 in Book C, p. 550 at the Charleston County Office Building, Charleston, South Carolina. T.J. Mellard surveyed and drew the plat describing 3971 acres in 1872. Langdon Cheves inherited and managed these properties for more than forty years in partnership with others. The Crowfield tract consisting of 1,464 acres was purchased from John Middleton on February 5, 1840. The Bloomfield tract consisting of 1364 acres was purchased from Arthur Gibbes in 1855. The north-western section of the Oaks and all of the 17, 18 and 19-mile tracts consisting of 1143 acres were purchased from Captain Carsten Vose on May 18, 1871. The original plat was recorded April 1873 in plat book B, p. 40. Manuscript letters were added for this publication to illuminate the description: A- De La Plaine's Main House, B- Crowfield Main House, C- Crowfield Avenue, D. Road to Dorchester, E- Bloomfield Main House, F-Bloomfield Main Avenue, G- Bloomfield Second Avenue, H - The Oakes Plantation, I – Eighteen-Mile House Tract, J – Seventeen-Mile House Tract, K – Back River Upper Road, L – Northeastern Railroad, M - Road to Moncks Corner, N – Nineteen –Mile House Tract, O – State Road (Road to Wassamassaw), P – Compass Rose indicating north. Henry A.M. Smith

During the first decades of the twentieth century, motor vehicles and improved roadways enabled more workers to commute to jobs in Charleston County, but farming persisted as the only livelihood for many and an important supplemental source of income for most.[385] Langdon Cheves

---

385. Langdon Cheves, 1848-1939, Cheves property papers, 1844-1935. The Cheves

appreciated the potential profitability of fertile land and he traveled to Goose Creek regularly to manage his properties. He seldom traded the convenience of automobile for train travel and he often rode a rail coach from the city station near his Bull Street home in Charleston to the Otranto and Mount Holly Depots, his favored doorways to his rural domain.

Born in 1848 to Isabella and Dr. Charles Manly Cheves, son of a President of the United States Bank, Langdon Cheves grew up among the landed and privileged class of Carolina. As a youth, he was an avid naturalist and an accomplished wildlife artist, and after graduating from the College of Charleston with advanced mathematic skills, he worked briefly outdoors as an engineer. Unhappy applying his engineering skills to surveying, he successfully apprenticed with General James Conner (1829-1883) at a Broad Street Law practice, where he eventually assumed partnership status. In that capacity, he combined his math, surveying, and legal skills with his penchant for the countryside to become an astute land litigator and property manager.[386]

Langdon Cheves took a careful and abiding interest in his lands in Goose Creek and on a "sultry morning"[387] in May 1910, he disembarked at Otranto Depot to commence a familiar walk through his property to Mount Holly Station, four miles distant. Along the way, he measured the frontage of lots, evaluated the productivity of tenants, and searched for opportunities to consolidate his holdings. He made copious notes and tiny drawings of his properties, and at the age of sixty-two, a time when many consider retirement, Langdon Cheves sought ways to improve the yield of his rural demesne.

Langdon Cheves was well acquainted with the Otranto Hunting Club near the Otranto Station as well as the Goose Creek Club for the Preservation of Game, the sister association east of the Goose Creek Bridge. Since his youth, he frequented both places and serendipitously, his employer, General James Conner owned part of the Otranto retreat since it incorporated in 1872.[388] That spring morning in 1910, Langdon Cheves walked past the Otranto Club House, 350 yards north of the station aside the Atlantic Coast

papers, 1167.01.07.02 are among the collections of SCHS. Hereinafter this work cites it as Cheves Papers.

386. Robert B. Cuthbert, *The Picture Man, A Biographical Sketch of Langdon Cheves,* and Karen D. Stokes, *Langdon Cheves Goes to War,* Carologue, Fall, 2009, Vol. 25, No. 2, pp. 14-21 and 22, 23, SCHS.

387. Cheves Papers, One note stated, "May 19, 1910. Sultry Morning, a slight shower at 2:30, then a lovely afternoon. Walked down to Saxon [Hanahan Station], then on hand car to Ashley Junction & walked on to the station [Charleston]."

388. Langdon Cheves notations and sketches, Goose Creek, 5- 19- 1910, 7-2-1910, 1-21-1911, and 4-19-1913 among the Cheves Papers.

Line tracks in route to the wooden Goose Creek Bridge. Edward L. Wells built and furnished the little Otranto clubhouse for hunters and leased the dwelling for $3.00 per member each year.[389] The associates employed John Watson to stock the place and serve as gamekeeper and "deer driver," paying him $125.00 annually. Watson kept the house well supplied with firewood, canned goods and other essentials, such as playing cards and libations.

After Langdon Cheves crossed over the Goose Creek Bridge, he immediately approached John Watson's little clapboard home near the intersection of State Road and "Church Road" (Snake Road). Watson, a tall, straight and versatile man, grew up as a slave on James Island. Soon after the turn of the century, he found his way to Goose Creek to serve as a hunting guide and sexton for the old St. James, Goose Creek Church.[390] The Goose Creek Club for the Preservation of Game occupied the church property and in partnership with the Otranto Association, the club leased great amounts of acreage for the various deer, turkey and other bird hunting seasons. Additional arrangements extended the hunting territory beyond the boundaries of Otranto and the glebe.

Each year, on behalf of both clubs, Watson delivered bushels of peas to more than thirty-one nearby landowners as compensation for permission to shoot over their fields.[391] That year landowners such as Maggie Johnson and Hampton Pringle received peas as payment, and the hunting range expanded accordingly. However, tenant farmers such as Lee Bennett and Robert Barnwell received no compensation. They, Richard Bryant and dozens like them, leased farms on Crowfield, Bloomfield, Fredericks, Magnolias, 17, 18 and 19-mile tracts, Bees, Howe Hall, Ararat, Gadsden, and Blue House tracts and surrendered hunting rights to the club members as a provision of their lease agreement with the landowners.[392] Consequently, hunting club members roamed a huge expanse of natural and planted properties reaching along the banks of Goose Creek from the southern extreme of the old Schenkingh Plantation to the ruins of De La Plaine's house in Ladson.

389. Henry Workman Conner, 1890-1948, no.1256.02.05 and 28-235-1, SCHS. Also see "Mitchell & Smith," Records of the Otranto Club, 1916-1924, number 152.02.08 among the Conner Family Papers 28-235-3, SCHS. Hereinafter Conner Family Papers refers to this source.
390. Interview with Vermel Watson, daughter-in-law of John Watson, at Westview Elementary School, 12-28-83.
391. List of Lessors, 1909, among the Conner Family papers. The list gives the names of landowners and the amount of peas delivered as compensation for hunting rights.
392. Cheves Papers, 1166-01-01, 11-1-1913 (perhaps 1903), tenant contract between Langdon Cheves and James Nelson, John Jenkins witness. The contract reserved all hunting rights to the Goose Creek Club.

Figure 9.11: John Watson, in addition to other duties at the hunting clubs served as sexton for the St. James, Goose Creek Church during the early decades of the twentieth century. The photograph shows John Watson in his official church capacity wearing a sexton robe.

Soon after passing John Watson's home, Langdon Cheves paused where the State Road veered north. There, an intersection of three by-ways divided his attention. He peered north along the dirt State Road that was his intended route, but the perspective also granted a long view toward Edwin Parson's large and elegant home at the terminus of the shady Avenue of Oaks. Cheves also looked east, along Howe Hall Road reaching far beyond his vista where the ancient Howe Hall main house stood overlooking the headwaters of Foster Creek. In all his days, neither Langdon Cheves nor any of his family owned Howe Hall lands.

James Vidal owned those properties for decades and now many claimed sections of it. Prior to the Civil War, James Vidal purchased 1,505 acres of land between Liberty Hall, Brick Hope Plantations and Foster Creek. Most of his tract spanned the boundaries of renowned Howe Hall Plantation, the countryseat of influential and wealthy families of the colonial era, but at the time Cheves passed near, most whites avoided the place, and some derisively labeled it, "Hog Hall."

James Vidal created "Hog Hall" when he retired in the early 1870s and sold Howe Hall Plantation in sections. He conveyed relatively large segments to two white farmers, Edwin J. Wright and William Tennent, but he also conveyed eleven smaller parcels to African-American farmers.[393] These eleven Howe Hall property sales to African-Americans provided rare opportunities for freedmen to obtain property in Goose Creek. William and John Gaillard, two African-American agents with the Bureau of Freedmen, Refugees and Abandoned Lands, helped fledgling land buyers like Daniel Wood and William Durant purchase their little farms from Vidal, but other freedmen and women, such as Caroline Dawson struck

---

393. The following fourteen citations list Howe Hall Plantation lands conveyed to two white and twelve black purchasers: James Vidal to Edwin White and William Tennant, RMC Book E, number 16: 7, Mortgage, March 4, 1869, James Vidal to William Gaillard, Trustee, Book N, number 15: 282, December 1, 1869, James Vidal to Iden Butler, RMC Book P, number 15: 141, May 16, 1871, James Vidal to Caroline Dawson RMC Book P, number 15: 143, May 16, 1870, James Vidal to Richard Yeadon, RMC Book P, number 15: 145, May 16, 1870, James Vidal to John Gaillard Jr. Trustee, RMC Book S, number 15: 145, June 4, 1870, and Book O, number 15, 154, February 25, 1870, James Vidal to Daniel Wood, RMC Book A, number 16: 260, April 5, 1871, James Vidal to Frank Ladson and James Rivers, RMC Book A, number 16: 188, October 4, 1871, James Vidal to William Durant and Russell Moultrie, RMC Book J, number 16: 132, December 3, 1872, James Vidal to Samuel Middleton and John Denny, RMC Book N, number 16: 168, December 3, 1872.

deals of their own. James Vidal eagerly sold the land and black families emerged as Howe Hall landlords.

During that era, landowners rarely sold outside their race, but Vidal, a son of a German immigrant, was a first generation South Carolinian[394] and he did not feel obligated to abide by the unwritten social mores that compelled most. Consequently, he sold "white land" to black farmers. When he retired from Goose Creek to the comforts of Charleston, many conceived the division of the old plantation as a sign of despair and most derided the small Howe Hall farmsteads as "Hog Hall," because little clapboard homes with hogs replaced the manor.[395] Conceivably, such derision was credible from the perspective of landowning wealthy white families of bygone days, but the liberated African-Americans cherished their homes and livestock. The Howe Hall hogs were private property of liberated families and the hams, shanks and bacon from "Hog Hall" did not portend desperation to them, but shone as long anticipated slices of freedom.

That freedom also shone in the halls of small sacred places emerging throughout Goose Creek during the decades following emancipation and onto the era of Langdon Cheves. When Cheves turned sixteen years-old and marched off to the front lines of war in 1864, Reverend L. Philips, Minister of St. Stephen's Church in Charleston retreated from the bombarded city to offer services in the St. James, Goose Creek Church. After each service, he traveled farther into the countryside to spread the gospel and baptize new Christians among the workers in the slave villages. He prayed with the African- American Christians at Howe Hall and baptized many. He felt energized by the vibrant spirit of Christianity among the bound workers who worshipped each Sunday under spreading oaks. When Cheves paused in 1910 to peer down Howe Hall Road, that rutted wagon path led one mile to a whitewashed sanctuary near the same shady oaks. There, a vibrant congregation of African-American Christians regularly worshipped at the Greater Mount Zion AME Church. That assembly ascended from the Howe Hall slave prayer groups when Reverend T. Smalls officially

---

394. "Federal Naturalization Oaths, Charleston, South Carolina 1790-1860" SCHM. v. 66, no. 4, October, 1965, 226 John Vidal, father of James, took the Naturalization Oath of Citizenship on 4-23-1807.

395. Samuel Gaillard Stoney, *Plantations of the Carolina Low Country* (New York: Dover Publications Inc. Carolina Arts Association, Charleston, South Carolina: 1938), 76 and the Cheves Papers, 34/320.

established the church in 1885. At the time Langdon Cheves passed near, Reverend R. Weatherspoon and Bishop, James A. Shorter presided.[396]

Departing the three-way intersection, Langdon Cheves continued on the graded State Road past "Mr. Parson's back gate," and beyond a clump of bushes that marked the footprint of the 17-Mile House Tavern. That tavern stayed busy during the heady era of rice and riches, but no one reestablished the business after it burned during the Civil War and the ugly lot remained barren. Across from the bushy ruins of the tavern sprawled a "huge tar kiln, 150' r[adius]," an ugly and obsolete industry that marred the landscape as Cheves approached the railroad crossing. Near the crossing, another "negro church (Mt. Carmel)," and Cato Jefferson came into view.[397]

Cato Jefferson, a fellow land manager of sorts, "came out" that day to greet Mr. Cheves. Langdon Cheves employed Cato from time to time to collect rent and he paid Cato for the right to hunt over his little farm near the railroad crossing, but Cheves did not condone Cato's real estate ventures. Some African-Americans in Goose Creek used innovative funding methods to acquire real estate and Cato Jefferson was an early visionary. He and Frederick Mitchell concerted the dreams of landless tenant farmers by pooling the farmers' dollars in a trust. The two financiers used the trust money to buy land and then granted shares of the land to the members of their joint ventures called, "societies." The contributors to the society each worked a section of the tract and gleaned the harvest, but they unknowingly surrendered ownership because their names never appeared on the registered deed.[398]

In an identical arrangement, Frank Ladson, a 26-year-old black farmer teamed with James Rivers to buy a 200-acre section of Howe Hall from James Vidal. This purchase originated a "Hog Hall" society similar to the one that Cato Jefferson worked. Cheves called these pyramid investment schemes, "grape vine trusts," and he doubted their legality. The society arrangements clouded land ownership in several sections of Goose Creek and

396. Michael J. Heitzler, *Boochawee Plantation Land and Legacy in Goose Creek*, South Carolina Historical Magazine, January-April 2010, Vol. III, No.1-2, pp. 62,63. Also see, African-Methodism in South Carolina, *A Bicentennial Focus, Seventh Episcopal District* (Tappan, New York: Custombrook Inc., 1987). See, the Greater Mt. Zion AME. Church, 142nd Anniversary Program Publication. Also, author interview with Vermell Watson, at Westview Elementary School, Goose Creek, South Carolina, 11-4-1980.
397. Cheves Papers. See Langdon Cheves notes and comments, May 19, 1910. He states, "Cato Jefferson came out..." Cato Jefferson rented three acres for $1.00 in 1880, US Agricultural Census, St. James, Goose Creek Parish, 73.
398. Cheves Papers, May 19, 1909, March 10, 1925.

as Cheves predicted, long running disputes persisted. Thus, Cheves avoided purchasing land from most minority owners unless they kept clear titles, such as the registered land papers Richard Myers and his heirs possessed.

Figure 9.12: The photograph shows the State Road at the Eighteen-Mile Marker near the home James Nelson rented in the early twentieth century. William Henry Johnson (1871-1934) produced the photograph. The image is in the William Henry Johnson Scrapbook, circa 1920-1923, among the photographic collections of the South Carolina Historical Society (34/293), Charleston, South Carolina.

Forthright freed persons, Richard and Margaret Myers purchased 200 acres of farmland from Mary Austin in 1875. Cheves sought their property for years because the heirs possessed a clear title. Also, Back River Upper Road accessed all of it and it lay contiguous to Cheves' Eighteen-Mile Tract near the intersection of State Road and the railroad. After Richard Myers died in 1898, "the year of the great snow,"[399] his heirs subdivided the tract until the "little house" at the intersection of Back River Upper Road and Liberty Hall Road remained. Langdon Cheves purchased Myers home and a parcel, upon which it stood in 1909, to consolidate further his Eighteen-Mile Tract.

399. Census of Population of the United States of America, 1870 and Census Production of Agriculture for St. James, Goose Creek Parish, 1870. 394. See Cheves Papers, 34/320.

The Eighteen-Mile Tract cleaved from Button Hall Plantation after the Civil War and a four-hundred yard railroad trestle transected the central wetlands of that property. Those wet grounds once produced a fortune in rice but by the turn of the twentieth century, the shallow waters sheeted uselessly across its expanse from the State Road toward Foster Creek until Langdon Cheves carved parcels of the higher ground along the floodway into farms. Tenants built clapboard homes and lesser shacks and used the floodway for irrigation. Cheves employed J.P. Clarke to collect $10.00 annual rents from thirty-one tenants residing at Button Hall as well as James Nelson, who occupied a house at the Eighteen-Mile Stone.[400]

Langdon Cheves rented the nearby farmhouse and eight acres to James Nelson, farmer and family man. The Nelson house stood on the site of the razed Eighteen Mile House Tavern near the western shoulder of State Road, one half mile from the rail crossing where a semblance of a rural center appeared.[401] James Nelson enjoyed the convenience of the small ponds near his house that once refreshed ponies loaded with frontier trade essentials, but now the puddles watered his plow mules and milk cows.

His house lay within a short walk to the rail crossing where a steam-powered saw and gristmill operated in a barn. By way of his rental agreement with Langdon Cheves, Nelson promised to pay eight dollars a year for the right to live upon and farm the land. The lease agreement also obliged Nelson to pay Cheves by way of a lien on all crops he grew on the property and the agreement directed any ginner or factor who may receive his crops to deliver sufficient money to Langdon Cheves. Thus, a tight network of renter, lord and intermediary protected Cheves from default. Lee Bennet, with a similar lease agreement resided across the railroad track from the gins and John Jenkins lived next to him. Jenkins collected the Crowfield tenant rents for Langdon Cheves and sometimes, on behalf of the farmers without reliable conveyance, he carried dried corn in his wagon to the gristmill. The gristmill operated for many years turning dried corn into meal and grits for home use or sale and the sawmill cut logs into boards. Several converging pathways and barely discernable dirt paths connected dozens of farms to the mills and the location saved many farmers from the two-mile trek to similar facilities at the Mount Holly Station.

---

400. Charleston, S.C. 4-10-1905, Statement of rents collected by J.P. Clarke for the year 1903-1904 for Langdon Cheves, Charleston, S.C. among the Cheves Papers.
401. Memorandum of Agreement (lease), 1-1-1913 between Langdon Cheves and James Nelson. See Michael J. Heitzler, *Goose Creek, A Definitive History, Volume Two Rebellion, Reconstruction and Beyond*, the History Press, 2006, Appendix XVI, Tenant Farmers, 256, 257.

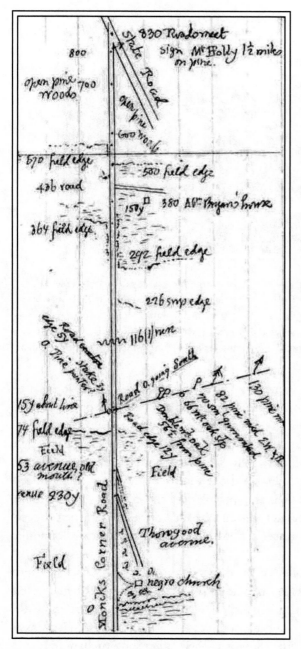

Figure 9.13: Langdon Cheves drew this sketch entitled, "went to Mt. Holly" April 19, 1913. The drawing shows Moncks Corner Road at the top, diverging from its intersection with the State Road. Moncks Corner Road passes "Abm [Abraham] Bryan's House" and the "negro church" (Casey Methodist Church). Thorogood Avenue branches from the "Moncks Corner Road" and two footpaths connect the church to the roadway.

Figure 9.14: The photograph shows Casey Methodist Episcopal Church, erected circa 1870 on the Road to Moncks Corner, one mile south of the Mount Holly Railroad Station. The author took this photograph in 1977 after someone removed the windows and doors and eleven days before it burned to the ground. Today a copse of trees between the Casey cemetery and the Goose Creek Branch of the Berkeley County Library mark the location.

A few of the families in nearby Casey preferred to bag their meal at the mill near the Nelson house, but one half mile south of the Nelson home, someone nailed a wooden sign to a thick pine tree. There, at the intersection of State Road with the Road to Moncks Corner, the sign indicated the way to Mount Holly Station, due north, one and one half mile distant. Many, including Nelson, ventured to Mount Holly to sell dried corn when a sufficient amount justified the extra travel. At Mount Holly, the miller purchased the grain, crushed or minced it, then bagged it and sold some to the grocer and loaded the rest on train cars bound for grocers in Charleston.

Langdon Cheves followed the directional sign down Moncks Corner Road to Casey to assess his land and tenants. That day in 1910, he greeted Abraham Bryant (sometimes Bryan), resident of a wooden house at the top of the rise. Abraham Bryant began a multigenerational and extended Casey family when he married Alice Sumpter. Their oldest son Abraham Jr. reared five children and his brother and sister-in-law, Ben and Daisy Bryant reared Herman and Jennie Mae. Each generation of Bryants contributed much to Casey including Sampson Bryant Sr. He made caskets and tombstones in the 1930s and 1940s, and shod horses, shaped wagon wheel rims, and fashioned hinges, fasteners and other metal implements.

That morning Abraham Bryant Jr. carefully followed his mule through his newly plowed field that reached to "the run." The run drained much of the defunct Button Hall rice lands and there a wooden wagon bridge delivered Cheves over the muddy water toward the divergence of "Thorogood Avenue."

Thorogood Avenue bordered Casey Cemetery, Church and School with a cool tunnel-way of foliage that followed a dry ridge for a mile through the center of the agricultural neighborhood. The important roadway reached from the ancient site of Joseph and Jane Thorogood's frontier cabin on high ground north of the Casey community to the emerging twentieth century world of roads and rail. Casey residents especially sought that cool tunnel-way during the hottest days of summer and followed it to Sunday worship at Casey Methodist Church.[402]

The Casey Methodist Church was a beautiful white, large, wooden structure with stained glass windows, a chorus loft, and an elegant ministry dais.[403] It was the center of a God-fearing community and more than a hundred worshippers typically filled its walls on Sunday mornings. Eventually, a school and an assembly hall ascended nearby, partly due to the dynamic leadership of Reverend William Evans. He founded Casey Church and brought carefully crafted sermons until his death in 1885 at the age of sixty-five, not much older than Langdon Cheves, when he passed by that day in 1910.

Langdon Cheves managed the Casey lands that were once part of Mount Holly Plantation, but now where black women leased one third of the divided properties. Mothers such as Minda Harley, Martha McGill, and Celia Clinton led one third of the renting families at Casey and the women, with few conveniences ruled over extended clans that included nieces, nephews and grandchildren.[404] However, every morning a small convenience appeared in the form of the "water man." He arrived downstream of Casey Spring to fill numerous containers. He rode atop a wagon behind a huge black ox carrying water jugs and buckets of every description for delivery to the homes stretched along the rutted road. The

---

402. Parson interview, October 14, 1980.
403. Parson interview, October 14, 1980. Loretta Parsons attended Casey Church from 1934 until 1974.
404. Cheves papers, 34-0320.

people paid him with turnips, tobacco, corn, poke salad, "pot magic" (a wild herb) and anything else in season. The waterman and Joseph Bryant, the "weekend butcher," who delivered hams, shanks and roasts on Saturdays, ate better than most throughout the year.[405]

Numerous minority settlements like Casey emerged as viable communities in the parish during the first half of the twentieth century. Each featured a place of worship from where ministers led from the pulpits. Mount Carmel Church (established 1880) assembled close to the rail crossing, St. Paul's appeared on the old Springfield lands, and African- American houses of worship such as Grove Hall broke off from white institutions along the State Road as far as Wassamassaw and Sandridge.[406]

Figures 9.15: The image shows a Ford automobile owned by William Henry Johnson on the State Road one mile north of the Goose Creek Bridge circa 1923. Langdon Cheves used this roadway to access much of his property. The image is in the William Henry Johnson Scrapbook, circa 1920-1923, among the photographic collections of the South Carolina Historical Society (34/293), Charleston, South Carolina.

---

405. Parson interview.

406. Russell J. Cross, *Historic Ramblin's Through Berkeley*, Cross-Williams FamilyLimited Partnership (Columbia, South Carolina: Reprinted by the R.L. Bryan Company, for the Berkeley Historical Society, 1985), 176.

Once past Casey Church, Langdon Cheves diverted from the Road to Moncks Corner along "Gibbes Path." Since the colonial period, that path reached east from Crowfield to Back River, and for many years John Gibbes from Broomhall (Bloomfield), as well as landowners of other bordering properties, kept the road passable for wagons. It ran atop a narrow ridge separating the Foster Creek and Back River drainage fields, crossing the railroad track, and skirting Springfield Plantation to intersect Old Back River Road. By the twentieth century, the overgrown pathway was suitable for horsemen and pedestrians only and it often led Cheves to Springfield where he rented properties annually to J.H. and J.G. Harmon, W.H. Bell, Joel Huff and Joseph J. Driggers for $2.00 an acre. Those families produced vegetables, corn, peas, beans, sweet potatoes and hay for themselves and their animals,[407] but that day, after emerging from the lowlands, he stepped onto the railroad track and followed it north to the Mount Holly Train Station.

Mount Holly attracted families to its convenient businesses and farms and some land speculators divided larger tracts in that vicinity into smaller parcels for sale to working families. For example, James S. Simmons bought a 200-acre section near the station for $3,400 in 1905 and sold parcels to farmers such as Toney Gilliard and Josiah Green.[408] Langdon Cheves refused to sell his tracts or parcels, preferring to supervise the tenant farmers and walk through the countryside for more decades. That afternoon in 1910, a "slight rain at 2:30..." convinced him to shelter inside the Mount Holly Station but when the storm surrendered to a "lovely afternoon" the spry senior "...hiked down to Saxon [Hanahan], then [rode]on a handcar to Ashley Junction & walked to the [Charleston] station."[409]

Langdon Cheves regularly "stepped the line[s]" in Goose Creek many more years, witnessing significant changes in the parish before he died in 1939 at the age of ninety-one. He saw the creation of the Goose Creek Reservoir, the discontinuation of regular passenger train service, the appearance of "motor cars" sputtering over the Goose

407. Cheves Papers, a letter from J.H. Knight to HAM Smith and Langdon Cheves dated 3-2-1910 reporting names and amounts of land rents, and plat of four tracts of land owned by Toney Gaillard, Richard Myers, James Stephens and John Green, in1874. Also, see the United States Census, 1880, Mount Holly District, Productions of Agriculture, St. James, Goose Creek.
408. Berkeley County Deed Book, C #13 p. 7, Mitchell & Smith. Otranto Club records, 1916-1924, 152.02.08, SCHS.
409. Cheves papers, section 1, 2 and 3, handwritten on a single sheet of paper dated 5-19- 1910.

Creek Bridge, the regular use of motor graders on the unpaved State Road, and workers laying miles of paved highway through his precious farmland.

When Langdon Cheves diverged from Gibbes Path that day in 1910 to follow the railroad tracks toward Mount Holly Station, he unknowingly traced part of the route of the future "King's Highway" (State Highway 52) and a few years hence, he unwittingly set a series of events in motion that facilitated that project. In 1915, Cheves consented to flood some of his low-laying creek-side lands when the Charleston Light and Water Company erected a dike across Goose Creek to create a potable water reservoir for families and businesses in peninsular Charleston. That manmade basin spurred municipal, military and industrial activity that produced new wealth, created new jobs and sent a new highway through the center of the Cheves farmlands.[410]

In 1917, the City of Charleston purchased the Goose Creek Reservoir and pumping station from the private company and formed the Commissioners of Public Works to expand the municipal water system. A long drought and severe water shortage the following year sullied the early successes of the commissioners, but opportunity harkened. The United States Navy requested a larger and more reliable water supply for the expanded military base on Charleston Neck, and the West Virginia Pulp and Paper Company needed large amounts of water for a new industrial plant on the Cooper River. As a result, the commissioners envisioned a grand scheme. The Charleston Water Commissioners employed men and boys, some from the Saxon, Otranto and Mount Holly areas, to excavate by hand, a twenty-three mile long, seven-foot high tunnel from the basin in Goose Creek to the Edisto River. The plentiful water supply from the Edisto River mitigated the municipal shortages, sated the military and industrial needs and spurred the expansion of economic activity from peninsular Charleston to the homes of workers in the northern sectors of the county.

Many workers continued to walk or ride the train to work, but motor transport, including carpooling to the naval and industrial facilities increased in popularity and prompted state and local officials to undertake ambitious road projects. In 1922, the Berkeley County Highway Commissioners negotiated with Langdon Cheves to chart a route through his properties. Cheves reluctantly negotiated with the commissioners, perceiving potential

---

410. A plat of Goose Creek showing the Goose Creek Dam, McCrady Plat 2992, C3184. Also see map showing the flood waters created by the Charleston Light and Water Company Dam on lands owned by Henry A. M. Smith, 1907, 32-84-07, SCHS.

damages to his precious tenant farms, but eventually consented to a 75-foot highway right-of-way contiguous to the railroad track from "Goose Creek [waterway] to Mount Holly Depot."[411]

Before the commission paved the new road in 1923, motorists in increasing numbers sought the gravel-surfaced South Carolina Highway 52. Workers of many professions, including the "Ladies of American Tobacco Company" shuttled to jobs in Charleston and the fast highway encouraged urbanites to venture outside of the City. Some motorists sought hunting diversions and other recreations in the countryside, while a few entrepreneurs, such as H. Smith Richardson discovered lucrative investment opportunities.

Figure 9.16: The faded image shows the waters of Goose Creek between the Goose Creek Bridge and the 2,200- foot-long railroad trestle spanning the creek. The image shows the waterway after a dam created the Goose Creek Reservoir. The Oaks main house appears in the distance. William Henry Johnson (1871-1934) produced the photograph. The image is in the William Henry Johnson Scrapbook, circa 1920-1923, among the photographic collections of the South Carolina Historical Society (34/293), Charleston, South Carolina. The trestle is described in, *Bonsal Road Near Completion, Train to Cross Goose Creek Trestle Next Wednesday,* The Watchman and Southon, Sumter, South Carolina, September 16, 1914, among the collections of the University of South Carolina Library.

---

411. Langdon Cheves, letter to Berkeley County Highway Commissioners, Moncks Corner, South Carolina, February 15, 16, 1922, and letter from unknown author to William H. Dennis, 2-21-1922, 1167.01.07.03 among the Miscellaneous land papers, 1735-1932 with the Cheves Papers, SCHS.

Figure 9.17: The photograph shows (from left to right) Cleo Bowers, Maggie Singletary, Florence Driggers, Lorean Thompson, "Lokey" Driggers and Celena Harmon, "Ladies of American Tobacco Company." The women wear white dresses with green trim and collars, their work uniforms in 1934. The ladies commuted by automobile via the State Road and the Goose Creek Bridge to make cigars at the tobacco company on Meeting Street in Charleston. The new South Carolina Route 52 improved their daily commute. The "Smith General Store" on Myers Road near Carnes Cross Roads appears in the background. The image is courtesy of Mrs. Lorean Thompson.

H. SMITH RICHARDSON

After retiring, H. Smith Richardson sought the diversion of the southern forests and fields. A resident of Green Farms, Connecticut, he arrived in Mount Holly by automobile on the new highway projecting north from Charleston's Meeting Street. He began his career as a sales clerk for his father who invented Vicks Vaporub ® and became a successful entrepreneur. He substantially increased his family fortunes, coming south when he recognized the investment potential of the undervalued properties in the old St. James, Goose Creek Parish. He amassed 7,910 consolidated acres, including all of Thorogood, Tom Hill, and Old Barn tracts. His largest transaction occurred in 1937 when he purchased 5,874 acres for $27,000. His large consolidation extended north and west of the Atlantic Seaboard

Coastline right-of-way near the Mount Holly and Strawberry Depots and predictably, he named his land, "Mount Holly Plantation." He resided on the property much of the year in a modest, single-story, ranch style house and toured his domain by automobile and foot. He enjoyed stalking deer and turkey, but he also grew tobacco, harvested timber and leased parcels to farmers. The tenants spoke highly of him testifying, "...he kept a direct interest in people ...there was a rich complexity to him that impressed everyone."[412]

Figure 9.18: The photograph shows the obsolete Five Towers Motor Inn in 1963. Max Baker built the popular Five Towers Motor Inn in 1930 with four rooms in each two-story tower. The second such establishment in the Greater Charleston Region, it was intended to serve a rapidly increasing motoring public using Highway 52. The "one stop" motor inn located across the road from the Otranto Railway Depot sat next to Baker's general store, automobile garage and filling station. The inn featured a long covered shed for parking open roof automobiles. Edward M. Baker, son of Max, assumed management of the successful enterprise (Charleston News and Courier Newspaper March 11, 1963).

The new gravel roadway transecting the "Cheves lands," avoided the Goose Creek Bridge and consequently relegated the St. James, Goose Creek Church site to the lesser-used State Road. Nonetheless, the vestry never abandoned the sacred place. In 1931, the churchmen painted the exterior of the sanctuary in a soft rose hue, in accordance with a sketch

412. Author interview with Eloise Gowder at Goose Creek Library, 5-1-1982.

made by Charles Fraser 128 years earlier. They followed that renovation with regular annual services that renewed interest and inspired sufficient contributions to employ contractors to attach metal sheeting over the window shutters and doors and install a slate roof to retard forest fire flames. Although circumstances stabilized for the mother church, the two chapel sites faded further from memory in the countryside that increasingly attracted land speculators.[413] However, H. Smith Richardson was the last individual to invest in large amounts of land in the defunct parish. As the middle decades approached, 1940-1950, wealthy individual investors and interests of the old southern families gave way to large conglomerates. The first among those larger financiers were government agencies seeking deep-water tracts on Goose Creek for military applications. Soon, the infusion of federal money sparked the interests of industrial leaders who coveted the great expanses of inexpensive forests and abundant fresh water. Residential and commercial development followed until the old parish transformed into modern suburbia.

---

413. *The News and Courier*, 4-20-1925. William Henry Johnson visited the Chapel of Ease at the camp in Strawberry in 1927 and measured 62 feet from end to end of the ruins of the "red cross" type cruciform foot print.

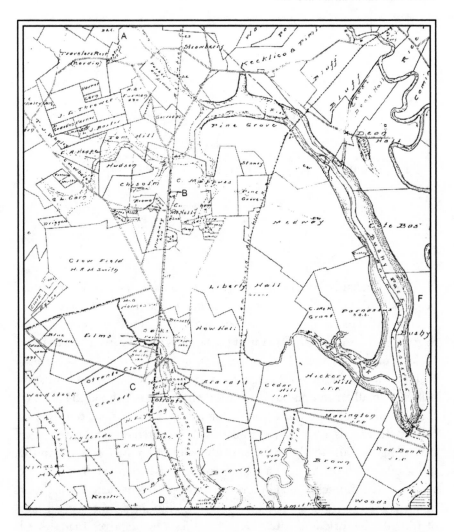

Figure 9.19: This detail of the *G. Palmer Gaillard Map of Berkeley County and Parts of Charleston and Dorchester Counties, SC, circa 1940,* shows the boundaries of farms near the Saxon, Otranto, Mount Holly and Strawberry Railroad Stations. The author added manuscript letters for orientation: A- Groomsville Baptist Church near the Strawberry Railroad Station, B- Mount Holly Station, C-Otranto Station, D- Saxon Station, E- Goose Creek Reservoir and F- Bushy Park (Back River) Reservoir.

CHAPTER 10

Goose Creek and its Sacred Places

H. Smith Richardson's Mount Holly Plantation and the families residing near the rail stop of the same name, composed the most significant neighborhood in the St. James, Goose Creek Parish until the second half of the twentieth century, when many of the families joined with others to form the City of Goose Creek. The story of these people and their land contrasts strikingly as their little rural neighborhood transformed into a robust sunbelt city. Small farms and businesses near the rail stop defined the place at the beginning of the middle decades, but by the end of that era, the families melded their lands into a municipality that dominated the landscape. After chartering in 1961, the boundaries of the City of Goose Creek expanded to include much of the eastern parish, relegating Mount Holly to one of several dozen municipal neighborhoods, and erasing evidence of its prior importance. No trains stopped at Mount Holly during the second half of the 20th century, and after 1986, the diesel locomotives that slowed every day to snatch the mailbag off its hook at the tiny Mount Holly Post Office ceased the duty. A regional mail delivery complex in the center of the City, with a consolidated postal zip code, supplanted the Mount Holly office. Soon the last general store at Mount Holly closed too and most remaining structures vanished when locals salvaged the wood. However, as the City of Goose Creek surges into the twenty first century, Mount Holly may ascend as one of several important thresholds to the burgeoning municipality. Contemporary talk of multi-modal transportation for the Berkeley, Charleston and Dorchester Region renews interest in passenger rail service. Conceivably, trains may stop again at modern Mount Holly,

Otranto and Strawberry Stations in the heart of the ancient parish, and commercial activities spinning from those locales may beckon residents to the gateway bridge, its antique church and sacred places.

THE MIDDLE DECADES - 1940-1960

James Rozier and his bride, Agnes Jaudon opened the Rozier General Store in Strawberry near the old chapel of ease at the camp in 1939, and that year Hilton Waring Bunch arrived with his family at nearby Medway Plantation to manage timberland. The sparse white communities near the Strawberry, Mount Holly and Otranto Depots did not support a school and the few children commuted to academies in Moncks Corner or Charleston, while the black scholars attended one or two-room schools locally. Most white families attended Groomsville Baptist or nearby Smyrna Methodist Church and interred loved ones outside the walls of those sanctuaries, while black families packed Casey Methodist, Mount Zion, St. Paul's and other houses of prayer.

During the middle decades, families in the eastern parish formed quasi-institutions, such as the Mount Holly Home Demonstration Club. Women members of the association participated in chair caning and rug making, and mothers taught daughters food preservation techniques and recipes. The members attended club meetings to engage socially and to receive the latest news arriving twice daily with the trains. As late as 1930, no one in the obsolete parish possessed a radio[414] and residents gleaned most current information from depot gossip. The train passengers transmitted information to the general stores, from where the hearsay broadcasted to the social circles. The first radio in the parish tuned-in near 1935 at the mercantile in Mount Holly. Television debuted twenty years later when "the entire community,"[415] gathered to witness the newest phenomenon at Gowder's General Store.

George and Eloise Gowder purchased the Morning Star Grocery at Mount Holly from Tom Addison in 1946 and managed it for ten years.[416] Their best customers included two teachers at Casey Elementary School, who bought supplies for hot school lunches. Near the Gowder store, the

---

414. United States Enumeration Census, St. James, Goose Creek Township, 1930.
415. Gowder interview 1982, and author interview with Eugene Bryan at his home in Strawberry (sometimes called, "Twenty-two") on 6-7-05. The State Highway 52, kept a gravel surface on some sections into the 1950s.
416. Gowder.

Tokio Kodama family resided on the second floor of their mercantile shop. They relocated to Mount Holly when Federal authorities purchased their home at Marrington Plantation and annexed the land to the Naval Weapons Station.[417] Mrs. Hilma Watkins opened a grocery at the Mount Holly Post Office in the 1930s and later Mrs. C. B. Linder managed it.[418] As mid-century neared, Mount Holly persisted as the most vibrant commercial center in the parish. In addition to the railroad station, stores and post office, it featured a mill saw, gristmill, sugarcane press, fertilizer merchant, casket maker and five houses. Mount Holly resembled a small agricultural town, but by mid-century most of the farmsteads no longer sustained families, but merely supplemented the incomes of fathers working at the military installations expanding nearby.

World War II brought employment to Greater Charleston when defense related industries employed workers and by 1950, the population of the greater Charleston Area, including southern Berkeley County, exploded to 225,000 people.[419] Most heads of households commuted by way of the Naval Ammunition Depot (N.A.D.) Road that traversed the new and wider Goose Creek Bridge and from there followed Red Bank Road toward the Cooper River. That road provided the most convenient land access to the increasingly important weapons depot hidden in forests overlooking Goose Creek.

As more civil servants found employment at the Naval Ammunition Depot in southern Berkeley County and the naval facilities in the northern section of Charleston County, newly arrived families sought homes within easy commutes. In response, Jack Etling began building two and three bedroom block, brick, or wood-sided houses on his family chicken farm carved from the Oaks Plantation. "I laid out the first lots in October 1953," Etling recalled, and his modest, well-constructed homes sold quickly.[420] Families accessed Etling's sturdy little houses in Pineview Acres and Pineview Terrace subdivisions by way of dirt streets featuring the names of his daughters and their friends. When his real estate successes blossomed, others commenced building homes in nearby Forest Lawn and Greenview subdivisions.

---

417. Gowder. General Highway Map 1951 shows 10 structures at Casey including a church and school

418. *Berkeley Democrat* (Moncks Corner, South Carolina), 9-14-32.

419. Edgar, 1998, 57.

420. Jack Etling interview with the author at the Etling residence in Pineview Subdivision, 10-12-1982 and Goose Creek Gazette, 8-29-84.

Figure 10.1: The photograph shows James H. Rozier Sr. in the center with his wife, Agnes Jaudon Rozier and their sons Robert H. Rozier on the left and James H. Rozier Jr. on the right. James H. Rozier Sr. operated the store for forty-two years. The image is courtesy of James H. Rozier, Jr.

Near the end of the middle decades, more millions of investment dollars flowed to nearby military bases and to new industries expanding nearby at the Bushy Park Industrial Complex on the Cote Bas Peninsula. In addition, the Navy erected the Polaris Missile Facility, United States Atlantic Fleet Area (POMFLANT), near Back River. There, skilled workers assembled the latest missiles and warheads and many of these skilled employees sought family homes in nearby Goose Creek.

During this dynamic growth period, community leadership faltered. The recently- arrived residents knew too little about their emerging neighborhoods to take charge of decision-making, and no Berkeley County official stepped up to the challenge. County officials possessed no experience in dealing with population surges nor did they feel any kinship with the outsiders arriving in large numbers to the farthest southern extent of their rural domain. Thus, gravely inadequate supervision permitted haphazard development to continue until the rural infrastructure collapsed.

The new Goose Creek families found feeble water, sewer and sanitation services. They found no police, no firefighters, no emergency personnel, no sanitation workers, and worse - they found no one in charge. Deteriorating conditions resulted in low pressure and foul tasting water from shallow wells, smelly and unhealthy sewage from malfunctioning septic tanks, rotting and unsightly garbage cluttering the forests, and traffic snarling substandard and unregulated intersections. Worse of all during the 1950s, residents perceived no signs of relief and conceived no plans for recovery.

Figure 10.2: The image shows Thomason's Store and Gulf ® Station circa 1960. Today this sleepy way station is the busy intersection of St. James Avenue and Thomason Boulevard. The image is in the possession of the author.

THE CITY OF GOOSE CREEK

The worsening circumstances prompted leading men of the new subdivisions to step forward. At first, Jack Etling and Waring Bunch met routinely along their abutting property lines between Bunch's Trailer Park and Etling's rising Pineview Subdivisions. A serious man, Hilton Waring Bunch believed in order, regulations and rules and successfully employed that code as a family man, land manager and owner of a successful sixty-unit mobile home park. His multi-generational family hailed locally. The Hilton, Waring and Bunch clans planted and farmed the St. James, Goose Creek Parish since the colonial era, and the middle decades of the twentieth century found Bunch managing the long-leaf pine forests of Medway Plantation. However, in 1957, he relocated with his bride and two children to five acres of property he purchased at the intersection of State Highway 52 (Goose Creek Boulevard) and State Road (Red Bank Road/ St. James Avenue). He built a tidy, white asbestos shingled, single story home in a copse of pines and carefully lined five dozen mobile homes on his sprawling back yard.

The Hilton-Etling meetings widened to include others such as J.B. Brown, Jr., and Lonnie B. Holland, and the meeting-place shifted from the shade trees to the nearby Etling home. Mr. Etling recalled "....those men kept sitting on my porch..." searching for solutions to increasingly deteriorating circumstances and "...someone had to pay for an ad..."[421] Finally, the founders pooled their dollars to advertise in the Charleston newspaper for an incorporation election. Those early leaders concluded that a town (municipality) was the best way to garner resources required to bring order out of chaos and they offered that option in the form of an incorporation election to a skeptical populace.

The Goose Creek municipal incorporation election occurred Tuesday, March 14, 1961 when almost 500 citizens joined the municipality. They elected Hilton Waring Bunch, Mayor, and Edgar Neis, Roger Anderson, Edgar Binnar and E.W. (Jack) Etling as Councilmen. They also selected "Goose Creek" as the name of the newest town in South Carolina.[422] Three weeks later, at 7:00 pm, April 6, 1961, Mayor Hilton Waring Bunch sounded a wooden gavel, calling the first meeting of Council for the "Town

---

421. Jack Etling interview 10-12-1982. Author interview with Mayor Hilton Waring Bunch, Jack Etling, and Orvin Thompson at the Thompson home at the Thompson Trailer Park, 7-20-1980.
422. *Berkeley Democrat*, 3-22-61.

of Goose Creek" to order. That single action commenced a journey toward a vision until the place emerged as a leading South Carolina municipality. At the helm during the formative years were hesitant but willing leaders compelled by forces stronger than each was, but manageable by them collectively.

Figure 10.3: The photograph shows Turner's Barbershop. Officials used it as the first City Hall and Municipal Court. It sat on the western corner of the intersection of Marilyn Avenue and St. James Boulevard (State Road/State Highway 176).

Figure 10.4: The photograph shows the charter members of the Pineview Baptist Church in July 1961. Mayor Hilton Waring Bunch, standing in the center at the front door of the church, called the first meeting of the Town Council to order on April 6, 1961.

Year	South Carolina Population	Berkeley County Population	St. James, Goose Creek Parish Population	Parish Percent of State	Parish Percent of County
1950	2,117,027	30,251	6,715	.3%	22%

Year	South Carolina Population	Berkeley County Population	Mount Holly District*	Mount Holly % State	Mount Holly %County
1960	2,382,594	38,196	11,573	.5%	30%

Year	South Carolina Population	Berkeley County Population	City of Goose Creek Population	City Percent of State	City Percent of County
1970	2,590,713	56,199	3,656	.1%	7%
1980	3,120,729	94,727	17,899	.6%	19%
1990	3,486,703	128,776	24,692	.7%	19%
2000	4,012,012	142,651	29,208	.7%	21%

The table shows census tracts for selected years. The Census Bureau did not use the St. James, Goose Creek Parish tract after 1950, but instead, divided the tract into divisions, with most of the St. James, Goose Creek Parish included in the Mount Holly Division. The 1960 Mount Holly Division included all of Berkeley County west of the Cooper River and south of Moncks Corner.

Figure 10.5: The photograph shows from left to right: Congressman Mendel Davis, Goose Creek City Councilmen Jack Etling and William Infinger, Mayor Malvin Mann and the first Mayor Hilton Waring Bunch at the dedication of City Hall, at 125 St. James Avenue, on February 12, 1974.

Figure 10.6: The photograph shows the façade of the third Goose Creek City Hall, after workers installed front windows in 1989.

Figure 10.7: The photograph shows City Hall at the Marguerite H. Brown Municipal Center, August 11, 2012. The image is courtesy of the City of Goose Creek.

At first, Mayor Bunch and his Council met every week in "Turner's Barber Shop," a wooden building at the intersection of Marilyn Avenue with State Road (St. James Avenue). Clinton L. Turner cut hair there, but he opened it for other community purposes when church members, scouts, and others vied for the space. In 1961, the barbershop converted to the first City Hall, and when town officials appointed Turner as the sole municipal judge, they arranged a corner for a judicial bench. Jack Etling recalled, "I saw that place [Goose Creek] change from woods to a town..." in Turner's Barbara Shop and from that humble location, two hundred yards south of the Eighteen-Mile Mark, the City of Goose Creek awakened.

Consistent expansion and improvement followed. The municipal leaders experienced an unprecedented 58% population surge in one year in 1969, then averaged more than five percent population growth in the 1970s,[423] and enjoyed a comfortable 3% average expansion of population in subsequent decades.[424] Today, almost forty thousand residents come

423. Berkeley Democrat, August 18, 1971.
424. Alumax (later Alcoa) bought most of the Mount Holly property in two transactions in 1978 and 1979 from H. Smith Richardson Jr. who acted as trustee for his father. Since

home to the City of Goose Creek, the tenth most populated municipality in South Carolina.

Contemporary residents of the City of Goose Creek dutifully remember their humble beginnings and the spiritual underpinnings that sustained their forefathers through every era. In 2006, hundreds of residents converged at the St. James, Goose Creek Church to commemorate the tri-centennial founding of the parish, and five years later more than one hundred City residents returned to the church and to the site of the first City Hall to recall the naissance of their parish and fifty-year-old municipality. Today, a reliable municipal foundation underpins the community, preserves the heritage of the ancient places and provides a unique historic context where families thrive.

TRI-CENTENNIAL 2006

At eleven o'clock in the morning, on the Sunday after Easter (Low Sunday), April 23, 2006, John Barnwell, Senior Warden of the St. James, Goose Creek Church, accompanied Reverend William Paterson Rhett, Jr., into the ancient sanctuary to offer the memorial service recognizing the 300th anniversary of the creation of the St. James, Goose Creek Parish. In 1712, six years after the "Church Act" established the parish, John Barnwell, the immigrant mustered young militiamen to ride against the Tuscarawas in North Carolina. His actions on behalf of the Colonial Assembly initiated a series of native engagements that culminated three years later when Captain George Chicken and his militia, charged into the center of a war party during the Yamassee conflagration. Chicken's successful attack reinforced the British hold on South Carolina and emboldened the royal bequest at a time when the dominion of the crown was in peril. Now the vestry recounts and celebrates that legacy each spring with an annual Christian service in the St. James, Goose Creek Church near the gateway bridge. The priest dutifully adheres to the Anglican Canonical Rites, and in doing so, retells the long story of Goose Creek and South Carolina in which John Barnwell, George Chicken's neighbor and contemporary, stands at the beginning of the three hundred year story, and John Barnwell, Senior Warden reports at the end.

---

then, Alcoa Mount Holly created the Mount Holly Commerce Park in its northern sector as a showcase for modern industry.

Figure 10.8: The photograph shows the interior of the St. James, Goose Creek Church. A central aisle approaches the elevated pulpit where a spiral staircase ascends. The author took the photograph on April 22, 2007.

ST. JAMES, GOOSE CREEK CHURCH

The St. James, Goose Creek Parish was one of the original ten colonial subdivisions organized more than three decades after the first Europeans with their native and African bondsmen traversed nearby Goose Creek. The parochial and civil subdivision provided a legal setting for ecclesiastical and governmental institutions. However, the Yamassee War did not occur for another nine years, and only within that harsh context, did a sufficient number of people seek solace in sacred places, and raise the sturdy church and chapels from the wilderness.

Across more than three centuries, names of low-country families and their sanctuaries remain intrinsic to the legacy of the St. James, Goose Creek Parish, and the section that chartered a dynamic municipality. The architecture and amenities of the St. James, Goose Creek Church partially explains the heritage, speaking of its Barbadian roots and new-world fortunes. Additionally, dozens of parishioners repose and twenty-seven tombstones testify within a cemetery outside the thick bulwarks of the church building.

The sacred graveyard, listed in the United States National Register of Historic Places, is a protected and preferred repository for relocated memorials from neglected parish cemeteries. Once "open to the beasts of the field..."[425] a brick enclosure and an iron gate now protects the sacred repository. Family members re-erected the tombstone marking the grave of Dr. Robert Brown (Broun) from the St. James, Goose Creek Chapel of Ease to the St. James, Goose Creek Church Cemetery after 1927.[426] Charles Manigault, grandson of Peter, moved the testimonial stone for Thomas Bromley, a close friend of Peter Manigault. He conveyed it from Steepbrook Plantation to his townhouse at 6 Gibbes Street, before the rising Goose Creek reservoir inundated the Steepbrook cemetery early in the twentieth century. A subsequent owner of the townhouse transferred the stone to the St. James, Goose Creek Church Cemetery thirty years later. Family members moved the "Parker Monument," from the Hayes family memorial park to the St. James, Goose Creek Church Cemetery. It was once visible from the front door of the Hayes Plantation mansion. When the ancient home crumbled from neglect, the family relocated the monument in 1955 to its present location near the main entrance to the Goose Creek Church.

Conceivably, others will transfer memorials to the church grounds when stewards neglect isolated burial sites or the property surrounding those places develop beyond propriety. One such obscure cemetery lies in dense forests at Woodstock Plantation,[427] and another stands nearby among scattered bricks in a plowed field of the obsolete Spring Grove Plantation in Ladson. Preservationists may move those remnants someday to the St. James, Goose Creek Cemetery as they did with the remains and relics at Windsor Hill in 1978.

---

425. Dalcho, 252

426. *South Carolina Gazette*, 8-26-1765. William Henry Johnson noted the marker for "Dr. Robt. Brown, Esq. d. 1757 AE 43," during his visit to the chapel cemetery on 5-29-1927. See the William Henry Johnson Scrapbook. SCHS.

427. Robert Behre, "Long Lost Patriot Found in N. Charleston," *Charleston, Post and Courier*, 3-29-2010. The Weber and Weiser Companies are developing the area around the isolated cemetery with the graves of important contributors to the Revolutionary and Civil War eras.

Figure 10.9: The Bulline/Bee Cemetery at Woodstock Plantation features notables such as Thomas Bee 1739-1812, who served many important offices including Speaker of the House of Representatives. The photograph is among the collections of the author.

The remains of Major William Moultrie, son of Major General William Moultrie, as well as the souls and soil of his Ainslie and Braisford family members, lay together in a re-internment grave in the St. James, Goose Creek burial ground. Preservationists relocated the markers and remains from the tiny Windsor Hill family cemetery hidden in dense forests above the farthest reach of the Goose Creek headwaters.

In 1798, two years after burying Major William Moultrie at Windsor Hill, the family interred his stepmother Hannah Lynch Moultrie, second wife of the immigrant, John Moultrie. John and Hannah reared one son, Alexander, who rose to prominence in government service similar to his four half brothers. He rose to the position of Attorney General for the new State of South Carolina. Alexander planted rice at Richmond Plantation in the St. James, Goose Creek Parish, where his main avenue intersected the Road to Moncks Corner near the chapel of ease at the camp. Undoubtedly, he attended his mother's burial merely twelve miles from his rural home, and during the solemn graveside conversations, the general expressed to

Alexander, his desire to be buried next to William, his son and namesake. Alexander and the family honored that request when the general perished seven years later.[428]

Figure 10.10: The main house at the Elms Plantation sat empty for years and the earthquake of 1886 severely damaged it. Almost all evidence of the beauty of the place was gone by the dawn of the 20th century. During the first half of the 20th century, brick thieves who used the slightly oversized blocks to underpin their cabins and support their hearths, mined it. Developers built upon the plantation cemetery that was long obscured and forgotten. The photograph circa 1936 is among the collections of the Library of Congress, 308417.

In 1978, well-intentioned preservationists moved the remains of Major General William Moultrie, counter to his "earnest wishes," from the side of his son on Windsor Hill. Archaeologists recovered scant bone slivers and dark soil from the sunken graves of several family members, their caskets long collapsed and their ashes awash by two centuries of seepage. The scientists dutifully attempted to separate the general's remains from the other family members and re-interred the handfuls of family vestigial in the St. James, Goose Creek cemetery, marking the site with engraved

428. Alexander Moultrie kept the family Bible that recorded General William Moultrie's desire to be buried aside his son, William.

stones. During the same time, they re-interred the bone slivers of the general at Fort Moultrie on Sullivan's Island - more accessible to tourists.

Sadly, and notwithstanding the best of intentions of preservationists and the limits of forensic science, there is little doubt that disturbed remains of General Moultrie lay mixed with his deceased family in the churchyard at Goose Creek. Understandably, a stone memorial to Major General William Moultrie stands next to the grave marker of his son, Major William Moultrie in the Churchyard. There, the stalwart vestry cares for the final resting places of the Moultrie family as they do many others, ever cognizant of the importance of their charge. However, no one oversees the two chapels of ease that remain sorely neglected and subsequently vanished into the landscape in two corners of the ancient parish.

THE ST. JAMES, GOOSE CREEK CHAPEL OF EASE

Chapel Creek flows six miles north of the St. James, Goose Creek Church, washing near the souls resting in marked and unmarked graves at the St. James, Goose Creek Chapel of Ease.[429] For centuries, the hallowed ground embraced the remains of volunteers who mounted the breastwork against a war party during the late spring of 1715. That holy place also received the remains of patriots of a revolution,[430] rebels of a great civil divide and Christians of a later era, as the headstones denote.[431] Barely discernable in the forest floor, is a cross-shaped trench filled with earth and broken bricks that outlines the crumpled cruciform chapel. Thieves dug that depression to salvage foundation bricks from the ruins with which to build chimneys and footings for 19th century cabins, and stalwart Baptists sold some to pay for the relocation of the St. James Baptist (Bethlehem Baptist) Church to Groomsville. By doing so, they unintentionally left a faint scar in the earth – the footprint of a Christian cross.[432] That impression is all that remains

429. Chicken died in 1727. His widow probably buried him at the Chapel of Ease cemetery near or possibly within the walls of the cruciform structure.
430. Families interred Aaron Loocock, John Deas and Archibald Brown of the Revolutionary War era in the cemetery.
431. Baptists built the Bethlehem Baptist Church (later St. James Baptist Church) on the site and used the ground to bury church members for eighty years.
432. The statement, "Sale of the old brick.....$16.00," is an itemized account of revenue collected to offset the cost of moving the wooden Baptist Church from the camp to Groomsville. The itemization is in the church minutes among the collections of Reverend Samuel Lynes. He notes "Record in the will book I and J, 1839-1845: 422." The statement is among the Lynes Family Papers. The easement for the Chapel of Ease at the camp

of the cruciform chapel. Nonetheless, the impression is a durable memorial to Francis LeJau - the missionary priest who prayed in the woods, Captain Chicken - the frontier warrior, and the gallant black and white men atop the breastwork. Furthermore, the story imbued in the surrounding forests, tells of the fortunes wrought from inland rice fields, the moral conundrum of the American Revolution, the savagery and zeal of the Civil War and the immense reticence to racial equity. The 21st century brings renewed marvel to the story resounding in this haunting place.

Figure 10.11: A row of brick crypts line the eastern edge of the cemetery at the Strawberry Chapel of Ease. The author took the photograph on 5-26-08.

WASSAMASSAW CHAPEL OF EASE

The Wassamassaw Chapel of Ease evolved from a tiny log and chinked cabin to a clapboard structure that doubled as a school. It stood twelve miles west of the St. James, Goose Creek Church on high ground immediately

---

appears on public record again in 1972 and thereafter. See Nina J. Marlowe, 7-17-1972, BCDB A242:86.

above the creek and wetlands. By the end of the Revolutionary War, it was the only sanctioned chapel of ease in the parish. In the early 19th century, the Baptists worshipped there, and later built upon its ground, unintentionally obscuring the original chapel grounds with the Wassamassaw Baptist Church and cemetery.[433] Although today its exact place is not discernible, the rugged little sanctuary stood conscientiously at the center of a frontier community on the edge of the British Empire for sixty years. Near there, Captain Chicken and the Goose Creek militia pushed a large party of warriors into retreat through the wet thickets, ending the native assault and terminating the indigenous threat to British rule in South Carolina.

Once a bulwark to the dangerous frontier, Wassamassaw emerged as a bustling colonial village, but stayed aloof from the busiest eastern section of the parish until the 19th century. Then the State Road spanned the parish and transformed Wassamassaw into an important political crossroads on the busiest byway from Charleston to Columbia and beyond for the next one hundred and fifty years.[434] The Wassamassaw community thrived as a bastion of European-American rule and a final place of resistance to the passage of the "Old South" after Reconstruction. Now, the vibrant historic district is re-emerging in the 21st century with comfortable homes and amenities for families who re-discovered the abundant gratuities of the Wassamassaw section of the ancient parish.

---

433. Ballentine.
434. South Carolina Highways 16 and 176 intersect near Wassamassaw Lane, the entrance road to the Wassamassaw historic site.

Figure 10.12: A four- rifle salute marks the adjournment of a ceremony that properly disposed used Confederate flags at Wassamassaw Cemetery on 5-10-08. Interred at the cemetery are at least twenty Confederate veterans.

THE CONGREGATION

The annual assembly on the Sunday after Easter personifies the epic by bringing together the vestrymen, who are the long-term caretakers of the St. James, Goose Creek Church, and descendants of the ancient congregation.[435] Some ancestors settled surrounding grounds when the Middletons, Schenckinghs, Thorogoods, and Fleurys forded the creek during the earliest frontier era. Other relatives crossed the wooden Goose

---

435. Vestry members attending in 2006 included John Barnwell, Senior Warden, Bradish J. Waring, Junior Warden, Ford P. Menefee, Secretary, Vestrymen Frank L.P. Barnwell, William E. Martin, Jr., E. Horry Parker, Donald F. Parker, William H. Priouleau, Jr., Richard W. Salmons, Jr., Julian M. Simons, Cotesworth P. Simons, and Charles W. Waring, III. Robert Simmons serves as sexton. Michael J. Heitzler, Mayor of the City of Goose Creek, memorialized the three hundredth anniversary of the establishment of the parish with an address before the chancel of the St. James, Goose Creek Church on 4-23-2006.

Creek Bridge with the second-generation of immigrant families including the Howes, Hyrnes, and LeJaus. Vestrymen and congregants converted the rugged Huguenots to the Anglican fold, pushed back the bounds of the wilderness, and set the stage for heady lifestyles that prompted the Colonial Assembly to create the parish soon after the turn of the 18th century.[436] Two family members from Boochawee Hall rose to the Provincial Governor's office and Howe Hall sent a Speaker to the Common House of Assembly during the turbulent years when predecessors joined Vestrymen James Moore and George Chicken to oust the hapless Proprietors.

Contemporary vestrymen boast names that memorialize the era of inland rice dominance when invention and discipline were common virtues and grand fortunes shone in elegant homes and fine carriages that pattered across the Goose Creek Bridge to Sunday worship or beyond.[437] Families including the Prioleaus, Warings, Allens, Gibbes, Barkers, Izards, Parkers and others, planted rice in miles of wetlands, some within sight of the gateway bridge and reaped impressive fortunes from the soggy soils. During the second revolution, the Avenue of Oaks leading to the Middleton home sheltered British Colonel Banastre Tarleton and his troops when they pursued bands of wily patriots. The shady avenue of oaks also sheltered forefathers of republican laws at the time when clans such as the William Johnson family, the Smiths and the Manigaults stiffened to the challenges of the rising republic. Vestrymen recall familial conflicts and bitter resistance when armies marched along the causeway, and across the bridge to impart their will onto a rebellious land during the desperation of civil war and the internecine conflict that followed. No ancestor invited Henry Orlando Marcy or Frederick W. Liedtke to stand watch over the liberated souls, and impart distant justice upon a prostrate land, but families such as the Stoneys and Parkers, energetically hailed Wade Hampton III and hurried his ascent to the statehouse.

Finally, as steel rails and new roads severed old property lines, some family heads such as Langdon Cheves held tightly to great swaths of Goose Creek forests and fields where liberated souls of varying complexions toiled until the advent of the modern era. Then, a new generation of ancestors, some hailing ancient names, such as Mayor Hilton Waring Bunch initiated a renewal that persists today.

436. Bradish J. Waring, Junior Warden, and Charles W. Waring, III trace lineage to James Moore, Sr. of Boochawee Plantation.
437. Ancestors of the current vestrymen, E. Horry Parker, Donald F. Parker, and William H. Priouleau, Jr., were innovative rice planters on Goose Creek and Back River.

THE GOOSE CREEK BRIDGE, GATEWAY TO SACRED PLACES

Today, residents and visitors from many corners of the world cross over the Goose Creek Bridge on NAD (Naval Ammunition Depot) Road pursuing opportunities and enjoying bountiful lives in a section of Carolina that is the City of Goose Creek. The people who come home to the burgeoning municipality represents forty-two ethnic groups,[438] somewhat similar to the diverse humanity of the frontier who waded across the shallows, leading pack horses in pursuit of new-world bounties - unfathomable in their distant homelands. Unlike their predecessors, fording the waterway in search of sustenance, those passing over the modern concrete structure on four lanes of asphalt, barely notice the ancient creek that flows beneath. That waterway nourished frontier families, supplied the bounties of an empire, and washed lands from which a prominence successfully emerged. However, time erodes memories of buckskin-clad frontiersmen, and great social transitions across numerous eras obscure most of their stories, but the flow way continues. It persistently drains tepid waters from corners of Carolina lowland, and when the stream turns south against a gentle bend of cypress knees, it flows unfailingly beneath the Goose Creek Bridge, gateway to sacred places.

---

438. City of Goose Creek, South Carolina, zip code 29445, United States Enumeration Census for the year 2010. There are forty-two ethnic groups represented among the 37,000 residents of the City of Goose Creek, South Carolina.

Sources

PRIMARY SOURCES:

Barnwell, Catherine O. Compiler. *Barnwell Letter Book*, Charleston, South Carolina: South Carolina Historical Society.

Bethlehem Baptist Church, Ledger of the Solemn Covenant of the Bethlehem Baptist Church in St. James, Goose Creek Parish, 1811-1871. Charleston South Carolina: Charleston Museum.

Cheves, Langdon. 1848-1940: *Miscellaneous land papers, 1735-1932*. Papers deposited with The South Carolina Historical Society. Charleston, South Carolina.

Cheves, Langdon. 1848-1940: *Financial Papers, 1860-1925*. Papers deposited with The South Carolina Historical Society. Charleston, South Carolina.

Chicken, George, d. 1727, Langdon Cheves ed. *George Chicken Journal, 1715-1716, A Letter from Carolina in 1715, City of Charleston Year Book, 1897*. Charleston, South Carolina: South Carolina Historical Society.

Chicken, George, d. 1727, *Colonel George Chicken's Letter of Administration to Catherine Widow*, Will Book 61-A, Works Project Administration (WPA): Charleston County Library, Charleston, South Carolina.

Chicken, George, d. 1727. *Inventory of Colonel George Chicken*, Will Book 61-B, WPA. Charleston, South Carolina: Charleston County Library.

Chicken, George, d. 1727. *Will of George Chicken*, Will Book 52, WPA. Charleston, South Carolina: Charleston County Library.

Donnely, John, Last Will and Testament, 1860, Box 165, number 2, Charleston District, proved September 5, 1865.

Dordal Family papers, in the private collection of the Roland Dordal family, 204 Easy Street, Goose Creek, South Carolina.

Graves, Charles W., Plantation Journal, 1846-1875, 34/0183, Charleston, South Carolina: South Carolina Historical Society.

Graves family papers, 1853-1854, 43/0530, Charleston, South Carolina: South Carolina Historical Society.

Grooms, George, Last Will and Testament, September 4, 1848, Will Book K, 1845-1851, Charleston District, Charleston, South Carolina: Charleston County Office Building.

Keckley family papers, 1816-1977, Charleston, South Carolina: South Carolina Historical Society.

Letters of the Society for the Propagation of the Gospel in Foreign Parts to the Ministers of St. James Church, Goose Creek, 1702-1765, Charleston, South Carolina: The South Carolina Historical Society and Columbia, South Carolina: South Carolina Department of Archives and History.

Lynes Family Papers, Charleston, South Carolina: Charleston Museum.

Manigault Family Papers, Charleston, South Carolina: South Carolina Historical Society.

Marcy, Henry O. *Diary of a Surgeon, US Army, 1864-1892*, February 26-March 1865, Charleston, South Carolina: South Carolina Historical Society.

Miscellaneous Communications, Number 3, Records of the *Board of Soldiers Relief, 1863*, Columbia, South Carolina: South Carolina Department of Archives and History.

Office of the Register of Mesne Conveyance, Charleston, South Carolina: Charleston `County Office Building..

Poppenheim Family Legal Papers, 1854-1876, Charleston, South Carolina; South Carolina Historical Society.

Porcher family Papers, 1793-1960, Charleston, South Carolina: South Carolina Historical Society.

Turnbull Family Legal Papers, 1856-1865, Charleston, South Carolina: South Carolina Historical Society.

Records of the Assistant Commissioner for the State of South Carolina, Bureau of Refugees, Freedmen and Abandoned Lands, 1865-1870, Microfilm Publication 'M869, Roll 34 "Reports of Conditions and Operations, July 1865 - Dec. 1866" 'Washingon, D.C.: Department of National Archives and History.

Return of Men Liable Under the Recent Call for each of the four-militia companies in the St. James, Goose Creek Parish on September 1864. The records describing the 18th Regiment of South Carolina Militia are among the papers of the Adjutant and Inspector General Office no. 43/679, Charleston, South Carolina: South Carolina Historical Society,

Smith, Henry A.M., Smith papers, Charleston, South Carolina: South Carolina Historical Society.

Society for the Propagation of the Gospel in Foreign Parts, Letter books, 1702-1786, Charleston, South Carolina: South Carolina Historical Society.

Southern Campaign, American Revolution Pension Statements and Rosters, http://www./southerncampaign.org, Pension Application of Archibald Brown, W21740, Transcribed by Will Graves.

St. James Church, Goose Creek. *Minutes of the Vestry, 1872 – 1925.* Charleston, South Carolina: South Carolina Historical Society.

Tennent Family Papers, Charleston, South Carolina: South Carolina Historical Society.

Traunter, Richard, *Travels of Richard Traunter of the Main Continent of America from Appomattox River in Virginia to Charles Town in South Carolina*, Two Journals 1698, 1699, Richmond, Virginia : Virginia Historical Society.

United States Enumeration Census, St. James, Goose Creek Parish, 1790, 1800, 1810, 1820, 1830, 1840, 1850, 1860, 1870, 1880, 1890, 1900, 1910, 1920, 1930.

United States Census, Products of Agriculture, St. James, Goose Creek Parish, Charleston District, 1860, 1870, 1880.

United States Census, Products of Industry, St. James, Goose Creek Parish, Charleston District, 1850, 1860, 1870 and 1880.

William Henry Johnson, (1871-1934), William Henry Johnson Scrapbook, Circa 1920-1923, Charleston, South Carolina: South Carolina Historical Society.

SECONDARY SOURCES:

PERIODICALS, PAMPHLETS, REPORTS AND OTHER SOURCES

Ball, Elias, Bull Papers, "Poor white farmers, St. James, Goose Creek Parish." and Forfeited Lands List, Sinking Fund Commission, Columbia, South Carolina: W.B. McDaniel, General Book and Job Printers, 69 Main Street, Charleston, South Carolina: South Carolina Historical Society,

Ballentine, George H. *Church Record Book of Wassamassaw Baptist Church, Wassamassaw Section, Berkeley County, South Carolina, 1875-1919.* Private Publication by George H. Ballentine, 2714, Phyllis Drive, Copperas Cove, Texas, 2001.

Berkeley County Deed Books, Berkeley County Office Building, Moncks Corner, South Carolina.

Berkeley Democrat Newspaper, on microfilm at the Berkeley County Library, Moncks Corner, South Carolina. 9-14-1932, 11-24-1938.

Carroll, B.R. Historical Collections of South Carolina...New York, Harper & Brothers, 1836.

Charles, Tommy. *An archaeological reconnaissance of the St. James Church properties of the diocese of South Carolina in Goose Creek, Berkeley County, South Carolina.* University of South Carolina Institute of Archaeology and Anthropology, Columbia, South Carolina. 1988.

Cheves, Langdon. 1848-1939: *Abstracts of Titles, 1694-1850.* Papers deposited with The South Carolina Historical Society. Charleston, South Carolina.

Cook, John B. P.E. *Goose Creek Reservoir, Berkeley County, South Carolina*, Report of Findings and Recommendations, Goose Creek Task Force, Berkeley County Soil and Water Conservation District, June 1, 1995.

Cote, Richard, *City of Heroes, The Great Charleston Earthquake of 1886*, Corinthian Books, Mt. Pleasant, South Carolina, 2006.

Dutten, Captain Charles Edward, U.S. Ordnance Corps, *The Charleston Earthquake of August 31, 1886*, Ninth Annual Report, 1887-88, U.S. Geological Survey, Washington D.C., 1889.

Fraser, Walter J., *Lowcountry Hurricanes*, The University of Georgia Press, Athens, Georgia. 2006.

Hill & Swayze's *Confederate States Rail-road & Steam-boat Guide, Containing the Time-Tables, Fares, Connections and Distances on all the Rail-roads [sic] of the Confederate States,* also the Connecting Lines of Rail-roads [sic] , Steam-boats and Stages. J. C. Swayze, 1862. Rare Book Collection, University of North Carolina at Chapel Hill.

Keowee Courier, *Acts of the Legislature, An Act to Raise Supplies, 1866*, Keowee Courier, Pickens Court House, Pickens, South Carolina, R.A. Thompson and Company Publisher, University of South Carolina Library.

Kirk, Francis Marion, *The Yamassee War, a paper prepared by Francis Marion Kirk for the Annual Court of the Society of Colonial Wars in the State of South Carolina*, April 15, 1950, among the collections of the South Carolina Historical Society, Charleston, South Carolina,

Lansdell, Brent , Charles F. Philips and Ralph Bailey Jr., Brockington and Associates Incorporated, Cultural Resources Survey and Testing of the Weber Research Tract, Charleston, South Carolina, July 2006.

Articles Published by the South Carolina Historical and Genealogical Society

Cuthbert, Robert B. *The Picture Man, A Biographical Sketch of Langdon Cheves*, Carologue, Fall, 2009, Vol. 25, No. 2

Heitzler, Michael J. *Boochawee Plantation Land and Legacy in Goose Creek*, January-April 2010, Vol. III, No.1-2.

Smith, Henry A.M. *The French Huguenot Church of the Parish of Goose Creek, South Carolina. Transactions of the Huguenot Society of South Carolina*, Volume 16: p. 43. 1915.

Stokes, Karen D. *Langdon Cheves Goes to War,* Carologue, Fall, 2009, Vol. 25, No. 2.

Thomas, J.P. Jr. *"The Barbadians in Early South Carolina"* Volume 31, pp. 75-80. Charleston, South Carolina.

Waterhouse, Richard. *Economic and Changing Patterns of Wealth Distribution in Colonial Lowcountry South Carolina*, Volume 89: pp. 203-217. 1988.

INTERVIEWS

Author interview with: Mrs. Gertrude Trescott via telephone to her home in Moncks Corner, South Carolina, June 1, 2007.

Author interview with: Mrs. Loretta Parsons at Westview Elementary School, July 1984.

Author interview with Mrs. Eloise Gowder, Berkeley County Librarian at the Berkeley County Library, Moncks Corner, South Carolina, May 1, 1972.

Author interview with: Mr. Eugene Bryan at his home in the Strawberry Community (also called Twenty-two), South Carolina, 6-7-05.

Author interview with: Jack Etling at the Etling residence in Pineview Subdivision, October 12,1982.

Author interview with: Hilton Waring Bunch, Jack Etling and Orvin Thompson at the residence of Orvin Thompson, July 20, 1980.

MAPS

Abernathie and Walker, *A Specimen of the Intended Traveling Map of the Roads of the State of South Carolina,* From Actual Survey by Walker and Abernathie, Protracted from a scale of one inch per Mile, 1st. Sept. 1787. This map is among the collections of the United States Library of Congress.

Bowen, Emmanuel, *A New & Accurate Map of the Provinces of North & South Carolina, Georgia &c. Drawn from late surveys and regulated by astronl [sic]. Observatns* [sic]. By Emanuel Bowen, 1747. Among the Collections of the Library of Congress.

Burr, David H. *Map of North and South Carolina, Exhibiting the Post Offices...1839* From his *The American Atlas,* London, J. Arrowsmith, 1839.

Gaillard, J. Palmer, Compiler, *Map of Berkeley County and parts of Charleston and Dorchester Counties S.C.,* among the collections of the Berkeley County Museum and at the Berkeley County Office Building.

Mills, Robert. *Mills' Atlas of South Carolina.* 1825 Easley, South Carolina, Southern Historical Press, 1980.

Moll, Herman, *A New and Exact Map of the Dominions of the King of Great Britain...,* 1732, London, among the map collections of the University of North Carolina, Chapel Hill.

Moll, Herman, *A new map of the north parts of America claimed by France under ye names of Louisiana, Missisipi [Mississippi], Canada, and New France with ye adjoining territories of England and Spain*: to Thomas Bromsall, esq., this map of Louisiana, Missisipi [Mississippi] & c. is most humbly dedicated, H. Moll, geographer / laid down according to the newest and most exact observations by H. Moll, geographer, 1720.

Tanner, Henry Schenck, 1786-1858. *Tanner Map* 1833. Act of Congress, *A new map of South Carolina with its canals, roads & distances from place to place along the stage & steamboat routes.* From his *A New Universal Atlas* (Philadelphia,1836). Library of Congress.

South Carolina General Highway and Transportation Map, 1940, South Carolina Department of Highways and Transportation, Columbia, South Carolina.

Plats traced from the originals among the Henry A.M. Smith Collection at the South Carolina Historical Society, Charleston, South Carolina.

Goose Creek Church: Plat of a tract of land situate in St. James, Goose Creek, containing 270 acres and belonging to the Goose Creek Church. It was surveyed May 1888 by (name not legible). Plat is on microfiche and among the Henry A. M. Smith Papers. The plat shows the location of the "Old School House" at a point N50 S 11.70 and N 14 ½ S 22.

Matthews, M. Copy of a plan of a body of land in Goose Creek, part now forming part of the glebe of St. James Church and part now belonging to the estate of Benjamin Coachman, dec'd. 1 plat, 2 pages: tracing; 46 x 61 cm. Request #: 32/120/A027

Other Plats on microfilm among the collections of the South Carolina Historical Society.

Goose Creek Church, 1888.

Lands Adjoining Goose Creek Reservoir, 1917.

260 acres on Back River Road in St. James, Goose Creek Parish "property of Mr. Beiling [Behling] now C. Voses [Vose] to be conveyed to Henry A. Middleton, 1871.

JOURNALS

Charleston City Gazette, South Carolina Historical Society and on microfilm at the Charleston County Library, Charleston, South Carolina.

Charleston News and Courier, 8-28-1876, September 1 and 7, 1876, 6-11-1877, 10-17-1876, 10-18-1876, 9-1-1876 and 9-7-1876, April 22, 1900. April 17, 1904. April 23, 1906. April 20, 1925. Cainhoy Race Riots, Records Chiefly Consisting of Affidavits of a disturbance at a meeting in Cane Hoy, South Carolina in which several persons were killed by gunfire on October 16, 1876. The newspapers are on microfilm at the Charleston County Library, Charleston, South Carolina.

Journals of the Governor's Council of South Carolina, 1671-1721. Transcribed by JohnGreen. South Carolina Department of Archives and History.

Journals of the Upper House of Assembly of South Carolina. Compiled bySouth Carolina Department of Archives and History, Columbia. (Cited as Upper House Records.) May 9/10, 1715.

Journals of the House of Representatives, 1783-1784. Theodora J. Thompson, Editor. Published for the South Carolina Department of Archives and History by The University of South Carolina Press, Columbia, South Carolina. 1977.

Journals of the House of Representatives 1785-1786. Lark Emerson Adams, Editor. Published for the South Carolina Department of Archives and History by the University of South Carolina Press, Columbia, South Carolina. 1979.

Journals of the House of Representatives 1787-1788. Michael E. Stevens, Editor.

Published for the South Carolina Department of Archives and History, The University of South Carolina Press, Columbia, South Carolina.1981.

Journals of the House of Representatives 1789-1790. Michael E. Stevens, Editor. Published for the South Carolina Department of Archives and History, The University of South Carolina Press, Columbia, South Carolina.1984.

Journals of the House of Representatives 1791. Michael E. Stevens, Editor. Published for the South Carolina Department of Archives and History, The University of South Carolina Press, Columbia, South Carolina. 1985.

Journals of the House of Representatives 1792-1794, Michael E. Stevens, Editor. Published for the South Carolina Department of Archives and History, The University of South Carolina Press, Columbia, South Carolina. 1988.

Official Records, http://ehistory.osu.edu/osu/sources/records/ Official Records, Series 1, volume 47, part 2, Columbia, Chapter LIX.

Records of the British Public Records Office Relating to South Carolina. Vol. 6. Transcribed by W. Noel Sainsbury. South Carolina Department of Archives and History, Columbia.

BOOKS

Bailey, Louise N. *Biographical Directory of the South Carolina House of Representatives:* Volume III, IV, 1775-1815. Columbia, South Carolina: University of South Carolina Press, 1988.

Ball, Edward, *Slaves in the Family,* Farrar, Straus and Giroux, New York, 1998.

Bates, Susan Baldwin and Harriot Cheves Leland, Editors, *Proprietary Records of South Carolina,* V. III, Abstracts of the Records of the Surveyor General of the Province 1678-1698. Charleston, South Carolina: The History Press, 2007.

Bridges, Anne Baker Leland , and Roy Williams, *St. James Santee, Plantation Parish, History and Records,* Reprint Company, Spartanburg, South Carolina, 1997.

Brown, Douglas Summers, *The Catawba Indians, People of the River,* the University ofSouth Carolina Press, 1966.

Campbell, Jacquelin Glass, *When Sherman Marched North from the Sea: Resistance on the Confederate Home Front,* Chapel Hill, University of North Carolina Press, 2003.

Crane, Verner W. *The Southern Frontier, 1670-1732,* Ann Arbor Books, The University of Michigan Press 1956.

Cross J. Russell, *Historic Ramblin's Through Berkeley*, Cross-Williams FamilyLimited Partnership, 1985, Reprinted by the R.L. Bryan Company, Columbia, South Carolina for the Berkeley Historical Society.

Dalcho, Frederick. *A Historic Account of the Protestant Episcopal Church in South*

Carolina. Charleston: A.E. Miller, 1820, reprinted 1969.

Dhalle, Katherine, History of the 55th Massachusetts Volunteer Infantry, LWF Publications, with "Lest We Forget," Volume 3, Number 2, April, 1995.

Edgar, Walter, *South Carolina: A History*, University of South Carolina Press, Columbia, South Carolina, 1998

Ford, Arthur Perroneau and Marion Johnstone, *Life in the Confederate Army: Being Personal Experiences of a Private Soldier in the Confederate Army; Some Experiences and Sketches of a Southern Life,* the Neale Publishing Company, New York and Washington, 1905.

Foster, Lisa, *Janie Mitchell, Reliable Cook, An ex-slave's recipe for living, 1862-1931,* Evening Post Publishing Company, Charleston, South Carolina, 2011.

Fraser, Charles. *A Charleston Sketchbook, 1796-1806,* Rutland, Vermont: Charles E. Tuttle Co.1940.

Gibbes, Robert Wilson, *Documentary History of the American Revolution,* Volumes II and III 1776-1782, Spartanburg, South Carolina: The Reprint Company, 1972.

Headlam, Cecil ed. Calendar of State Papers, Colonial Series, American and the West Indies, 1716-1717, London, 1922.

Heitzler, Michael J. *Goose Creek, A Definitive History, Rebellion, Reconstruction and Beyond,* The History Press, Charleston, 2006.

Hirsch, Arthur Henry, *The Huguenots of Colonial South Carolina*. London: Archon Books, 1962.

Hudson, Charles. *The Southeastern Indians*. Knoxville: University of Tennessee Press,1976.

Johnson, Joseph, *Traditions and Reminiscences, Chiefly of the American Revolution in the South,* Charleston, South Carolina, Walker and James, 1851.

Klingberg, Frank J. *The Carolina Chronicle of Dr. Francis LeJau, 1706-1717.* Berkeley and Los Angeles: University of California Press, 1956.

Leiding, Henriette Kershaw, *Historic Houses of South Carolina*. Philadelphia: J.B. Lippincott, 1921.

Martin, Margaret Rhett, *Charleston Ghosts*, Columbia: University of South Carolina Press, 1963.

Mathew, William M. Editor, *The Private Diary of Edmund Ruffin, 1843, Agriculture, Geology & Society in Antebellum South Carolina,* The University of Georgia Press, Athens and London, 1992.

McCrady, Edward, *History of South Carolina*, 4 vols. New York: McMillan, 1897-1901.

McCrady, Edward, *The History of South Carolina Under Proprietary Rule, 1670-1719*. New York: Mcmillan, 1897.

Milling, Chapman J. *Red Carolinians*, Chapel Hill, the University of North Carolina Press, 1940.

Nelson, Louis P. *The Beauty of Holiness, Anglicanism and Architecture in Colonial South Carolina*, University of North Carolina Press, Chapel Hill, 2008.

Porter, Kenneth W. 1948 *Negroes on the Southern Frontier, 1670-1763, Journal of Negro History* 33:53-78.

Oatis, Steven J. *A Colonial Complex, South Carolina's Frontier in the Era of the Yamassee War 1680-1730*, University of Nebraska Press, Lincoln and London, 2004.

Orvin, Maxwell Clayton, *Historic Berkeley County, 1671-1900,* Printed by Comprin,Charleston, South Carolina 1973.

Pierre, C.E. *The Work of the Society for the Propagation of the Gospel in Foreign Parts in the Colonies.* Washington, D.C. From The Association for the Study of Negro Life and History, Inc. From the Journal of Negro History 1, no. 4 (October 1916).

Poyas, E. A. *The Olden Times of South Carolina.* Charleston: S. G. Courtenay & Co 1855.

Schmidt, James D. *Free to Work, Labor, Law, Emancipation and Reconstruction 1865-1880,* University of Georgia Press, Athens, 1998.

Schmidt, James D. "A Full-fledged Government of Men:" *Freedmen's Bureau Labor Policy in South Carolina, 1865-1868,* Paul A. Cimbala and Randall M. Miller, Editors. New York: Fordham University Press, 1999.

Policy in South Carolina, 1865-1868, in The Freedmen's Bureau and Reconstruction, Reconsiderations, Paul A. Cimbala and Randall M. Miller, editors, Fordham University Press, 1999.

Sellers, Leilla, *Charleston Business on the Eve of the American Revolution,* Chapel Hill,North Carolina: University of North Carolina Press, 1932.

Solomon, Robert S. M.D. *The CSS David, The Story of the First Successful Torpedo Boat,* The R. L. Bryan Company, Columbia, South Carolina, 1970.

Wallace, David Duncan. *The History of South Carolina.* 4 vols. New York: American Historical Society, Inc., 1934.

Waring, Joseph Ioor, *St. James Church, Goose Creek, South Carolina: A Sketch of the Parish from 1706-1898,* Charleston, South Carolina, Lucas and Richardson Co. Printers and Engravers, 1897.

Williams, Alfred Brockenbrough, *Hampton and His Red Shirts: South Carolina Deliverance,* Walker Evans and Cogswell, Charleston, 1935.

Index

A

Allen, Andrew 49, 151
American Revolution 14, 19, 116,
    122, 126, 134, 142, 148, 283,
    291, 299–301
Anderson, Roger 271
Andrews, William 50
Ararat 220, 248
Austin, Robert 228

B

Back River 24, 31, 36, 38–40, 71, 98,
    104, 108, 114, 138, 140, 169,
    170, 184, 186, 189, 192, 193,
    195, 196, 204, 208, 227, 228,
    242, 246, 253, 259, 265, 270,
    286, 296
Baptists 155, 158, 159, 166, 282, 284
Barbados 30, 33, 66, 93
Barker 52, 60–62, 63, 64, 66, 70,
    70–74, 78, 84, 92, 220, 221,
    286
barracks 121, 165, 233, 235
Binnar, Edgar 271
Bloomfield 27, 107, 110, 114, 191,
    245, 246, 248, 259
Bowman, Ralph 156
Bradwell, Isaac 164
Brick 14, 19, 23, 40, 42, 45, 67, 93,
    95, 100, 102, 105–107, 111,
    114, 116, 125, 129, 131, 146,
    151, 155, 158, 161, 164, 180,
    185, 186, 187, 194, 216, 232,
    234, 237, 242, 244, 245, 250,
    268, 279–281, 282, 283
bridge iii, v, 1, 3, 7, 9, 11, 17–22,
    24–26, 29–31, 35–46, 51–54,
    54, 56, 57, 73, 75, 76, 78, 84–
    87, 92, 97–99, 103, 104, 107,
    113, 115, 117, 118, 120–124,
    127, 132, 135, 141, 143, 144,
    146–148, 160, 161, 167, 168,
    172, 173, 174, 177–180, 184,
    192, 197, 205, 206, 212, 216,
    217, 227, 230, 235, 238, 244,
    247, 248, 257, 258, 260, 261,
    262, 263, 267, 268, 277, 286,
    287, 298
Brogdon, Jonathan 236
Broom Hall 26, 48, 107, 117, 130,
    131, 163, 245
Browning, William 145
Brown, J.B. 9, 11, 13, 23, 51, 126,
    128, 271, 279
Bunch 267, 271, 273, 275, 276, 286,
    295
Bunch, Hilton Waring 267, 271, 273,
    275, 286, 295
Bun, Douglas 236
Bushy Park 265, 270

C

Campbell, Cuffy 122, 207, 208
Cantey, Joseph 145
Carnes Cross Roads 210, 213, 226,
    262

Pinopolis 118, 144
Poyas, Elizabeth 158
Pringle 248

R

Red Bank 30, 36, 53, 54, 114, 138,
    141, 155, 166, 220, 268, 271
Red Bank Road 30, 36, 138, 155, 166,
    220, 268, 271
Rhame, Dr. O.C. 229, 237
rice 48, 67, 78, 91, 96–98, 102, 104–
    109, 111, 115, 122, 129, 133,
    138, 140, 141, 144, 164–166,
    184–186, 187, 190, 194, 205,
    211, 213, 228, 242, 244, 252,
    254, 257, 280, 283, 286
Richardson, Smith H. 41
rivers 29, 46, 59, 65, 76, 110, 144,
    250, 252
Rutledge, John 137

S

Santee 15, 46, 52–54, 56–60, 64, 66,
    72, 73, 76, 80, 85, 89, 135, 147,
    200, 298
Schenckingh, Barnard 30
Schenckingh, Benjamin 34, 41, 72,
    80, 89, 90
Shiver, Magnus 236
Simmons, James S. 259
Singletary 166, 262
slave 30, 37, 40–42, 44, 48, 50–53,
    64, 66–68, 70, 77, 78, 83, 97,
    98, 101, 103, 104–108, 110,
    113, 114, 121, 125, 131, 134,
    139, 140, 144, 145, 151, 153,
    159–161, 164, 168, 170, 172,
    180, 181, 183, 185, 186, 187,
    191, 194, 198, 204, 207–209,
    212, 213, 216, 223, 229, 248,
    251, 298, 299
Smith, Henry A.M. 31, 49, 79, 102,
    246, 291, 294, 296
Smith, Maria 163

Smith, Thomas 33, 39, 40, 41, 51, 52,
    88, 90, 102, 130, 156
Smith, William 146
Smith, William Laughton 133, 147,
    163
Smyrna Methodist Church 267
SPG 42, 74, 81, 86, 94, 96
St. Andrew 102, 172
St. Bartholomew 115
St. James 3, 10, 12, 14, 15, 18, 19,
    21, 23–27, 38, 40–42, 45–47,
    53, 54, 57, 70, 71, 77, 80, 85,
    93, 94, 100–103, 105, 108–110,
    111, 117, 118, 120, 123, 126,
    128, 132, 141, 143, 145, 147,
    150–152, 154, 156–158, 160,
    161, 164–167, 170, 172, 176,
    180, 183, 191, 193, 196, 197,
    200, 202, 207, 211, 212, 216,
    219–222, 224, 226, 228,
    230–233, 235, 236, 238–243,
    244, 245, 248, 249, 251–253,
    259, 262, 266, 267, 270–272,
    274–283, 285, 289–292, 296,
    298, 301
Stone, Robert 112
Strawberry 14, 21, 22, 62, 64, 71,
    121, 159, 162, 166, 169, 170,
    179, 191, 192, 196, 202–204,
    220, 221, 223, 229, 230, 236,
    263–266, 283, 294
St. Stephen 64, 70, 168, 169, 177,
    179, 180, 200, 251
Summerville 144, 173, 189, 190, 213
Sumter 123, 166, 194, 261

T

tanner 104, 158, 296
Taylor, Peter 110, 112, 114
Tennent, William 204, 208, 250
Thomas, Samuel 40, 241
Thorogood 10, 13, 30–32, 32, 35, 38,
    49, 76, 77, 78, 98, 114, 126,
    128, 138, 140, 162, 163, 166,

The Author at the Wassamassaw Baptismal

Author, Michael Heitzler reflects next to a five-foot deep Baptismal Spring, lined with cypress boards on the forest edge near the Wassamassaw Cemetery. Full immersion baptism is a central tenant of Baptist Churches and reliable springs or other water sources are preferred at worship sites. The photo taken July 4, 2011 is among the author's collection. See Ballentine, 60, "Bro. [sic] Dangerfield moved that a committee be appointed to arrange for and build a Baptistery at spring, near the Church…"

Finale

Friends remember me

When sitting at thine ease

Speak of me often, though it be

Only to tell my faults

For better that some hearts be taught

Even of my follies than of naught

Oh! yes, remember me

In gentleness and love

Mid all the changes of this life

Its thousand joys and fears

But grant me still that little spot

Friends! dearest friends! forget me not

Anonymous author inserted this poem onto the last page of the *Book of the Covenant, Bethlehem Baptist Church*

CPSIA information can be obtained at www.ICGtesting.com
Printed in the USA
LVOW05s0524200813

348639LV00003B/6/P